Our Great War Heroes:
Seven Param Vir Chakra Recipients

Volume 1

Our Great War Heroes:
Seven Param Vir Chakra Recipients

Volume 1

(True Stories of Seven Flaming Warriors of Indian Army)

Shyam Kumari

Vij Books India Pvt Ltd

New Delhi (India)

Published by

Vij Books India Pvt Ltd
(Publishers, Distributors & Importers)
2/19, Ansari Road
Delhi – 110 002
Phones: 91-11-43596460, 91-11-47340674
M: 98110 94883
e-mail: contact@vijpublishing.com
web: www.vijbooks.in

Copyright © 2021, *Shyam Kumari*

ISBN: 978-93-90439-70-6 (Hardback)
ISBN: 978-93-90439-71-3 (Paperback)
ISBN: 978-93-90439-72-0 (ebook)

All rights reserved.

No part of this book may be reproduced, stored in a retrieval system, transmitted or utilised in any form or by any means, electronic, mechanical, photocopying, recording or otherwise, without the prior permission of the copyright owner. Application for such permission should be addressed to the publisher.

Also by Shyam Kumari

English:

Vignettes of Sri Aurobindo and the Mother
More Vignettes of Sri Aurobindo and the Mother
Beautiful Vignettes of Sri Aurobindo and the Mother
How They Came to Sri Aurobindo and the Mother, Volumes 1 to 4
Musings on the Mother's Prayers and Meditations, Volumes 1 to 3
Sunlit Days
Sweet Steps
Towards Light
Teacher's Guide to Sunlit Days, Sweet Steps and Towards Light
Lights from Nolini Kanta Gupta (compilation)

Hindi:

Bharat, Vishwa aur Manavta ka Bhavishya – Sri Aravind evam Sri Ma kay Alok may
Bhagwan Ki Oar, Parts 1 and 2
Sri Arvind Aur Sri Ma Ki Divya Lila, Parts 1 and 2
Gulab Ki Pankhuriyan (21 stories)
Aparajita (24 stories and 2 plays)
Prem Divani (35 stories and 2 plays)
Jeenay Ki Kala, Parts 1 and 2
Anupam Kahaniya Arambhik, Part 1
Anupam Kahaniya, Parts 1 to 4
Madhur Kahaniya, Parts 1 and 2
Shishu Rang Tarang, Part 1
Nav Bal Rang Tarang, Parts 1 and 2
Nav Rag Anurag
Shri Arvind Sahitya – Jyotirmaya Tarange

OUR GREAT WAR HEROES: SEVEN PARAM VIR CHAKRA RECIPIENTS (VOLUME 1)

The following books are available both in English and Hindi:

Our Great Revolutionaries (1): Chandrashekhar 'Azad'
Our Great Revolutionaries (2): Kanailal Dutt
Param Vir Chakra Recipients (1): Major Som Nath Sharma
Param Vir Chakra Recipients (5): Second Lieutenant Rama Raghoba Rane
Param Vir Chakra Recipients (8): Major Shaitan Singh
Param Vir Chakra Recipients (9): Colonel Dhan Singh Thapa
Param Vir Chakra Recipients (10): Coy Quartermaster Havildar Abdul Hamid
Param Vir Chakra Recipients (11): Lt. Col. Ardeshir Burzorji Tarapore
Param Vir Chakra Recipients (12): Lance Naik Albert Ekka
Param Vir Chakra Recipients (13): Second Lieutenant Arun Khetarpal
Param Vir Chakra Recipients (16): Hon. Captain Bana Singh
Param Vir Chakra Recipients (18): Captain Vikram Batra
Param Vir Chakra Recipients (19): Captain Manoj Kumar Pandey
Param Vir Chakra Recipients (20): Grenadier Yogender Singh Yadav
Param Vir Chakra Recipients (21): Rifleman Sanjay Kumar

Contents

Dedication	ix
Acknowledgements	x
Foreword by (Late) Maj. Gen. K. K. Tewari, PVSM, AVSM	xiii
Foreword by Maj. Gen. (Dr.) G. D. Bakshi, SM, VSM (Retd.)	xv
Foreword by Maj. Gen. Mrinal Suman, AVSM, VSM, PhD. (Retd.)	xviii
Foreword by Maj. Gen. Ian Cardozo, AVSM, SM (Retd.)	xx
Foreword by Maj. Gen. Satya Swaroop Sharma, KC, VSM (Retd.)	xxii
Foreword by Maj. Gen. Suresh Thadani (Retd.)	xxiii
Foreword by Air Vice Marshal Vishwa Mohan Tiwari (Retd.)	xxiv
Farewell to a Martyr	xxv
Preface	xxix
1. Major Som Nath Sharma	1
2. Lieutenant Colonel Ardeshir Burzorji Tarapore	32
3. Second Lieutenant Arun Khetarpal	55
4. Hon. Captain Bana Singh	81
5. Captain Vikram Batra	113
6. Captain Manoj Kumar Pandey	138
7. Grenadier Yogender Singh Yadav	165

Appendices 193

Appendix 1	Forgotten By History	193
Appendix 2	PVC Som Nath Sharma Remembered By His Sister (Late) Major Dr. Kamla Tewari	197
Appendix 3	PVC A. B. Tarapore Remembered By His Daughter Zarin Boyce and His Son Xerxes Tarapore	199
Appendix 4	PVC Arun Khetarpal Remembered By His Brother Mukesh Khetarpal.	204
Appendix 5	The Ice Warriors of Siachen Glacier	205
Appendix 6	PVC Manoj Kumar Pandey Remembered By His Mother Brijmohini Pandey	211
Appendix 7	Homage to PVC Vikram Batra By His Father, Girdhari Lal Batra	212
Appendix 8	The Param Vir Chakra	214
Appendix 9	Three Schemes By Shyam Kumari	217

Author 223

Dedication

I dedicate this book at the lotus feet of Sri Aurobindo

who renounced all personal comforts and bore unimaginable hardships for India,

who declared in unambiguous words that India was a "Godhead" and the "Mother",

who, by his mantric words, infused a new life in the youth of the almost dead and depressed nation, through his journals "Bande Mataram" and "Karmayogin",

who, while imprisoned in the Alipore Jail by the British, had the realisation of "Vasudev",

who was foremost amongst the revolutionaries and shook the throne of the British Empire by his yogashakti.

And also at the lotus feet of the Mother

who, unbeknown to the world, is guarding India

and leading the whole Creation towards a golden future.

Acknowledgements

Many people have helped through inputs and encouragement in the making of this book.

Firstly, I thank heroes PVC Honorary Captain Bana Singh and PVC Havildar Yogender Singh Yadav who have lived to tell the tales of their glorious exploits. I thank them both for visiting me in Pondicherry and recounting to me their stories. Secondly, I thank my sister Raka, her husband Satya Prakash and daughter Kumari Taru, who interviewed several PVCs and their families on my behalf. Thirdly, I thank (Late) Maj. Gen. K. K. Tewari, Param Vishisht Seva Medal (PVSM), Ati Vishisht Seva Medal (AVSM), who gave me constant and unstinted support in this project.

I thank the families of the martyred heroes of this book who opened their hearts and told me the stories of their hero sons and brothers, even though it must have been painful for them to relive those moments, to reveal those precious memories. They are: (Late) Maj. Gen. K. K. Tewari; (Late) Major Mrs. Kamala Tewari; Mrs. Zarin Boyce; Xerexes Tarapore; (Late) Brigadier M.L. Khetarpal AVSM; (Late) Mrs. Maheshwari Khetarpal; Mukesh Khetarpal; Shri Girdhari Lal Batra; Mrs. Kamal Kanta Batra; Vishal Batra; Mr. Gopichand Pandey; Mrs. Brij Mohini Pandey and Pratibha Pandey.

I also thank the following for their help and support: Lt. Gen. Jagdish Chander PVSM, AVSM, VSM, ADC (Retd.); Maj. Gen. Ian Cardozo (Retd.); Maj. Gen. Mrinal Suman, AVSM, VSM, PhD (Retd.); Maj. Gen. Raj Mehta (Retd.); Maj. Gen. Suresh K. Thadani (Retd.); Maj. Gen. G. S. Bal, VSM (Retd.), General Officer Commanding, 36 Infantry Divison; Colonel Lalit Kumar Rai, VRC (Retd.); Colonel Mahip Tomar; Colonel Ashok Chowdhury (Retd.); Dr. Larry Siedlitz; Dr. N.K. Kalia; Shri Arun Churiwal; Shri Shankar Poddar;

Shri O.P. Dani, Shri Satish Deora; Ms Maria Jain; Ms Vilas Patel and Shri Rakesh Oza. Most of all I thank my son Kim for his constant support.

Publication of these hero stories for adults will bring the Army heroes closer to many more Indians.

Listed below are sources of information which have helped me write this book:

Claude Arpi, author of "Braving the Heights" in *The Pioneer*, 28 February 2007.

Lt. Col. Yashpal Singh Rana (Second-in-Command, 8 J&K LI), author of a typewritten report about the 1987 Siachen battle.

Maj. Gen. Ian Cardozo (Retd.), author of *Param Vir - Our Heroes in Battle*.

(Late) Maj. Gen. K. K. Tewari PVSM, AVSM, author of *A Soldier's Voyage of Self-Discovery*.

(Late) Lt. Gen. Hanut Singh PVSM, AVSM, MVC author of "*Fakhr-E-Hind*" The Story of the Poona Horse.

Lt. Gen. Dr. M. L. Chibber PVSM, AVSM, PhD (Retd.) author of Pakistan's Criminal Folly in Kashmir.

Lieutenant Colonel Rajkumar Pattu and Brigadier Man Mohan Sharma, authors of Indian Prisoners of War in Pakistan.

Brigadier L.P. Sen, author of *Slender Was the Thread*.

Lieutenant Colonel A. Asthana, commanding Officer 1/11 Gorkha Rifles.

T. Samphel, author of *Unsung Heroes of Kargil War*.

Srinjoy Chowdhury, author of *Despatches from Kargil*.

Gaurav Savant, author of *Dateline Kargil*.

Vinayak Parab author of an article in *Salam Sainik*.

Hira Lal Yadav, author of *Salam Sainik*.

Shobita Asthana, author of 'Reminiscences of Manoj Pandey' in *the Indian Express* 10 September 1999.

Archana Masih: interviewer of Shri Girdhari Lal Batra.

Onkar Nath: interviewer of Shri Girdhari Lal Batra.

Search Engines – Internet.

wikipidia.org/924/893/Battle of Longewala-India.

en.wikipedia.org/wiki/The_Poona Horse.

'Heroism' Bharat Rakshak.

Web-site Poona Horse Regiment Association.

Foreword By

(Late) Maj. Gen. K. K. Tewari, PVSM, AVSM

I consider it a privilege to be asked to write a 'Foreword' to this series on 'Our Heroes'. This series of books on modern Indian Heroes serves an important and long overdue need. Stories of valour and heroism can awaken a spirit of emulation in others. There is nothing more precious than life. And yet, a soldier in the country's service may be called upon to offer this most precious of all things as if it were a mere trifle.

In five decades since India's Independence, the Indian soldier has repeatedly made the supreme sacrifice. India owes an immeasurable debt to the untold thousands of soldiers who have died uncelebrated in her service. The 21 recipients of the Param Vir Chakra are the few acknowledged symbols of the unknown soldiers and their many exceptional acts of courage and sacrifice.

A wilful act of self sacrifice performed as an act of duty can only come from a tremendous training in character. What high training engenders the fortitude and bravery which converts ordinary boys, and increasingly now, girls into selfless heroes? Were it possible to adapt this training in character and bravery to the needs of civil life, India would be an extremely effective society. The need of the hour is to find the methods and means to generalise this capacity for heroism, routinely demonstrated by soldiers defending India's borders, into the youth of India who constitute the largest segment of India's population and are the hope of her future.

The author Shyam Kumari of Sri Aurobindo Ashram deserves to be complimented on this laudable project she has undertaken. The political leadership and the academicians in the country would do well to introduce such stories of gallantry in the service of the nation in all schools, colleges and other training institutions of the country.

Sri Aurobindo has described the need for awakening a spirit in the service of the nation in an article titled "The Bourgeois and the Samurai" written in the early 20th century while comparing India and Japan, which should be read by all thinking Indians.

Foreword by

Maj. Gen. (Dr.) G. D. Bakshi, SM, VSM (Retd.)

Why do men fight? More importantly, what impels them to willingly lay down their lives for a piece of tattered silk or for a desolate and frozen peak in the back of beyond? Philip Mason, the famous chronicler of the British Indian Army wrote, "Men may come to the Colours [flags representing units of the Armed Forces] for the pay, but it is not for the pay alone that they win the Victoria Cross."

What is that vague and indefinable something that turns a man into a hero, one who overcomes the greatest fear of all: fear of death, wounds and darkness? Was there an ancient race of hero-men who were such warriors? Do they exist anymore? As you turn the pages of this book, you will actually meet them face to face, the military heroes of India of today, young men who willingly sacrificed themselves that you and I may live as free citizens. For your tomorrow they gave their today. You will see these heroes in the flash and fury of the modern battlefield, in the shriek of the diving and strafing jet fighters, in the thundering barrage of the big guns, in the angry growl of tank engines, in the deadly chatter of the machine guns. Amidst the shrieks of the stricken and dying, you will see that charging hero leading his men in action – in the face of certain death.

I have had the proud privilege to serve with such men in the face of certain death. 2nd Lt. Arun Khetarpal was a batch mate of mine from the NDA days. We all remember him – tall and handsome, always having a gentle smile on his face. He laid down his life when he was just 21 years of age – he was then the youngest recipient of the nation's highest gallantry award. Before dying, this handsome young man with the innocent face of a child had fought like a tiger and destroyed six enemy tanks single-handedly. Captain Vikram Batra, the young man whose exultant victory cry – *"Yeh Dil Mange* more" –

had echoed through the country during the Kargil war was from my Regiment, the Jammu and Kashmir Rifles, which has a long tradition of valour and sacrifice. Both these young men had become the iconic faces of the wars they fought and won.

When you go through these sensitive thumbnail sketches of the lives and heroic deeds of seven recipients of the Param Vir Chakra, you will see a thread of commonality that runs through these narratives. All these heroes had some sterling qualities in common:

- **Self-Transcendence:** Without exception, they all seemed to transcend the limited consciousness of the body and the great fear of death and dying. They displayed great courage, and their primary credo was '*Abhayata*' or fearlessness. It is this transcendence that makes them great and worthy of our respect.

- **A Desire to Lead:** They greatly cared for the esteem of their men and went to great lengths to earn it. They did not order their men into action, but led them personally instead. Their abiding mantra was 'Follow me'. These heroes inspired their men to achieve seemingly impossible goals in the face of death.

- **A Sense of Destiny:** Each of them was imbued with a sense of being a man of destiny, a chosen being with a mission, one who was born to do something big. Each of them had a premonition that he would not die an ordinary death, and this led to an overpowering commitment to his duty.

- **Generosity and Kindness of Spirit:** You will see in all of them a great generosity, an innate kindness of spirit. They almost always sacrificed themselves to save their comrades in the battlefield. They put their own lives on the line, not once but again and again and again, to save others.

An educational system must not just transmit knowledge. Above all, it must impart values, abiding values like courage, altruism, compassion, a great love of the country, a great sense of mission and duty – the abiding values, in fact, of 'Duty, Honour, country'. All these abiding values enable us to transcend our petty selves, our fear, our greed, our selfishness. They teach us self-transcendence.

The pity is that most of our textbooks these days have no mention of such values. Our schools are focusing instead merely on cramming knowledge to pass exams. They do nothing whatsoever to inculcate these essential values. That is why today we are faced with the all-pervasive stink of corruption. The news headlines unearthing scams in every walk of life advertise our moral decay and the complete loss of values.

That is why books like these are exceedingly important. They bring us face to face with men who were living embodiments of the values of 'Duty, Honour, Country', men who taught us to rise above ourselves and sacrifice our lives for what was for the highest good. We sorely need such men and women who are inspired by ageless and immortal values. Of them one can say with pride, as Robert Laurence Binyon did of the martyrs of World War 1, in his poem "For the Fallen":

>They shall grow not old,
>
>As we that are left grow old:
>
>Age shall not weary them,
>
>Nor the years condemn.
>
>At the going down of the sun
>
>And in the morning
>
>We will remember them.

There were warriors who fought the Mahabharata War, and there were sages who recorded their deeds for history and posterity. Ms. Shyam Kumari is one such sage. In recording the inspirational lives of our modern military heroes in such a sensitive manner, she has done the country, and the generations to come, a yeoman service.

Foreword by

Maj. Gen. Mrinal Suman, AVSM, VSM, PhD. (Retd.)

Our God and soldiers we alike adore ev'n at the brink of danger; not before: After deliverance, both alike requited, Our God's forgotten, and our soldiers slighted.

– Francis Quarles

Soldiering is not a profession. It is a commitment. Soldier's dedication to duty, loyalty to the nation, and willingness for the supreme sacrifice are driven less by material considerations and more by an overwhelming urge to earn the love and respect of their countrymen. A grateful nation's recognition of their contribution to national security acts as the strongest motivator.

No country has understood this aspect better than Britain. With a view to honour the 'unique service' rendered by members of the armed forces and their families, the military covenant (nation's promise that troops will be cared for in return for the sacrifices they make) is being converted into a law. It will put the covenant on a statutory basis for the first time in world history. While introducing the proposal in the House of Commons in May 2011, the UK Defence Secretary stated, "The government has no higher duty than the defence of the realm, and the nation has no greater obligation than to look after those who have served it . . . The obligation we owe to our service men and women, set against the commitment and sacrifice which they make, is enormous." No wonder its armed forces have remained undefeated for centuries and the sun never set on the British Empire.

Apathy for matters concerning national security had been a bane of the Indian psyche. Indian military history is a saga of defeats and failures. Starting with Alexander the Great, legions of invaders emerged victorious and plundered the subcontinent, turn by turn. Despite individual acts of bravery, Indian kings almost always suffered defeat. Unfortunately, our centuries of slavery and foreign rule have taught us nothing. We continue to remain mired in internal dissensions. Our concern for national security and the armed forces is limited to singing the national anthem in cinema halls.

In the recorded Indian history of over 2000 years, the 1971 Indo-Pak War stands out as the most astounding military feat. Indifference for national security concerns was so widespread and insidious that the media, which went berserk celebrating the 25th anniversary of Indian cricket world-cup win of 1983, forgot to commemorate the outstanding military victory that gave birth to Bangladesh. India had no time to remember its martyrs and show gratitude for their sacrifices. Though India has fought five wars since Independence and over 40,000 soldiers have made the ultimate sacrifice, shamefully, the country did not have a national war memorial for nearly seventy years.

In the above environment of appalling neglect of the Armed Forces, author Shyam Kumari's efforts to honour the memory of India's brave soldiers and to instil a sense of pride in its citizens can only be described as stupendous and remarkable. It is hard to believe that a single individual can strive to achieve so much in a lifetime. By paying tributes to the winners of bravery awards, she has been trying to create awareness amongst people, especially school children, regarding the sacrifices made by India's valiant soldiers to safeguard national sovereignty. It is often said that any country that does not care for its soldiers loses the moral right to expect them to die for its security. One hopes we shall not have to face that fate.

Ms. Shyam Kumari is an inspirational person. One hopes and prays that many more will emulate her, to stimulate and arouse the Indian psyche from its slumber. With a sense of deep gratitude, and on behalf of all Indian soldiers, I salute her. We wish her a long and healthy life and many more years of service to our nation and society.

Foreword by

Maj. Gen. Ian Cardozo, AVSM, SM (Retd.)

This book *Our Great War Heroes of India – 1: 7 Param Vir Chakra Recipients* is remarkable for the manner in which it brings to life the stories of seven of India's most celebrated heroes. This book has broken the boundaries of conventional military writing by taking the reader into the intricate details of the lives of these heroes, thereby helping us to understand what motivated these men to do the unthinkable. It helps to also bring into focus for the common man what the life in the Armed Forces is like. These stories tell us how these men lived and behaved both in peacetime and in war. And they help us understand that it is a character which is the mainspring of the actions of these military heroes, and it is the manner in which the Armed Forces live their lives in peacetime that helps them to fight and die in war.

I hope that those who read this book, particularly the youth of our country, will pick up some of the values that motivated these heroes who sacrificed their lives so that we may live. The conduct of the 21 recipients of India's Param Vir Chakra set an example that the nation can with benefit follow. If India is to take its rightful place in the comity of nations, then each and every one of us has to do his or her bit to make this happen. This can only happen if we are prepared to put 'Country First' and 'Self Last'.

Shining examples of such ideals illuminate the pages of this book: how these heroes put their lives in the line of fire for a higher purpose, how love of the country and of its people motivated them, and how they were willing to even make the supreme sacrifice for our sake.

These stories should motivate all of us to do the same in every action of our daily lives. If this happens, we can do no wrong, and India will be a brilliant example for the world to follow.

Foreword by

Maj. Gen. Satya Swaroop Sharma, KC, VSM (Retd.)

Ms. Shyam Kumari, a person herself committed to spirituality and social service, has taken so much trouble to provide the detailed life sketch and acts of the gallantry of each of these heroes that the book written by her, in my opinion, is a historical document which, besides describing these heroes and their brave acts, also covers many historical facts of these wars that have otherwise been forgotten. For her great contribution of creating awareness in the new generation, she deserves the highest appreciation and this nation will always remain grateful to her for her research and superb effort. I recommend that this crucial book should form part of the prescribed or recommended reading for every child in every Indian school.

Foreword by

Maj. Gen. Suresh Thadani (Retd.)

Shyam Kumari has been touched by the lives of those who have displayed a spirit of sacrifice for high and noble causes, especially our freedom fighters and military heroes. She has a natural affinity for the military, and has, over the years, made serious efforts at the personal level to highlight the courage, patriotism and sacrifice of its heroes who fought bravely in India's wars. She has also made it a point to reach out to the nation's youth, through her real-life stories of gallant soldiers and courageous freedom fighters and inspire them to live and work for higher causes. In this volume, she has written about seven gallant men of the Indian Army who were awarded the Param Vir Chakra, the nation's highest wartime gallantry medal, for fighting bravely above and beyond the call of duty, in the wars and skirmishes that India has fought since 1947. Their stories are truly inspiring.

Foreword by

Air Vice Marshal Vishwa Mohan Tiwari (Retd.)

I am happy that Shyam Kumari has bravely yet sensitively attempted the task of documenting the lives and actions of these Param Vir Chakras. This literature has become richer for her unique portrayals. As an example, she, inter alia, writes that the parents of PVC Bana Singh were very religious and taught their children to be honest and of noble character, and that his two brothers became *'ragis'*, singers of Guru Granth Sahib. These may appear to be small details and many other writers may have skipped them, but they are vital in creating the picture of Bana, in the reader's mind, as a person as well as a Param Vir Chakra Vijeta who, through sheer grit and perseverance, removed the intrusion by the adversary perched on the 21,000-foot peak of Siachen Glacier. The author has covered the lives of these seven PVCs in just such wonderful, convincing, and inspiring detail that I have not found in many other books of the same genre. After reading these true stories, there can be no doubt left that our real heroes are our soldiers. Shyam Kumari has fulfilled a vital service that will help in moulding today's children in tomorrow's ideal citizens and brave warriors. I am sure that her readers, young and old alike, will be inspired by these true, loving and daring deeds of our War Heroes, and will be filled to overflowing with the same love for the Motherland.

Farewell to a Martyr

Speak not, speed not
O traveller! Softly pass
On this flower-strewn road,
For here in repose,
On his way to an eternal abode,
Lies the body of a young martyr,
Ready for the funeral pyre.
Thick is the jasmine odour,
Red the flame
Of burning camphor,
Plaintive the notes
Of the bard's sad lyre
As he sings the tale
Of heroic valour
Of this son of India
Who traversed a way
Most arduous.
In a grief-warp,
The frail mother is caught

From a pain so sharp,—

O how can solace be sought?

From her stunned heart

Escapes no sigh,

As she clings to him

Who was her life.

Whose eyes were

Two lamps of light.

The mother devastated,

A monument of sorrow

Pleads with death,

Alas, in vain,

To let her borrow

Just one moment

Of her son's brief life,

O, let him speak

Some loving last words

To his broken mother,

His shattered father,

His bereft sister,

His stunned brothers.

Ah, this sweet boy

She suckled,

Farewell to a Martyr

A toddler, in her arms who nestled,

With loving care, whom she nurtured:

Her brave son, so intensely loved.

Wife stunned, her heart riven torn as under.

Hopes dead, future bleak,

Day her enemy, night a torture.

Child forlorn, orphaned, bewildered.

For the journey's last leg

On the gun-carriage

His body draped in a flag

They reverently lay.

How cruel this march

How cruel this way

Their feet traverse

As their arms they reverse

The bugles' plaintive notes

To the heavens form an arch.

The father tries to hold back

His spilling tears

Proud of his son

As he sets alight the pyre.

In state after state

In cities and villages

Across the land of India
Thousands keep vigil,
As burn radiant with valour's
Eternal light
The mortal remains
Of India's martyrs.
Proud is Mother India
Of its worthy sons,
Of them she will not
Forget one.
Vain is not their sacrifice,
Vain is not the snuffing
Of their precious lives.
Their great deeds
Will steel and light
Our hearts and minds
Calling us to play our parts
As well, to die willingly
In India's defence,
To win at whatever cost
Mother India's battles.

Preface

For a nation to preserve its Independence and protect itself against foreign domination, it is imperative that it awakens the spirit of bravery and establishes the ideal of the Kshatriya in the hearts of its citizens.

At a particular epoch of Indian history, due to the influence of the Buddhist doctrine of the unreality of life and the theory of Mayavad or Illusionism, India lost her strength. Indians forgot the ideals of bravery as embodied by her ancient heroes, Lord Ram, Lord Krishna, Arjuna and Bhima, to name only a few. Due to an excessive stress on the life beyond, the Life-Instinct in the Indians dwindled. The number of warriors and soldiers decreased, while those of Sannyasins and mendicants increased. It is said that at one time in Bihar alone there were nine lakh monasteries.

Belief in the unreality of life caused India to lose her grip on the outer world. As a result, foreign invaders and barbarians marched into India and looted and crushed the country repeatedly. Lakhs of Indians were butchered and millions were forcibly converted to the religion of the invaders. The matchless bravery of India seemed lost. For centuries India remained a slave nation, exploited by different conquerors. Indians lost the right to walk with their heads held high; worse still, the nation lost its self-confidence and self-respect.

After centuries of torpor, the spirit of nationalism awoke in the 19th century. The real battle for freedom of the country began in 1857 with the sacrifice of Queen Lakshmi Bai of Jhansi. Thousands of freedom fighters and countless soldiers died in the battle of liberation or languished in British jails for decades. They bore the terrible atrocities of the Cellular Jail in the Andamans and fearlessly faced the batons, bayonets and bullets of the British police and the British

Army. Many were killed or exiled. As a result of the sacrifice of these martyrs the great day of 15th August 1947 dawned, the chains of slavery were severed, India regained her freedom and once again we could hold our heads high.

Unfortunately, we seemed to forget the story of the subjection of our country. On the one hand, for decades the political arena became a dark field where the lowest universal forces became active. On the other hand, forgetting the shameful centuries of slavery, forgetting the sacrifice of those who gave their lives so that the country might gain freedom, we became enamoured of wealth and comfort. Our young men receive very high, almost undreamed of, salaries from multinational corporations while, sadly, the Indian Army is short of thousands of officers. Though with the advent of Shri Narendra Modi India has taken a patriotic orientation. The sacred slogans of "Bharatmata Ki Jai" and "Vande Mataram" are being chanted by millions of Indians again.

Today India is surrounded by hostile neighbours. China and Pakistan seem to have become our eternal enemies. From Tibet, scores of China's nuclear missiles are targeted towards India. In the present circumstances, no weak nation can hope to remain safe. Powerful nations can crush any weak nation. If India becomes weak, she can be dominated and conquered by other powers.

To safeguard her Independence, India needs to keep the flame of nationalism and bravery burning brightly in the hearts of her children. To kindle the flame of self-sacrifice, it is necessary to imprint in the hearts of the youth the stories of our revolutionary heroes who suffered terrible atrocities and even climbed the gallows with a smile and the cry "Bharatmata Ki Jai" on their lips. Also, we should tell them the stories of our brave soldiers and officers who have sacrificed their lives in the defence of the country after Independence.

We have to imprint in the hearts of each child, teenager and youth of the nation the sacred life stories of our martyrs. If this is done, the spirit of the Kshatriya will reawaken in the children of India. They will become burning flames of nationalism. They will compete to be the first to sacrifice his life for the country. Then, no nation, however powerful, will dare to invade India. An independent India, a great India, will establish the rule of Truth in the world, and will fulfil the prophecy of Sri Aurobindo by becoming the guru of the world.

The Divine Mother of Sri Aurobindo Ashram had always supported the Indian Army. Once she had said, ". . . Army is the only hope for India."

Lord Wavell had predicated the survival of India as one entity on the preservation of the Indian Army as an effective and irreproachable instrument.

Below I quote from a prayer written by Sri Aurobindo, which I hope will become the constant prayer of numerous children of Mother India:

"Mother Durga! India lies low in selfishness and fearfulness and littleness. Make us great, make our efforts great, our hearts vast, make us true to our resolve. May we no longer desire the small, void of energy, given to laziness, stricken with fear."

With humble Pranams to Sri Aurobindo and the Mother.

Shyam Kumari

Sri Aurobindo Ashram, Pondicherry

Major Som Nath Sharma

"I shall not withdraw an inch but will fight to the last man and the last round."

When the Kargil war began in May 1999 in Kashmir, the booming guns, the loud explosions of bombs, the whistling bullets and the flying shrapnel were all reminiscent of the 1947-48 War. In fact, war has been going on almost continuously in Kashmir since 1947 – sometimes as a pitched battle, but more often as clandestine skirmishes.

Among the first martyrs to lay down their lives in defence of Kashmir was Major Som Nath Sharma, whose story is recorded in golden letters in Indian military history. The nation showed its gratitude for his exceptional bravery by posthumously honouring him with its first Param Vir Chakra (PVC).

Som Nath was born into a household steeped in devotion and heroism. His mother, Lila Devi Vasudeva, a woman of deep faith, and his father, A. N. Sharma, an officer in the Medical Corps of the British Indian Army, rejoiced at the birth of their handsome, healthy and cheerful son in Kangra on 31 January 1923.

Very few people know that Maj. Som Nath's connection with Kashmir was deep-rooted. His maternal grandfather, Pandit Daulat Ram Vasudeva, had been the Accountant General to the Maharaja of Kashmir. Som spent many happy days in his childhood with his grandfather in Srinagar, the city that he would later help defend with his life. He lived there whenever his father was posted in far-flung places where he could not take his family. While his father was posted in Waziristan among ferocious tribesmen, for instance, Som stayed in Srinagar, learning the Bhagavad Gita from his adoring grandfather, whom he respected no less than a guru.

Som Nath's early education was at Hampton Court School, Mussoorie, and Sherwood College in Nainital. His father was keen that he should join the ICS, but Som had made up his mind: he would follow in his father's footsteps and join the army. As a boy of ten, Som met the District Commander of Lucknow, Maj. Gen. Bruce Hey, and made an application to enter the Prince of Wales Royal Military College at Dehradun. The commander selected him, and Som's training for the army began.

Som was a good gymnast, a lifeguard at the collegiate swimming pool, as well as an ace student. When he passed out with distinction, Principal Scott wrote that Som was his most honest cadet, whom he was "always delighted to meet".

A born leader, Som would take charge of his close-knit family whenever he came home on vacations; his siblings and cousins instinctively accepted his authority. Well-built and handsome, dutiful and always cheerful, he was a favourite with all ages. When disputes or arguments arose in the family, he always took his mother's side, insisting that his brothers, sisters and even his father show her the same regard. One evening, his younger brothers wanted to watch a film at the cinema hall, but their mother was not in favour of it, as it was already quite dark. When one of his brothers tried to argue, Som told him, "If Ma doesn't agree, there must be a reason. We won't go." Every evening before dinner, their mother would do *puja* and *kirtan* (prayers and devotional singing), and Som would take part in it with great enthusiasm.

After completing his studies at the Prince of Wales Royal Military College, Som joined the Indian Military Academy (IMA) in Dehradun. Barely 19 when he was commissioned into the 19th Hyderabad Regiment on 22 February 1942, Som was soon sent off to active service in World War II, when he was just 20 years old.

Before leaving for Burma, Som went home on leave to recuperate from an illness. It was then that he heard of an Indian Army officer, Prem Bhagat, winning the Victoria Cross, the highest British military award for valour. Turning at once to his mother, Som said, "I too will win the Victoria Cross one day." She voiced her concern about such bravado. "Don't worry, Ma," Som reassured her. "The bullet meant for me has my name inscribed on it. I'm not afraid."

Cheerful by nature, Som always smiled, no matter how serious the situation. So popular was he with his subordinates that they affectionately called him 'Somi Sahib'. He was inspiring, honest and kind; strict yet fair, and himself a living model of the discipline and courage he expected from them. No wonder, the Kumaoni, Garhwali and Gorkha soldiers under him were ready to sacrifice their lives for him. His Kumaon regiment, which took part in the Burma war, was under the command of Lt. Col. Thimayya, who later became the Chief of Army Staff of the Indian Army. During the Burma war, a Japanese bomb landed in the trench where Som held position. By sheer luck, the bomb did not explode, and he made a miraculous escape.

At Arakan on the India-Burma border, Som and his men fought a fierce battle in the jungles. When his orderly, Bahadur, was seriously wounded, Som hefted him onto his shoulders and began walking, often lagging behind the rest of the detachment because of the weight. His commanding officer (CO), Lt. Col. Thimayya, called out to him: "Take that man off your shoulders, lay him down on the ground, and move back quickly to the camp."

"Sir, my orderly is badly wounded. He is losing blood and cannot walk," came Som's staunch reply. "How can I leave him like this?" Som carried Bahadur all the way to the camp on his shoulders and saved his life.

At the end of World War II, two battalions, 8/19 and 4/19 Hyderabad Regiment were combined into one, the 4 Kumaon Battalion. Som's uncle, Capt. Krishan Dutt Vasudeva, had belonged to that regiment. He had laid down his life while defending a bridge in Malaya in World War II, thus saving the lives of numerous comrades who could cross over the bridge to safety. Because of his deep emotional connection with this unit, Som had chosen to stay in the 4 Kumaon.

The 1947 Conflict

In 1947, India entered a new era, breaking millennial chains of slavery and bondage. A whole Himalaya of despondency had been lifted from the breast of our motherland. For most Indians, it was a time of jubilation and celebration.

But freedom did not bring unmitigated joy. The internecine quarrels between groups of Indians and the Machiavellian plotting by the British led to *Bharatmata* being sawn in two. Lakhs of Hindu and Sikh families had to leave their homes and properties in West Pakistan and migrate to India; communal riots broke out and soon went out of control. This hour of great joy also became one of darkest despair, of a plunge into fathomless abysses of indescribable horrors, of the destruction of decency and compassion. Man, the human, lost the battle to man the animal. Centuries of progress were belied; humanity was pushed under by a resurgence of the brute hidden in men's hearts.

Islamic radicalism came to the fore at the time of the Partition of India and threatens the world even today. It is tragic that its seeds were sown in that golden dawn of India's independence.

India's first Param Vir Chakra recipient, Major Somnath Sharma

Millions danced on the streets and waved tricolours in free India of August 1947. Processions marched on flower-strewn streets, strangers embraced each other, and people offered sweets to all and sundry. From the Himalayas to Kanyakumari, full-throated cries of *'Vande Mataram'* and *'Bharatmata Ki Jai'* pierced the air, chanted by countless elated Indians.

But the euphoria of tricolour-decked India contrasted with the gory horror of trains from Pakistan which daily arrived full of corpses of men, women and children of all ages, murdered mercilessly. There were two realities in India then, in stark contrast to each other: millions dancing versus millions butchered; lovers embracing in joy versus lovers sundered with bayonets; the exhilaration of *lasya* versus the demonic destructiveness of *tandava*. What Charles Dickens wrote of the French Revolution was equally true of India in 1947: "It was the best of times and it was the worst of times."

Brief History of Kashmir's Accession To India

Pratap Singh, the Maharaja of Kashmir, died in 1925, and his nephew, 30-year-old Prince Hari Singh, educated at Mayo College, Ajmer, ascended the throne. Maharaja Hari Singh dreamt of an independent Kashmir that would be the Switzerland of India. He took many steps to better the lives of his subjects, such as making primary education compulsory, giving preference to state residents for appointments in government services, and initiating the 'Agriculturalists' Relief Resolution' to free the farmers of the state from the clutches of unscrupulous moneylenders.

Yet there was manifest discontent in the mainly Muslim population of the Kashmir Valley. In addition to the usual reasons of poverty, high taxes and lack of employment opportunities, there were also doubts about the loyalty of their Hindu king, a controversy thought to be instigated by the British. There were demonstrations against the Maharaja's government; in one such incident on 13 July 1931, nearly 5000 Muslims staged a violent protest in front of a court building. To disperse the crowd, the police opened fire and 21 demonstrators were killed. The Muslims retaliated by attacking a good many Hindu citizens. Thus, were sown the seeds of a Hindu-Muslim rift in the Kashmir valley.

In 1932, after the Kashmir Muslim Conference, a political party of the same name was formed, with Sheikh Abdullah as its first president. In June 1938, the Working Committee of the Muslim Conference opened its doors to all citizens of Kashmir, irrespective of religion, caste or creed, thus giving it a national character in place of a Muslim one. In 1939, the Muslim Conference was renamed the National Conference. This popular Kashmir party was going to play an important role during the Partition of India in 1947.

The National Conference supported the 'Quit India' movement in 1942 and raised, in 1944, the demand for a democratic government in Kashmir. The Maharaja conceded some of the public demands and inducted two popular ministers into his cabinet. In 1946, the National Conference launched the 'Quit Kashmir' movement, but Maharaja Hari Singh used force to suppress it. At this stage, Jawaharlal Nehru tried to go to Srinagar to support Sheikh Abdullah and the National Conference, but the Maharaja had him detained at Uri and then expelled from Kashmir. Some of the party leaders were imprisoned as well, including Sheikh Abdullah.

On 17 June 1947, the British Government passed the Indian Independence Act. But the prickly issue of the future of the 562 princely states, which were not ruled directly by the British, had to be resolved. The Government of India Act of 1935 and the Indian Independence Act of 1947 allowed the princely states to join either India or Pakistan through an Instrument of Accession executed by the ruler. A Pandora's Box had burst open.

In the interim period from 17 June to 15 August 1947, the ruler of a princely state could enter into a Standstill Agreement with either or both of the independent dominions of India and Pakistan. The leaders of Pakistan felt that Kashmir, with its majority of Muslims, should join them. Also, unlike Hyderabad and Junagarh, whose rulers wanted to join Pakistan but had no common borders with it, Kashmir had common borders with both India and Pakistan. Maharaja Hari Singh, who still dreamt of an independent Kashmir, acceded to neither India nor Pakistan, and sent telegrams to both, on 12 August 1947, for Standstill Agreements.

In early October, Sheikh Mohammad Abdullah, the leader of the National Conference, appealed to both India and Pakistan to give some more time to Kashmir to make up its mind and decide its future.

The Government of India accepted and honoured Kashmir's Standstill Agreement, but Pakistan had no compunctions in violating it and enforcing an economic blockade on Kashmir. In 1947, Kashmir consisted of two distinct regions: to the north of the Himalayan range lay Kashmir's three northern districts, Ladakh, Baltistan and Gilgit, and to the south, the Kashmir Valley and Jammu. Pakistan was now preventing vehicles carrying food, clothing, petrol, ammunition and other daily necessities from entering the state via Kohala (located on Kashmir's north-western border with Pakistan and linked by road to Srinagar) or via Sialkot (entry point on Kashmir's south-western border with Pakistan and linked by road to Jammu city). The object of this blockade was to force the Maharaja to merge Kashmir with Pakistan.

"These actions soured relations between Maharaja Hari Singh and Prime Minister Liaquat Ali Khan of Pakistan. The Maharaja made veiled threats that he would ask for assistance elsewhere if the needs of his state were not met. India, meanwhile, was grappling with the problems of Partition and was waiting for the state of Jammu and Kashmir to make up its mind in accordance with the Standstill Agreement. Pakistan, however, appeared in no mood to wait for the due process of law to take its normal course and organised an invasion to take matters out of the Maharaja's hands. Pakistan collected hordes of tribesmen from North-West Frontier, ex-soldiers, deserters from the Army, supposedly on leave – all under regular officers of the Pakistan Army. . . ." (Maj. Gen. Ian Cardozo, *Param Vir: Our Heroes in Battle*, 23)

In the meantime, instigated by Pakistan, a revolt had broken out in Poonch against the Maharaja. On 29 September 1947, Sheikh Abdullah, who had been in jail since 20 May 1946, was released, to help maintain communal harmony. The Maharaja, suspecting the loyalty of his Prime Minister, Ram Chander Kak, who was married to an Englishwoman and openly supporting Kashmir's accession to Pakistan, dismissed him and appointed Justice Mehr Chand Mahajan as Prime Minister on 15 October 1947.

Events moved at lightning speed thenceforth. Once Mahajan became Kashmir's Prime Minister, Maj. Shah, a secretary in the Pakistan government and a personal messenger from Jinnah, called upon him. Shah had been in Srinagar from the first week of October to negotiate the terms of accession to Pakistan. Shah urged Mahajan at length to advise the Maharaja to accede to Pakistan. Mahajan agreed to consider the matter on merits, with an open mind, provided the blockade was lifted. As Shah found this a reasonable request, he consulted Jinnah telegraphically and met Mahajan again that afternoon. Jinnah replied that lifting the blockade was not possible till accession was decided, and asked Mahajan to come discuss it in Lahore. Mahajan declined this coercive proposition. Shah turned aggressive, warning of the serious consequences if Kashmir refused to accede immediately. Mahajan replied, "A matter of this kind would throw the State into the lap of India." (Lt. Gen. [Retd.] Dr. M. L. Chibber, PVSM, AVSM, *Pakistan's Criminal Folly in Kashmir*, 64-66) But the invasion was no mere threat; the tribal *lashkars* were, on 15 October, already moving into their launching pad.

Meanwhile, in a Joint Defence Council meeting, both Mountbatten and Supreme Commander Auchinleck made their position clear: if Pakistan declared war on India, no other member of the Commonwealth would come to its help.

The terrible Hindu-Muslim riots of the period, and the consequent bloodbath, so shocked Som's grandfather, who truly believed in the freedom of all religions, that he died of heartbreak. Som's maternal uncle, Hari Dutt Vasudeva, came to Srinagar on 18 October in a military aircraft for the last rites. During the funeral ceremony, a renowned Muslim, their good family friend, warned Hari that suspicious activities were taking place on the banks of the Kishan Ganga River in Muzaffarabad. Hari must return without delay, he advised, as the Kashmir valley was in great danger. The warning was repeated by Hari's friend as well, Gen. Janak Singh, Kashmir's Inspector General of Police.

Tribal Invasion of Kashmir

On 20 October 1947, before Maharaja Hari Singh could send his representative to India, tribesmen from Pakistan invaded Jammu and Kashmir from different directions. K. H. Khurshid, personal secretary to Jinnah, called this invasion "a criminal folly which sealed the fate of Kashmir." The Maharaja's hand was forced – he had to accede to India to save Srinagar and the rest of Kashmir from the orgy of rape and loot that the tribesmen meted out to Baramulla (*Memoirs of Jinnah*, 23).

Jinnah, it appears, was informed of the tribal invasion only a few days before it was to be launched. He was invited to come up to Abbottabad to prepare for a 'triumphant entry' into Srinagar. Unaware of the impending tribal invasion, Jinnah had already sent his secretary, Khurshid, to Srinagar to facilitate the Maharaja's accession to Pakistan, which, to Jinnah, had seemed likely as both the Maharaja of Kashmir and Prime Minister Ram Chander Kak hated Nehru bitterly. But the rapid pace of events trapped Khurshid in Srinagar during the tribal invasion, and he was repatriated only on 1 January 1949, after the ceasefire.

It took only nine weeks, from 15 August 1947 (when India and Pakistan became independent) to 20 October (when the tribal *lashkars* entered Jammu and Kashmir) for this 'folly' to be prepared and committed. Pakistani scholars who later sifted the truth about the Kashmir problem recognise Khan Abdul Qayum Khan, the Chief Minister of North-West Frontier Province, as the key figure in organising this invasion. Of Kashmiri origin, he obviously had as emotional an attachment to Kashmir as Nehru. Qayum had a readymade set-up in the Frontier Scouts to help in this folly. He was ably assisted by Lt. Col. Iskandar Mirza, who later became the defence secretary of Pakistan and knew how to handle the Pathans. (Chibber, 51-52, 54)

This tribal invasion was code-named 'Operation Gulmarg' by Pakistan. The tribal *lashkars* were offered great incentives: all they could loot, and all the women they could violate. They were supplied with generous supplies of arms, ammunition and rations. They had 300 lorries with sufficient petrol and began their advance on the Muree-Srinagar road. It is now obvious to historians that this large-scale invasion could not have been organised without the full knowledge and tacit support of the British civil and military authorities.

In 1947, Col. Mohammad Akbar Khan was the Director of Weapons and Equipment in the Pakistan Army GH at Rawalpindi. He later revealed: "A few weeks after Partition, I was asked by Mian Iftikharuddin on behalf of Liaquat Ali Khan (Prime Minister of Pakistan) to prepare a plan of action for Kashmir. I found that the Army was holding 4000 rifles for the civil police. If these could be given to the locals, an armed uprising in Kashmir could be organised at suitable places; I wrote a plan on this basis and gave it to Mian Iftikharuddin. I was called to a meeting with Liaquat Ali Khan at Lahore, where the plan was adopted, responsibilities allotted and orders issued. Everything was to be kept secret from the Army. In September, 4000 rifles were issued at various places, the first shots were exchanged with the Maharaja's troops, and the movement gathered weight." (Chibber, 61)

Despite the care the Pakistanis took for secrecy, word of the planned invasion got leaked to India, particularly when transport was organised for the *lashkars* to reach various points on the border of Kashmir. Shiv Saran Das, the Deputy Commissioner at Dera Ismail Khan, the southern district of North-West Frontier Province, learnt of the plan and came on leave to India in late September to inform the government – a well-documented fact. Maj. Onkar Singh Kalkat, a Brigade Major at Bannu, also knew of this plan and warned the Indian Army. However, nothing could be done as J&K was still an independent State at that point. (Chibber, 69)

Brig. L. P. Sen writes about an event of that time in *Slender was the Thread*. A detachment of the 4th Jammu and Kashmir Light Infantry was located at Muzaffarabad. In this unit, half the soldiers were Dogra Hindus, and the other half Muslims of Poonch. Some of the latter had already started joining the Pakistan Army. Lt. Col. Narayan Singh had been in command of this unit for many years; but so confident was he of the loyalty of his troops that he had not accepted the offer to have the Muslim soldiers replaced by Hindus. The price he paid for this trust was a heavy one. On the night of 22 October 1947, the Muslim soldiers took control of the armoury, massacred the commander and his Hindu soldiers, and established contact with the tribesmen and the Pakistan Army soldiers on the far bank of the river. Seeing Muzzaffarabad lying undefended in front of them, the tribesmen attacked the same day and started looting, killing, raping, and setting the town on fire. A few Hindu soldiers, who had escaped the slaughter overnight, called and reported the situation to the authorities in Srinagar.

Muzaffarabad is connected to Srinagar by a pukka road – the invaders could have reached Srinagar in just two hours at a brisk march. The Chief of the J&K State Force, Brig. Rajinder Singh, immediately collected 200 men in Badami Bagh Cantonment and rushed out to stop the advance of the enemy. Well aware that the only way to stop their advance was to blow up the bridges on the way, he took along a large quantity of explosives, went as far as 72 miles from Srinagar and fitted them on the steel girders of the bridge over a seasonal river. He then took up position, awaiting the enemy's arrival.

The invaders reached there on the afternoon of 23 October; at once, a skirmish took place. As the enemy onslaught grew in momentum, Brig. Rajinder Singh ordered the bridge to be blown up and thus saved Srinagar. These Afridi tribesmen from the North-West Frontier Province were in Kashmir solely for loot and plunder, but now the route for their trucks and buses was blocked by the blown-up bridge. Not eager to leave behind their means of ferrying the loot home, the tribesmen scattered in small bands, and Srinagar was saved from their immediate advance. Brig. Rajinder Singh was badly wounded, but ordered his men to leave him and save themselves. Reluctantly, they left him under a small bridge. This brave officer was posthumously awarded India's first Mahavir Chakra. The remaining soldiers stayed on, hiding in the Badami Bagh cantonment and awaiting a new leader.

After the attack on Muzaffarabad, the Pakistanis advanced over the next two days and captured Uri. On 25 October, Baramulla was occupied. The Maharaja fled from Srinagar, acceding Kashmir to India. That evening, Liaquat Ali Khan held a meeting in Lahore to consider the action to be taken in view of the expected Indian intervention in Kashmir.

Col. Mohammad Akbar Khan, who was invited to that meeting, later wrote about the tribal invasion: "The performance of the tribal *lashkars* had been excellent where the ground was suitable for their sniping and hit-and-run tactics. It is not correct to say that they broke their ranks and went for loot just when they were within sight of Srinagar. It was part of their agreement with Major Khurshid Anwar of the Muslim League National Guards that they would loot non-Muslims in Kashmir. They had no other remuneration for this invasion." (Chibber, 61-62)

These three days of 24-26 would prove crucial for India. On 24 October, the Deputy Prime Minister of Kashmir went to New Delhi with a letter of Accession to India from the Maharaja as well as personal letters to Pandit Nehru and Sardar Patel, requesting military help. Mehr Chand, Kashmir's new Prime Minister, also wrote to them, pleading for the rescue of Kashmir from Pakistan's unjustified aggression.

On 25 October, Sheikh Abdullah went to Delhi, and sent his deputies, Bakshi Gulam Mohammed and G. M. Sadiq, to Pakistan to interact with Jinnah and Liaquat Ali, but neither leader consented to meet them. Meanwhile, on the same day, Baramulla was attacked by the tribesmen, indulging in an orgy of terror, loot and rape that delayed their march on Srinagar. The tribesmen were said to be unreliable when faced with adverse conditions because they would often run away from battle and start looting and plundering in just this manner. But the Pakistan Army had overlooked their unreliability and recruited them for the attack, an advantage for India that bought precious time now.

The Maharaja had realised that his dream of an independent Kashmir was irrevocably shattered. He asked for help from India, and Home Minister Sardar Patel promptly sent V. P. Menon to Jammu to meet the Maharaja. Menon reported that the usually bustling Srinagar now had the "stillness of a graveyard." He got the Maharaja to sign the declaration of joining India, and the Indian government accepted Kashmir's accession. (Menon, 16)

Meanwhile, sensing the danger of remaining in Srinagar, V. P. Menon and Mahajan persuaded the Maharaja to go to Jammu; it would be easier to negotiate terms with India from there. Considering the worsening situation, Maharaja Hari Singh and his family left for Jammu via the Banihal Pass on 25 October. "If you do not hear Indian planes tomorrow morning, shoot me in my sleep" is what Maharaja Hari Singh told his ADC, Capt. Diwan Singh, after signing the Instrument of Accession (Capt. Diwan Singh in an interview with Jupinderjit Singh, "Kashmir Accession Recalled," *Gaurav Ghosh*, June 2011: 19). On 26 October, V. P. Menon and Mahajan flew to New Delhi, going straight to Pandit Nehru's house.

Mahajan has given a vivid account of how it was a touch-and-go affair, of how Nehru was at first reluctant to send airborne troops to fight the *lashkars*, but after his initial hesitation, Sheikh Abdullah persuaded him to send the Indian Army to Srinagar. (For further details of this crucial meeting, the interested reader can refer to *Looking Back: An Autobiography* by Mehr Chand Mahajan)

Indian Army To The Rescue

With Kashmir officially becoming a part of the Indian Union, its defence now devolved on India. On 26 October, the government issued orders for the Indian Army to leave for Kashmir. Every moment was precious; orders were that the advance section of the Army should reach Kashmir the very next day.

The enemy was only 62 miles from Srinagar and the distance to Srinagar by road from the nearest point on the erstwhile Indian border was 300 miles, of which two-thirds was mountainous. Moreover, there were no bridges on some of the streams along the way. Therefore, it was decided to fly the troops in. By the evening of 26 October, troops from the 1 Sikh Battalion commanded by Lt. Col. Ranjit Rai were collected in Delhi, the first ones to be flown in.

The aerodrome at Srinagar was old, used only for the Maharaja's personal aircraft so far. There was no cemented runway; no space for big aircraft to land. Despite all this, the defence and safety of the airfield was of prime importance. Lt. Col. Rai was told to collect all available troops and fly to Srinagar to take charge of the airfield defence; more troops would be flown in as they became available.

A few civilian pilots volunteered to fly the smaller Dakota aircraft for the unusual task of ferrying the troops and material, even though there was no firm landing strip, no safety landing devices, and no fire-fighting facilities at the Srinagar airfield. The Dakotas were not even designed to fly that high or carry such weights, yet these pilots risked their lives again and again to carry out such a perilous task.

By divine grace and the help of 1000 totally dedicated volunteers of Rashtriya Swayam Sevak Sangh (RSS) (see Appendix 1) hundreds of sorties, loaded with troops and war material, were flown in on this earthen landing strip over the next few days, without a single untoward result. Clouds of dust billowed up while landing, affecting visibility, but the planes landed safely, time and again. This brilliant performance of the civilian pilots will remain a historic achievement.

Indian Troops landing at Srinagar Airport
Image Source: Ministry of Defence

The first in a continuous line of aircraft landed at the Srinagar airstrip at 9:30 a.m. on 27 October, carrying the first two companies. When these first Dakotas came in to land, the pilots were not quite sure if the airport was still in the hands of the state forces, or had fallen to the invaders during the night. If the airfield had been captured by the invaders, their orders were to fly back and land at Jammu. The Sikhs were then to move by road as far towards Srinagar as possible. However, the tribal invaders had wasted three precious days in loot, rape and arson at Baramulla, and this delay in their reaching Srinagar saved the city just in time. (Chibber, 55-56)

Lt. Col. Ranjit Rai, having collected his entire battalion, decided to move towards Baramulla to stop the enemy. He had moved his unit to just 34 miles from Srinagar, when they came under fire from the enemy's guns. The Pakistanis far outnumbered the Sikh battalion; both Rai and his deputy were killed while evacuating wounded soldiers. The unit moved back to Srinagar without its officers, but they had not sacrificed their lives in vain. Had they not moved towards Baramulla, the enemy would have taken possession of Srinagar before Indian forces had had time to organise a proper defence. But now the enemy were stalled at the outskirts of Srinagar, and there was some hope of saving the city.

The Army authorities in Delhi were not receiving accurate information about the battle in Kashmir, so Brig. Sen and Brig. Thapar flew to Srinagar on 29 October, assessed the ground situation, and returned to Delhi the same evening to brief Pandit Nehru and the Cabinet. Meanwhile, on 30 and 31 October, those courageous civilian pilots kept ferrying the troops and war material to that dusty airstrip, by now a pile of loose earth with constant clouds of dust hovering above.

The Army had its hands full in Delhi too. Communal riots were in full swing across the country. Som's Kumaon Battalion had been given the responsibility of maintaining peace and internal security in Delhi in 1946–47, and his D Company worked on it with zeal and impartiality. At the time of the Pakistani invasion of Kashmir, Som's left hand was in plaster up to the elbow, due to a wrist-injury sustained during a game of hockey. Nonetheless, he did not take even a day's break.

Som's Kumaon Battalion was now ordered to proceed to Srinagar, but he was told he could not accompany them, because of his plaster-encased arm. But how could Som allow himself to miss the great opportunity of fighting for his country? To the brave, the call for sacrifice is like the irresistible call of a sweetheart. No one understood his company better than him, Som stated emphatically to his superiors; his presence was essential.

Som had had few opportunities to be close to his father, who had been posted mostly in remote places such as Egypt, England, Karachi, Deolali, and Lansdowne, to name a few. It was quite a coincidence that when Som's unit was about to leave for Kashmir, his father, Maj. Gen. A. N. Sharma, visited him in Delhi. Som told him that he had volunteered to go to Kashmir and was flying there the next day. His father pointed out that his injured arm rendered him unfit for war.

"For the last five years, I've fought on behalf of the British government," Som replied stoically. "I'm not going to miss the opportunity to fight for my own country now, no matter what it costs me." During the Burma war, he had often talked passionately with his friends about India getting independence one day. His dream had become a reality now, and he had to be a part of it.

In the air manifest, the name recorded as commander of Som's sub-unit was that of a Sikh officer, but Som got it replaced with his own. He was the officer commanding that sub-unit, he argued, and so had the authority to do what he did. It is surprising that Som was permitted to go to battle, because an officer with a handicapped arm may become a dangerous liability not only to himself, but also to the soldiers under him. It was as though the goddess of war was asking for the sacrifice of this brave warrior.

Som met his mother on 31 October, before his flight. "Ma, aren't you proud of me, now that I'm going to fight for my country?" he asked.

She did try to dissuade him from going, because of his broken arm, but once she saw that he was firm in his resolve, she gave it up. Later, she brought something for him to drink in a glass. Suddenly, like a bad omen, it fell from her hands, shattering into pieces.

There was a stunned silence. Som tried to reassure his mother. "Why worry, Ma? It was only a glass." She hugged him, her eyes wet with unshed tears. "Ma, you are a soldier's wife and a soldier's mother," Som said, in a determined voice. "This isn't the first time I'm taking leave of you to go to war. Give me your blessings. You will always be in my heart."

It was a strange quirk of fate that Som was seen off, this time, by so many members of his family. His parents and his elder sister 'Cuckoo' had to leave for Ranchi the very next day, on his father's new posting. Som's closest friend, Maj. Krishna Tewari, had been posted to Delhi some months ago. They had fought together in Burma and Malaya. It was there that Som had suggested that his friend marry his elder sister. (In fact, Maj. Tewari would later marry Som's younger sister.) Before his departure to Kashmir, Som chatted with his old friend all night long, in the officers' mess. Tewari also tried his hand at dissuading Som from going to war with an injured arm, but it was no use.

Before taking leave, Som asked his friend for a personal memento to carry with him. "You can take anything you like," said Tewari. Som chose his friend's German Luger automatic pistol, which had been surrendered to Maj. Tewari by a Japanese officer at the end of the Burma war. Keen that their weapons should not fall into the hands of common soldiers in the victorious army, the Japanese officers had given up their weapons, including their Samurai swords, to the British Army officers.

The pistol had a sentimental value for Maj. Tewari. "Anything but that," he protested.

"You've no use for it in Delhi," countered Som. "I may need it in battle." Little did he know how true his words would prove to be.

The next morning, Som's uncle Hari arrived at the airport to meet his nephew. On reaching Willingdon Airfield (present-day Safdarjung Airport), Hari found Som very busy, despite his injured arm, in supervising the loading of arms and ammunition, mortars and machine guns onto the planes.

Hari, himself familiar with the Badgam area where they were headed, tried his best to dissuade Som from leaving. "Going to Kashmir with so few soldiers is like inviting defeat or death. Your arm is in a cast, as well. If you lead your soldiers in this condition, Som, you will put their lives in danger too. You can end up being court-martialled!"

"Only if I return, Uncle," Som laughed. "You know how devious the enemy is. My battle will last till the last man and the last round."

It is worth noting that a number of Som's relatives had a connection with the Army. His younger maternal uncle had lost his life in World War II in Malaya. His father, Maj. Gen. Amar Nath Sharma, would retire as the Director-General of the Armed Medical Services; Som's younger brother, Surindar Nath Sharma, would later rise to become a Lt. Gen. and the Engineer-in-chief; the youngest brother, Vishwa Nath Sharma, would retire as the Chief of Army Staff, 1988-90; and

Som's younger sister, Maj. Kamla Tewari, later became an Army Doctor.

Family Members of Som Nath Sharma

Som was himself a World War II veteran, but in this case, going to war with an arm in a cast was not mere bravado – it was a call to death. This was why his relatives were so intent on dissuading him from leaving for Kashmir.

Maj. Gen. S. K. Sinha, then a Major, who had helped in organizing the airlift of troops in those fateful days of October, recalled: "On 26 October, Lt. Gen. Sir Dudley Russel deputed me to arrange for an airlift of troops to Srinagar. Snow was expected within 15 days, which would ensure the airfield and roads would be closed to all further traffic. In those days there was no Banihal tunnel, and the 9,000-foot Banihal pass would be blocked by snow. The road journey normally took four days. There were only 15 days to lift a complete brigade of Indian troops to Kashmir with four months of stock for winter. On the first day only six Dakotas were available. But on the second day, all the Dakotas of all the private airlines were roped in. These had mostly European pilots. In 15 days, 800 sorties of Dakotas were flown from Safdarjung airport to Srinagar, without a single mishap.

Lord Mountbatten wrote of this effort, 'In my long experience of war, I have not come across such a massive airlift organised at such short notice and so successfully.'" ("Kashmir '47: How the day was won", *The Asian Age* [online edition], 2 November 2011)

Som Nath reached Srinagar on the morning of 31 October with about 80 men. On the same day, Brig. L.P. Sen was appointed in place of wounded Brigade Commander Katoch. Brig. Sen instructed Som to stay at headquarters and prepare a plan for defending the airfield and its surroundings in a 5-mile radius.

Maj. Gen. S. K. Sinha continued: "On 3 November, I was having a mug of tea with my friend Maj. Som Nath Sharma, sitting on a kitbag at Srinagar airfield. I had known Som in Delhi when he was with his battalion at Anand Parbat. He had met with an accident in Delhi and had his hand in plaster. Therefore, he and his company had been held back for local protection of the airfield. But he wanted a more active assignment." ("Kashmir '47: How the day was won")

Som was not keen on sending his men out for patrolling and action without accompanying them himself. The Indian Army was taking all possible precautions to protect the airfield, but they had too few men for this task. All the troops who had arrived earlier were by then busy facing thousands of tribesmen on the outskirts of Srinagar. The gravity of the situation was obvious. It was fortunate that the tribesmen had been distracted by the looting en route; else, they would have taken control of the Srinagar airfield by then.

The main thrust of the tribal invasion having been blunted by the fight with the 1 Sikh Battalion, the enemy was now trying guerrilla tactics to infiltrate Srinagar. Two companies of 4 Kumaon, along with one from another battalion, were ordered to hunt out and destroy the raiders.

Final Battle

At eight in the morning on 3 November, with about 80 soldiers under his command, Maj. Som Nath Sharma established a post three miles to the west of the airfield, on high ground above Badgam village and a forest. It was a burial ground, with white and blue crocuses in bloom. From this point, one could see the bottom of the valley, and beyond that, on the slope of the opposite mountain, the road to Gulmarg.

"Everything is quiet here," Som reported to Brig. Sen over the radio. "The villagers are going about their usual work."

Two of the three companies sent out to reconnoitre the Badgam area returned to the airfield without any confrontation with the enemy. As there seemed to be no enemy troops in the area, Maj. Som Nath was directed to pull back gradually after 2 p.m. with the remaining company. At the appointed time, Maj. Som reported to the brigade commander, confirming that he would follow the order to return.

It is not clear what impulse or information Brig. Sen was acting on, but he directed Maj. Som Nath to stay for one more hour. Som acknowledged the order. "I will start thinning out my troops at 3 p.m." Neither Brig. Sen nor Maj. Som had any real idea of what was to happen in the next hour, but it would later seem that divine grace had intervened to delay Som's company there and save the airfield.

At 2:35 p.m., Som reported to Brig. Sen that they were being shelled lightly from the direction of the village. "I am not returning fire, sir. There are many innocent women and children in the village," he explained. Even as he spoke, he observed some people coming towards his position, wearing long Kashmiri robes covering them from neck to feet.

When Maj. Som Nath challenged them, they replied that they were labourers working in the forest. Som was not convinced: their eyes and other facial features were unlike those of local Kashmiris. He sent some of his men to search them. Just then, the strangers pulled out weapons from under their robes – and the situation changed immediately.

A pitched battle began and the whole area was echoing with the bursts of mortar shells and the constant staccato of bullets. At 2:40 p.m., a force of more than 500 tribesmen advanced from the west, bringing the 4 Kumaon under heavy fire from small arms, mortars and heavy automatics. It was obvious that this force had come to capture the airfield and cut off the only link between Kashmir and the rest of India.

Som's company was soon surrounded by the enemy on three sides, and sustained heavy casualties from their artillery bombardment. Som realized the importance of holding this position – Srinagar, especially the airfield, would become vulnerable if this crucial position was lost. Though they were under heavy fire, and outnumbered seven to one, the undaunted Maj. Som urged his company to fight bravely, often exposing himself to danger as he ran across the open ground from post to post.

The legend of the twelfth-century Rajput king Prithviraj Chauhan claims that each officer of his army could single-handedly kill hundreds. As Prithviraj was returning from Kannauj with Princess Sanjukta, his army was chased by Jaichand's much bigger force. But Prithviraj's incomparable knights fought off the hordes of enemy soldiers, sacrificing their own lives to buy their king's safe return to Delhi.

A similar feat of unimaginable courage was demonstrated in Badgam by Maj. Som Nath and his matchless soldiers. Appreciating the seriousness of the situation, Som kept encouraging his beleaguered company as they fought against the heavy odds. Reporting to Brig. Sen on the radio, he requested more men, arms, ammunition, and air support. Additional help was not, however, immediately available. On being told so, Som assured his commander that he would not withdraw from his position and would continue to fight till the last man and the last bullet.

In spite of heavy shelling and bullets flying all over, Som ran around spreading out cloth markers for the air support to use when it would arrive. When the numbers of his men thinned to the point of affecting the company's firing power, Maj. Som, in spite of his fractured arm, began filling the magazines of the Light Machine Guns (LMGs) himself. Standing next to a LMG, he reported to the brigade commander that the enemy was then less than fifty steps away, his troops were heavily outnumbered, and they were under heavy fire, but they would not withdraw an inch.

In the middle of this conversation, a mortar shell landed on some ammunition close to him. Major Som Nath was killed on the spot by the resulting explosion.

Brig. Sen had ordered two fighter aircraft to give fire support. Som's men were so keen to avenge their beloved 'Somi Sahib' that they managed to keep at bay, for more than five hours, an enemy force ten times stronger, killing a large number of them. The men of 4 Kumaon demonstrated exceptional bravery and kept fighting even when they had run out of ammunition. About forty men followed the example of their brave leader, sacrificing their lives rather than giving an inch. Som's orderly, Bahadur, whose life Som had saved a few years ago in the Burmese jungles, was among those killed. Ultimately, the company was forced to fall back. In the meantime, Brig. Sen had sent a party from 1 Punjab to help them.

That was a critical night for the Indian Army. If the enemy had attacked Srinagar then, it could not have been defended. But it seemed that Goddess Durga herself was saving Srinagar. The enemy did not try to take the city during the night.

On 4 November, Home Minister Sardar Patel and Defence Minister Baldev Singh reached Srinagar and, considering the seriousness of the situation, promised to send additional reinforcements and weapons. The Army engineers had been building bridges over streams en route, and reinforcements started arriving in Kashmir in large numbers by road.

News of Maj. Som Nath's sacrifice spread like wildfire in the Kumaon Regiment. His soldiers wanted to bring back the body of their 'Somi Sahib' from the battle area so that he could be given a fitting funeral. In Delhi, his dear friend Maj. Tewari was given the delicate task of conveying the news to Som Nath's family. Maj. Tewari somehow controlled his own emotions and did so.

Som's sister and mother witnessed a strange incident at exactly the same time. Som's father had been transferred to Ranchi, but he was away in Calcutta on duty. Som's mother and sister, who had just moved to Ranchi to join Som's father, were sitting in the verandah of their new bungalow, waiting for the big truck that was bringing their luggage.

As the truck approached the house, a cow and newborn calf suddenly came in front of it. The driver swerved to avoid hitting them but collided with the gate instead. The cow was saved, but the calf was run over. The cow began to moan – a heart-rending cry that strongly affected Som's mother. "Cuckoo, my heart is sinking," she said to her daughter. "I fear something terrible has happened to my Som." Just then, they received the shattering news of his death.

After completing this tragic duty, Maj. Tewari sought the permission of his director, Brig. Akehurst, to journey to Kashmir and arrange for the recovery of Som's body. Brig. Akehurst was reluctant to grant his permission, but did so out of fondness for Tewari.

On the morning of 5 November, Tewari reached Srinagar and met Maj. Padamsingh, the officiating commander of the Kumaon Battalion. He also met the remaining soldiers of Som's company, who had returned to Srinagar after running out of ammunition. Many had been in the Burma War with Tewari, whom they had always regarded as Som's brother. They broke down when rebuked for coming back without Som's body. Despite the grim situation in Badgam, they volunteered to accompany Tewari and to help bring back the body of Maj. Som.

When Maj. Tewari sought Brig. Sen's permission, however, Sen flatly refused – Badgam was still under the control of the invading tribesmen. Maj. Tewari insisted, but Brig. Sen did not budge. Instead, he threatened to have Tewari placed under arrest and sent back to Delhi if he disobeyed his order. Maj. Tewari returned to Delhi that evening with a heavy heart.

Maj. Som Nath's body was recovered only on 7 November. It had been mutilated beyond recognition. All the bodies of the Indian soldiers killed at Badgam were found without their clothes. The tribesmen had mercilessly looted the clothes and the footwear of those killed, over and above their weapons. Some parts of Som's body were covered with pages stuck onto his body with thorns – pages torn from the copy of the Bhagavad Gita he had always carried in his pocket. These, and the empty holster of Tewari's German Luger, were the only means of identifying Som's body.

Half of that brave company had also given their lives, but not in vain – Indian troops found 200 bodies of enemy tribesmen who had been killed in the Battle of Badgam. And Kashmir had been saved.

The Kumaon troops gave a befitting farewell to Maj. Som Nath during a cremation on the spot. All had tears in their eyes, despite being in uniform. The Government of India awarded Major Som Nath posthumously with Independent India's highest medal for wartime gallantry – India's very first Param Vir Chakra – collected by Maj. Gen. Amar Nath Sharma on behalf of his brave son.

Citation

Major Somnath Sharma (Posthumous)

4 Kumaon (IC-521)

On 3 November 1947, Major Somnath Sharma's company was ordered on a fighting patrol to Badgam in the Kashmir Valley. He reached his objective at first light on 3 November and took up a position south of Badgam at 1100 hours. The enemy, estimated at about 500, attacked his company's position from three sides; the company began to sustain heavy casualties.

Fully realising the gravity of the situation and the direct threat that would result to both the aerodrome and Srinagar if the enemy attack was not held until reinforcements could be rushed to close the gap leading to Srinagar via Hum Hom, Major Sharma urged his company to fight the enemy tenaciously. With extreme bravery, he kept rushing across the open ground to his sections, exposing himself to heavy and accurate fire, to urge them to hold on.

Keeping his nerve, he skillfully directed the fire of his sections into the ever-advancing enemy. He repeatedly exposed himself to the full fury of enemy fire and laid out cloth strips to guide our aircraft onto their targets, in full view of the enemy.

Realising that casualties had affected the effectiveness of his light automatics, this officer, whose left hand was in plaster, personally commenced filling magazines and issuing them to the light machine gunners. A mortar shell landed right in the middle of the ammunition resulting in an explosion that killed him.

Major Sharma's company held on to its position and the remnants withdrew only when almost completely surrounded. His inspiring example resulted in the enemy being delayed for six hours, thus gaining time for our reinforcements to get into position at Hum Hom to stem the tide of enemy advance.

His leadership, gallantry and tenacious defence were such that his men were inspired to fight the enemy, by seven to one, for six hours after this gallant officer had been killed.

He has set an example of courage and qualities seldom equalled in the history of the Indian army. His last message to the Brigade Headquarters a few moments before he was killed was, "The enemy are only 50 yards from us. We are heavily outnumbered. We are under devastating fire. I shall not withdraw an inch but will fight to the last man and the last round."

Gazette of India Notification

No. 2 -- Press/50

Denoument

There can be no sadder example of defeating oneself and sacrificing one's national interests than India's inept handling of the Kashmir issue. It is a frustrating saga of a naive leadership stumbling from blunder to blunder, hoodwinked by its own idealistic view of human nature and politics.

As noted above, Hari Singh was the reigning monarch of the state of Jammu and Kashmir in 1947. He was vacillating between joining

India or Pakistan, when tribal marauders, backed by the Pakistan Army, invaded Kashmir in October 1947. Unable to counter them, Hari Singh appealed to India for assistance and agreed to accede to India. Indian forces blunted the invasion and reconquered vast areas at the huge cost of the lives of countless brave soldiers, but all in vain.

Maj. Gen. Mrinal Suman has succinctly summed up the political blunders that are largely responsible for the 'Kashmir mess':

"First, India erred by not insisting on unequivocal accession of the state to the Dominion of India and granted special status to it through Article 370 of the Constitution.

"Secondly, when on the verge of evicting all invaders and recapturing the complete state, India halted operations on 1 January 1949," and Vijaya Lakshmi Nehru Pandit rushed to appeal to the UN Security Council. "It is the only case in known history wherein a country, when on the threshold of complete victory, has voluntarily forsaken it in the misplaced hope of winning the admiration of the world community." For the humbled Pakistan Army, this step must have seemed an unexpected boon for saving face.

"Thirdly, and most shockingly, the Indian leadership made a highly unconstitutional offer of plebiscite in the UN."

As a result of these blunders, "forty percent area of the state continues to be under Pakistan's control, providing it a strategic land route to China through the Karakoram ranges. As a fallout of the unresolved dispute, India and Pakistan have fought numerous wars and skirmishes with no solution in sight. Worse, the politicians of Kashmir Valley are holding India to ransom by playing the Pak card. The so-called Kashmir issue is a self-created cancerous furuncle that defies all medications and continues to bleed the country" ("Seven blunders that will haunt India for posterity," *Indian Defence Review* [online edition], 17 October 2011).

Sometimes the heart cries out with unbearable anguish – Is it for this that Major Som Nath Sharma and so many other valiants of the Indian Armed Forces gave up their lives?

(L to R) Author Shyam Kumari, Maj.Gen. K. K. Tewari & Maj. Dr. Mrs. Kamala Tewari, brother-in-law & sister of PVC Somnath Sharma unveil the portrait of PVC Somnath Sharma at The Little Angels English School, Pondicherry, the first school to adopt a hero in 2005.

(Maj. Gen. K. K. Tewari launching the the first book of the series, "Our Heroes: Param Vir Chakra Recipients" on PVC Maj. Som Nath Sharma.

O Kashmir!

"However big the hordes
Of Pakistani marauders,
However daunting the odds,
And superior the enemy numbers,
Until I live, until I breathe,
This fair valley
They will have to leave.
O Mother Durga,
Grant me an iron will
Armoured with Thy blessings
Let me become invincible.
Bullets may shatter,
Bayonets may cleave,
But not for a moment,
Death I fear or for this
Ephemeral life grieve.
For my mighty nation
I'l fight to the last breath
And die with elation,
To this holy task
Is my total dedication.
My nation's future is the prize,
That my India may arise,
For this I wager my life
Today, willingly I will die

So that India may survive.
Victory to India' –
Cries my heart, my voice.
Oh, what a sublime choice.
For this battle glorious,
The blood in my veins
Courses with fervour.
Oh! to die for India,
I ask only this favour.
We will not flinch,
We will not retreat
With a fiery welcome
The enemy we will greet.
We will pound them
And roundly beat.
The Himalayas will be
A witness of our feat.
Not an inch of our land,
Will we cede,
To fight to the last man,
To the last bullet,
Is my creed.
If Gods take me
To their abode,
For a soldier's end
Is there a better mode?
A welcome in heaven

Awaits warriors,
A place near Gods
For country's martyrs."

Thus thought Somnath
As filled with a holy wrath
He fought fiercely
The foes of India.
A sudden explosion
Ripped him apart
And thus on the battle-field
Died this braveheart.

-Shyam Kumari
6th October 2006

Lieutenant Colonel Ardeshir Burzorji Tarapore

"The country always comes first!"

For Ardeshir Burzorji, who won the first Param Vir Chakra for the Poona Horse Regiment, country and service always took precedence over everything else. Born on 18 August 1923 in Bombay, he had plenty of role models in his own family. Witness their history – eight generations earlier, his ancestor General Ratanjiba had led the armies of the great Maratha leader Shivaji. For his bravery and loyalty, he was rewarded with a *mansab* of a hundred villages, Tarapore being the most important. Ever since, the male descendants of this family have affixed 'Tarapore' behind their name. Ardeshir's grandfather migrated to the Deccan and joined the Excise Department of the Nizam of Hyderabad; Ardeshir's father, Burzorji, a scholar of Persian and Urdu, also joined the same department and later became its Superintendent.

That Ardeshir had courage aplenty was evident even at the tender age of six. Playing in the backyard with his ten-year-old sister Yadgar, he saw the family cow break loose and charge towards her. Yadgar screamed for help, but Ardeshir was already springing to her defence. He picked up a stick and ran ahead of his sister to strike the cow on its nose. The animal veered away and Yadgar was saved.

At seven, Ardeshir was admitted to the Sardar Dastur Boys' School, Poona. Though average in academics, he excelled at athletics, gymnastics, boxing, swimming, tennis and cricket; he matriculated in 1940 as the School Captain.

Post-matriculation, Ardeshir applied for and received a commission in the Hyderabad State Army. After his initial training at the Officers' Training School at Golconda, he was sent to the one in Bangalore. On 1 January 1942, he was commissioned into the 7th Hyderabad Infantry as a Second Lieutenant, but Ardeshir longed to join the armoured regiment of the Hyderabad State Forces, equipped at the time with armoured Scout Cars. The military authorities were somewhat reluctant to sanction his request for this transfer. But then, men such as Ardeshir, destined for greatness, find their own way to blaze a trail on the canvas of time.

Courageous Young Man

Second Lieutenant Ardeshir's battalion was at one time being inspected by the Commander-in-Chief of the State Forces, Maj. Gen. El-Edroos. Ardeshir was carrying out routine training at the grenade-throwing range, when a recruit failed to throw the grenade correctly, and it fell back into the throwing bay. Twenty-year-old Ardeshir jumped into the bay, picked up the grenade and threw it to safety. The grenade burst in midair, its splinters peppering Ardeshir in the chest.

When he had recovered from his injuries, Maj. Gen. El-Edroos summoned him to his office to congratulate him on his presence of mind and bravery. Ardeshir requested the General to post him to the armoured regiment. His request was granted – Ardeshir was transferred to the 1st Hyderabad Imperial Service Lancers.

During the Second World War, the 1st Hyderabad Imperial Service Lancers saw service in the Middle East. The British CO of an Indian Army regiment also posted there had been in the habit of making derogatory remarks about the fighting abilities of Indian soldiers; on one occasion, he insulted the Nizam of Hyderabad. The fiery Ardeshir could not, and did not, allow these remarks to pass uncontested, though he knew he was probably jeopardizing his career. "You have insulted my country and my king – and I do not mean George VI," he retorted. This was deemed by the British commander to be an act of gross insubordination by a 'native' officer. Ardeshir's regiment was isolated and its ammunition withdrawn. Matters escalated to such a crisis that Maj. Gen. El-Edroos had to speak in person with Gen. Montgomery, the Commander-in-Chief of the British Indian Army, in order to resolve it.

Made For Each Other

After Hyderabad State merged with independent India, its armed forces were absorbed into the Indian Army. Ardeshir was posted to the Poona Horse on probation for two years. An armoured regiment founded in the nineteenth century, it is till 1999, the only regiment of the Indian Army to have won two Param Vir Chakras; one by the hero of this story, Ardeshir Tarapore, and the second by young Second Lieutenant Arun Khetarpal in the 1971 War.

Tarapore's first posting was to the B Squadron, but he was not made to feel welcome there, since the Hyderabad State Forces had fought against Poona Horse in 'Operation Polo' only a few months ago. It was Maj. 'Balli' Virk, Commander of A Squadron, who asked that Ardeshir be posted to his own squadron.

Capt. Ardeshir Tarapore truly bloomed in A Squadron. Known to his friends as 'Adi', he soon became an integral part of this squadron consisting mostly of Rajputs. He adopted its new recruits as the young sons of the squadron family, often calling these *sowars 'bacche'* (children); this became such a habit that he would even address elderly soldiers so, which amused everyone.

Impressed by the towering personality of senior non-commissioned officer Bahadur Singh, Adi grew a cavalry moustache like him. When Adi's probation period ended, Commander 'Balli' Virk gave a glowing report, which helped him get a permanent commission in the Poona Horse on 1 April 1951. Adi developed such a close rapport with A Squadron that he was often unofficially called 'Colonel of A Squadron', in later years.

In modern parlance, we might say that Adi and the Poona Horse were made for each other. "Adi was fiercely loyal to the Regiment," writes Adi's friend, Lt. Col. Shivraj Singh. "He could not tolerate even the slightest aspersion being cast on the good name of the Poona Horse. When the Regiment did well in any activity, particularly in sports, Adi would be in ecstasy; if the Regiment did not do as well as expected, Adi would be in a black mood and go round with a scowl on his face for days on end.

"Adi was 'an officer and a gentleman' in the true sense of the term. He was a loyal friend and was very sensitive to the moods and feelings of those around him. I remember an occasion in Jammu when I'd received news of the passing away of a favourite uncle of mine. I was sitting quietly under the mango tree outside our mess, and Adi must have sensed from my looks and mood that I was upset. He walked up to me and said, 'Shivji, what's wrong? Why are you so upset? Tell me. Sharing your troubles with a friend may lighten your heart.' He was so understanding and caring" (Lt. Gen. Hanut Singh, PVSM, MVC (Retd.), *Fakhr-E-Hind*, 219-222).

In The Footsteps of Napoleon

Adi greatly admired Napoleon -- he kept a bust of the French leader on his desk, and often quoted his words. Once, there was a party at the regimental mess. The mess staff had as usual filled a large silver bowl with water, rose petals floating on top. Adi, who had a fine sense of humour that helped him spot the lighter side of any situation, suddenly declared, "I am Napoleon's incarnation!" He struck a pose like his hero and, looking about for a suitable head-dress, seized the silver bowl and overturned it on his bald head, to represent Napoleon's hat. Of course, he became thoroughly drenched, but even that could not dampen his spirit.

Adi would match his hero in courage too. He had a Napoleonic quality of rising to the occasion, of taking unorthodox measures to fulfil the immediate objective. In 1962, when Adi was officiating as the Commandant, his regiment received orders to move to its new location within twenty-four hours. Normally, this would have been impossible to achieve in such a short time span, but Adi found a way: he ordered that the security fencing round the Quarter Guard, the regimental stores and the ammunition dump be broken. Vehicles were driven right up to the stores and loaded, and the tanks taken right up to the ammunition bays for their consignments of ammunition. Working through the night, the regiment was able to move on schedule.

Recognised for his perseverance and hard work in the regiment, Adi was selected in 1956 for an Automotive Course in England to be trained (and to later teach others in his regiment) on the use of the Centurion tanks newly acquired by the Indian Army. This knowledge later contributed to the Indian victory in the 1965 war, when these tanks were ranged against the formidable Pattons of Pakistan.

The Indo-Pak War (1965)

The Indian Army had suffered a considerable setback in 1962 when, ill-prepared and ill-equipped due to political miscalculations and wrong leadership, it had to face a well-prepared Chinese attack in high-altitude, mountainous locations. Emboldened by this contretemps, the President of Pakistan, Field Marshal Ayub Khan, and his Foreign Minister, Zulfiqar Ali Bhutto, made plans to annex Jammu and Kashmir through a military operation code-named 'Operation Gibraltar.' The Pakistanis planned to infiltrate trained and armed insurgents into Kashmir, who would provoke, organise and lead a local uprising, giving Pakistan a pretext for military intervention.

In April-May 1965, Pakistan began a large-scale border incursion into the Rann of Kutch. Pakistani leaders initiated this step, firstly, to test India's response under the leadership of Prime Minister Lal Bahadur Shastri, whom they considered a weak politician. Secondly, they wanted to assess the reactions of the major world powers, before implementing their planned incursion into Jammu and Kashmir. An added bonus was that it gave them the opportunity to test their new armour and equipment, so generously given by the U.S. government. India, with its characteristic restraint, responded only by countering the Pak incursion into the Rann of Kutch. Soon, a ceasefire was negotiated by the British government. Thereupon, Pakistan assumed that, in Kashmir too, India would give only a local response, and so went ahead with 'Operation Gibraltar.'

The Poona Horse had just returned from collective training to its headquarters at Babina in Madhya Pradesh, on 24 April. A party had been organized in the officers' mess to mark the end of a successful training season. At 9 p.m., when celebrations were in full swing, a coded order for operational deployment was received. That the Poona Horse was able to mobilize within the next few hours was in itself a marvel – by 4 a.m. on 25 April, within seven hours of receiving the orders, the regiment, with its huge tanks, armoured personnel carriers, trucks, ammunition, supplies and a hundred other tools of war, had been loaded on a train, ready to move to the front. And by that night, the Poona Horse had reached Upper Bari Doab canal near Jandiala Guru in Punjab, where it was deployed with other regiments of 1 Armoured Division. Pakistan was expected to launch an attack any day on this part of the border as well, and the battle-preparedness of the Indian Army was at its peak. But weeks and months passed, and there was no sign of battle here. The monsoon arrived, and Poona Horse was moved to barracks in nearby Kapurthala.

Indian leaders had accepted the Kutch ceasefire agreement in good faith, the central intelligence agencies and the military intelligence having no inkling of Pakistan's intentions. Around 30,000 Pakistani insurgents crossed the LOC from 2 to 5 August 1965, dressed as Kashmiri locals headed for various areas within Kashmir. The surprise element helped them capture the Thana Mandi area in Poonch Sector of Kashmir and the Kalidhar area of Jammu. Pakistan had planned to provoke local uprisings through these invaders but, as they closed in on Srinagar and Gulmarg, the locals, remembering the atrocities of 1947 committed by similar Pakistani *razakars*, alerted the Indian Army instead.

Indian military authorities decided to attack the bases and the supply routes of the invaders. Indian Army troops captured pickets in Kargil Sector posing a danger to the Srinagar-Leh highway, reclaimed the Pir Sahiba feature in Tithwal Sector, and advanced up Kishanganga River, blocking the possibility of infiltration from that route. By the end of August, Hazi Pir Pass was also captured.

All this time, Pakistan had kept up its pretence that the attack was not engineered by its regular forces but by 'freedom fighters' from Pakistan-occupied Kashmir. Surprised and discouraged by the reverses in Kashmir, and seeking to ease the pressure on their forces there, the Pakistanis now decided to stage a full-fledged military attack in Chhamb and Akhnur in 'Operation Grand Slam'. On 1 September 1965, they began an incessant artillery bombardment on Indian troops holding the Chhamb area and moved forward along the Manawar Tawi river (Lt. Gen. (Retd.) V. K. Singh, PVSM, "Winds of War – The 1962 & 1965 Conflict", *The Indian Army: A Brief History*, edited by Maj. Gen. Ian Cardozo, 113-114).

Supported by an armoured brigade and heavy artillery, the Pakistanis captured Chhamb and Jaurian, their offensive being finally stopped only six kilometres from Akhnur. Pakistani aircraft also attacked Indian military installations at Amritsar.

After nearly five months of waiting, the Poona Horse finally received news of the expected war on 3 September. The regiment had been out on a tactical exercise when the commandant, Lt. Col. Ardeshir, was summoned to Brigade Headquarters. The rest of the officers were asked to return to lines, where they received orders for the tanks and other vehicles to be made ready for battle along the Kapurthala-Kartarpur road.

"This is it," was Adi's curt comment to his officers, in a conference held after his return from Brigade Headquarters at 1:35 p.m. He gave orders for the move and deployment of the regiment in the general area of Madhopur. Loading of tanks onto the rake was to commence at the Kartarpur railway station siding by 4 p.m.; the officers had barely enough time to bid goodbye to their families.

The speed with which the regiment moved was astounding. The advance party, under the command of Maj. K. Girdhar Singh, left at 4:30 p.m. on 3 September, while the tank train of B Squadron under Maj. Narinjan Cheema moved from Kartarpur by 5:15 p.m. At each station, the local people gave the troops a rousing reception and presented them with food and flowers. The train's departure had been delayed by two hours, because the engine attached to it could not haul the rakes with such heavy loads; a more powerful engine had to be summoned, and in the meantime, a ramp to unload tanks had to be improvised. But such was the efficiency and speed with which these problems were resolved that the first train reached Madhopur at 4:30 a.m. on 4 September, where it was received by Maj. K. Girdhar Singh. By 5 September, the entire Poona Horse Regiment was concentrated in this area.

On 5 September 1965, the regiment moved to its forward concentration area on the road to Bajpur-Ramgarh, four miles north of the International Border. Everyone was alert, as there was a constant threat of hit-and-run strikes by Pakistani infiltrators. The regiment completed its deployment and dispersal before dawn. On 6 September, Pakistani aircraft carried out an attack. Both 6 and 7 September were devoted to reconnaissance, planning and preparation.

On the afternoon of 7 September, as the Commandant of Poona Horse, Lt. Col. Ardeshir Tarapore gave his orders for the regiment to secure the Tharoh crossroads by last light on 8 September.

The regiment's command structure was as follows:

- Commandant: Lt. Col. Ardeshir Tarapore (Adi)
- Second-in-Command: Maj. K. Girdhar Singh
- Headquarters Squadron under Maj. Sarab Ahluwalia
- A Squadron under Maj. D. V. Ghorpade
- B Squadron under Maj. Narinjan Cheema
- C Squadron under Capt. Ajai Singh
- Adjutant: Capt. Surinder Singh
- Quarter Master: Capt. Jasbir Singh

It is important to understand that a tank regiment functions as an integrated whole. The commandant is in charge of and responsible for all the squadrons of his regiment and their actions. And in battle, the different squadrons and branches work like extensions of his hands. On their collective effort depends the victory and glory of each battle.

Adi decided that the advance was to be with A Squadron under Maj. D. V. Ghorpade on the left, B Squadron under Maj. Narinjan Cheema on the right, and C Squadron held in reserve.

Lt. Col. Ardeshir seemed to have had a premonition about his end, though he was as always only too willing to die fighting for his country. Once he had given orders to his officers and determined the task of each squadron, Adi called Maj. Narinjan Cheema aside. Adi was always meticulous in planning everything to the last detail, be it in battle, in life or in death; now he instructed Narinjan about his last wishes: should he fall in battle, he was to be cremated, and his only son Xerxes, if he so desired, should be allowed to join the Army and get commissioned into the Poona Horse. He asked that his prayer book and ring be given to his wife, Perin, his watch to his son, and his favourite pen to his daughter, Zarin.

"Nothing will happen to you," Maj. Narinjan protested. "Please don't think about such things!"

"Narinjan, it is better to plan these things – one never knows," was Adi's serious reply. He would repeat these instructions after the capture of Phillora.

The Battle: 8–23 September 1965

Pakistan had deployed one infantry division for the defence of the Sialkot sector. Their new 6 Armoured Brigade was located at Gujranwala-Wazirabad; it had four armoured regiments, three of which were equipped with Patton tanks and one with Shermans. One armoured regiment of this division, 25 Cavalry, with two squadrons of Pattons and one squadron of tank destroyers, was deployed in support of the infantry division which initially opposed India's 1 Armoured Division. Indian intelligence agencies, however, were unaware that Pakistan had raised another armoured division.

On 8 September, the offensive by the Poona Horse Regiment commenced when Maj. Narinjan Cheema's tank fired a shot at the Pakistani post of Kadral. The heavy fighting on the left flank prompted Adi to let B squadron lead the charge. The regiment moved up to Rangre without any opposition but, once there, was heavily attacked by Pakistani aircraft. Luckily, no damage was done to the tanks, but the administrative wing of the regiment, which was stationed at Ramgarh, suffered considerable damage.

A rather ironical situation developed here. As Poona Horse marched into Pakistani territory, villagers streamed out of their houses and moved through the advancing columns of Indian troops. Some of them, who had taken shelter near Maj. Narinjan's tank, were cursing the air-force planes for attacking the tanks. These simple people had mistaken the Indian tanks for Pakistani tanks and the attacking Pakistani planes to be the Indian Air Force. In the highest chivalrous tradition of the Indian Army, the civilians were treated with kindness and were left unmolested.

Poona Horse fought its first battle in this war at a location south-west of Rangre. A platoon of Pakistan's Baluch infantry was seen huddling round a wall. Maj. Narinjan Cheema stopped his tank, laid his gun onto the wall and asked their *havildar* to surrender. The Pakistani refused; Indian troops had to shoot the detachment, even though they admired the enemy's courage.

Second Lieutenant Man Singh and Second Lieutenant Dhaliwal were now in the lead with their tanks. The Pakistani aircraft came roaring overhead again, supported by their artillery. For the second time, the enemy strafed Narinjan's tank, but their pilots were not shooting accurately. Their inefficiency bolstered the confidence of the Indian regiment.

After the attack on Maj. Narinjan's tank, Indian troops resumed their advance. Man Singh and Dhaliwal saw two troops of Pakistani Patton tanks about 1200 yards away and engaged them. Dhaliwal's tank was hit and went up in flames, but luckily the crew was able to bail out. B Squadron shot and burned two enemy tanks; the rest of the enemy retreated. At 5:15 p.m., the Pakistani aircraft attacked once more. Again, they picked out Maj. Narinjan's tank as target. However, despite their three repeated attempts, his tank was not destroyed.

That night, the regiment camped at the Sabzpir crossroads. Second-in-command Girdhar Singh gave orders that they were to make camp as they liked. But Adi, a perfectionist in such matters, was not pleased with the shoddy harbour layout of the regiment, when he arrived at 9:30 p.m. Poona Horse lined up and went into a perfect circular harbour in the next two hours, even amidst heavy enemy shelling.

A mistaken assessment of the events of 8 September by higher authorities meant that the Indian advance was halted for 48 hours. This gave the Pakistan Army time to regroup its forces; it moved 6 Armoured Division to this area.

Pakistan had 9 armoured regiments in this area to oppose India's 1 Armoured Division. India had only five regiments. Since they had a nine-to-five advantage of numbers over India, Poona Horse was asked to attack from the rear. It was planned that while other Indian forces would hold the enemy frontally, 1 Armoured Division was to outflank and strike from the rear. Poona Horse would thus fight in the Sialkot Sector against vastly superior numbers of Pakistani armour.

At 4 a.m. on 11 September, Adi gave his orders. The regiment was to advance from Rurki Khurd via Chak Ali to Libbe. The frontage of the advance passage was very narrow; Adi, therefore, decided to advance one up, with C Squadron leading, followed by the Regimental Headquarters, B, and A squadrons. The advance commenced at 6 a.m. The regiment met with no opposition until about 8:10 a.m. when they faced some enemy armour at a range of 800 yards. C Squadron destroyed five Patton tanks of the enemy, but three of its own Centurions were damaged due to enemy fire. Libbe was taken and the infantry was asked to clear the area.

Maj. Verinder Singh took a bold decision: having secured Libbe, he decided to capture Phillora as well, with 5/9 Gorkha Rifles. On their way, his squadron came upon a cluster of enemy tanks. In the ensuing fight, five enemy tanks were destroyed, and two were abandoned by enemy crews. C Squadron occupied the high ground, dominating Phillora from the north-east. On the slope, only 400 yards away, were seven Patton tanks. C Squadron destroyed two enemy tanks, while the others retreated towards Chawinda. Meanwhile, 5/9 Gorkha Rifles, under covering fire provided by C Squadron, proceeded to clear Phillora.

"If we must die, we'll die together!"

Even as Phillora was secured by C Squadron, Pakistani armour mounted a counter-attack on B Squadron, supported by two troops deployed in an orchard. B Squadron changed direction to take on the counter-attack, and A Squadron fought the enemy armour in the orchard. Adi destroyed two Patton tanks in this encounter. Five tanks of B Squadron were hit, but the crews bailed out to safety. A and B Squadrons destroyed six Patton tanks in all. Adi sustained an injury to his arm through a shell splinter, and Capt. Gurdial requested him to move back from the line of fire.

There, amidst the acrid smell of burning tanks and the hellish din of bursting shells, came Adi's famous reply. "Gordy, I will not leave you. If we must die, we'll die together!" When Capt. Gurdial insisted, Adi snapped, "Young man, don't tell me what to do."

Unable to withstand the fierce attack, the Pakistani Pattons began to withdraw. One of their intercepted radio transmissions instructed, *"Dushman ki taraf badho!"* ("Advance towards the enemy!")

"Nahin, wahan se kafi kargar fire aa raha hai aur hamara kafi nuksan ho chuka hai," answered the shaken tank commander. *"Ham ab Sialkot ja rahe hain."* ("No, there is very effective fire coming from that side and we have suffered considerable damage. We are now going to Sialkot.")

Maj. Sarab Ahluwalia of the HQ Squadron did admirable work, night after night, in replenishing the crucial supplies of petrol, oil, ammunition and food for the regiment. He had no clear details about the regiment's exact location and had to move by guesswork through enemy-held territory, yet he somehow managed to reach them unfailingly every night, braving danger and death each time. Without his unerring instinct and matchless courage, the regiment would have been stranded. The courage and devotion of the civilian truck drivers was also remarkable. Their presence in the forward area, where death could come at any moment, boosted the morale of the Indian troops.

At about midnight on 11–12 September, Pakistan launched a counter-attack on Phillora. Maj. Verinder and Capt. Ajai rushed to the spot. The enemy was engaged in hand-to-hand combat with Indian infantry. Verinder and Ajai halted their tanks 200 yards behind the infantry positions and started firing at the enemy over the heads of their own soldiers. As soon as the enemy came to know of the presence of Indian Centurions, they retreated. In the battles of Libbe and Phillora, at least fifty Pakistani tanks were destroyed while India lost only nine. The myth of the superiority of the Patton tanks was nullified, to the triumph of the Indian Centurions.

While C Squadron was at Phillora, a Pakistani helicopter landed south of Kalewali. Naib Risaldar Harbhajan Singh and Sowar Harbans Singh destroyed it with accurate sharp-shooting. The rotor blades of this helicopter are on display in the Regimental Quarter Guard.

At about 5 p.m. on 13 September, Adi called his 'O Group' to give orders for the following day. As he was doing so, the enemy attacked from south-west of Libbe, so his officers rushed back to their tanks. The Pakistani tanks halted about 1200 meters away and began firing. So deadly and accurate were the Indian shots that the enemy soon withdrew, leaving behind four burning Pattons. Pakistani commanders later wrote accounts of these operations, calling them 'kabaddi' – just as in that game, the opponents here entered each other's territory by turns and withdrew after doing some damage.

Seeing the restricted space in the terrain, Adi decided to move his squadrons one by one. The regiment commenced their advance at noon. C Squadron assaulted the Pakistani positions and killed thirty five men and destroyed three tanks. In just that day, the regiment annihilated eight enemy tanks without losing any of its own. Adi was injured in the fierce battle, but refused to be evacuated and got his wound bandaged using the first-aid box in his tank. Such was the confidence, courage and composure of his troops that, at night, while heavy shelling was going on, the soldiers of C Squadron gathered together for Ardas prayers in the open. One of them, brave Risaldar Kartar Singh, died while trying to save the crew of a burning tank.

In a clever move, Pakistan posted two Patton regiments to cover the gap between Badiana and Chawinda, thus turning it into a killing ground. Three Patton regiments were ready to take on two Indian Centurion regiments, in a bid to decimate their tanks.

On the Brigade Commander's orders, Adi asked B Squadron to advance and capture Jassoran. Maj. Narinjan destroyed three tanks, and Jassoran was taken. India's Gorkha troops came under heavy shelling. C Squadron, which had only seven tanks, destroyed three Patton tanks and, helped by their covering fire, 8 Garhwal Rifles, under their brave leader, Maj. Abdul Rafi Khan, conquered Butur Dograndi by 10:30 a.m. on 15 September.

Adi communicated with headquarters and with his colleagues on the battlefield via the field phone, but so cleverly that the Pakistanis were later forced to acknowledge the strength of his superior tactics: "Even when we managed to intercept his conversation, we could not understand its meaning."

Lt. Col. Shiv Raj Singh said, in later years, "After Poona Horse had captured Phillora, my brigade commander told me that Colonel Tarapore, the CO of my Regiment, was wounded and that I should arrange to evacuate him. Our brigade's Advanced Dressing Station was the forward-most medical unit in the sector. So I went around looking for the Regimental HQ of Poona Horse, amidst the chaos that prevailed in the battle area. Moving in my jeep in the general direction of the sound of the battle, I suddenly came across another jeep coming from an opposite direction on the same track. And who should I find in that jeep but Colonel Tarapore, his arm in a triangular sling taken from his tank's first-aid box, accompanied only by his driver and operator. As soon as he saw me, he stopped his jeep and in his usual jovial way said, 'Hello, Shivji! How are you? Where are you off to?' I was so happy and relieved to see him looking so fine. I told him I had come to evacuate him. 'What? For this scratch? Don't be stupid. I am not leaving the regiment and all the fun because of this minor thing.' And off he went to see the battle raging in another part of the sector where his regiment was fighting.

"That was the last I saw of good old Adi Tarapore. Next morning I heard he was killed in action." (Singh, 222)

When Pakistan lost its three heavily defended forward localities of Wazirwali, Jassoran and Butur Dograndi, its troops in Chawinda lost courage. They commenced evacuation of Chawinda. Aware of these developments, Capt. Ajai requested reinforcements to attack the retreating Pakistani troops. Commandant Adi asked permission from the brigade headquarters for moving A Squadron to reinforce Capt. Ajai, as there was no time to lose. On receiving permission from the brigade HQ, Capt. Gurdial moved the squadron forward with all possible speed.

"Hello 25, let us go and join them!"

In the best tradition of armoured regiments, the commandant leads from the front. When Capt. Gurdial reached the location of the Regimental Headquarters, the valiant Adi, ever ready for battle, sent a transmission to his Adjutant, words that have become famous in Poona Horse: "Hello 25, let us go and join them!" After all, Adi's motto had always been: "What my men do, I do. I must lead by example."

Courageous tank commanders prefer to move with their tank's cupola open; in spite of vision devices, it is very difficult, when the cupola is closed, to maintain orientation and ensure that the regiment is moving in the correct direction. However, although it is easier to locate and close in on targets with the cupola open, it is extremely dangerous when air attacks and artillery shelling are in progress.

Commandant Adi sported with danger and courted death, setting an example for his regiment, by moving forward with his tank cupola open, even though mortars and heavy shells were exploding all around. Following in their commandant's valiant steps, the whole regiment roared forward in their Centurions with open cupolas.

At 3 p.m. on 16 September, Commandant Adi, Capt. Surinder and Capt. Gurdial reached the spot where Capt. Ajai was heroically attacking the retreating enemy. The Regimental Headquarters, with Commandant Adi, Capt. Surinder, and the A and C Squadrons, were now right in the middle of the Pakistani killing ground. The whole area was exploding with tank fire, anti-tank missiles, mortars and heavy shells. The acrid fumes of cordite were stifling, making it difficult to breathe. Lying all over the field were tanks in various states – overturned, exploded, smoking, jammed, or turned turtle and lying on their sides, like huge prehistoric beasts.

The Pakistani shelling was so severe that two tanks of C Squadron were hit. Completely unconcerned about the rain of fire and the hellish din around him, Commandant Adi came out of his tank to check the infantry positions on the ground. It was at this time that his command tank 'Kooshab' was hit, injuring his intelligence officer Amarjit Bal, his gunner and his operator. It was not wise, Commandant Adi decided, to hold Butur Dograndi with the support of only a platoon of infantry, so he withdrew to Jassoran. 'Kooshab' could not be started; Commandant Adi moved to Capt. Surinder Singh's tank, when he discovered that Amarjit Bal was missing. Right in the midst of the fierce shelling, he ran back and carried Amarjit on his shoulders to Surinder's tank. He gave the wounded man a morphine injection and instructed the medical officer to carry Amarjit out of the battle zone.

"I didn't know that it was the last time I would see him," Amarjit later said.

The withdrawal to Jassoran was complete by 4:45 p.m., and 8 Garhwal Rifles had regrouped there to await orders. It was decided to recapture Butur Dograndi with A Squadron and 8 Garhwal Rifles. By that night, Capt. Gurdial Singh would report success.

For ten days, Adi had fought like a man inspired, pushing himself to be present wherever and whenever his regiment needed him on the battlefield. There were so many such instances that it seemed he was everywhere.

Adi's Premonition Comes True

Commandant Adi was upbeat and elated. He had seen his beloved regiment winning one battle after another. The second attack on Butur Dograndi was progressing well, and favourable reports were coming in. Such are the moments of glory for which a soldier lives and dies. In that moment of victory, Commandant Adi came out of his tank to get some fresh air and tea. Just as tea was being passed around, an enemy medium artillery shell landed on the off side of the tank. Adi died instantaneously.

Commandant Adi's death was kept secret for fear that the troops might be disheartened at the news. His body was kept at Jassoran; the constant and intense shelling made it impossible to cremate him immediately as per his last wishes. At 9 a.m. on 17 September, Risaldar Pyarelal of B Squadron was busy checking whether there was enough wood for cremation, when an enemy shell landed near the cremation site, injuring him critically. It was as if Pyarelal wished to follow his beloved commandant to heaven.

At 9:30 a.m., Adi was cremated at Jassoran. His ashes were taken to Poona and later immersed in the Sangam on 29 November 1965. Risaldar Pyarelal died on 19 September. "My brother went to heaven with his officer to serve him," said Pyarelal's brother later, when visiting Adi's wife.

Commandant Lt. Col. A. B. Tarapore had personally led his regiment into the fiercest fighting during the battle of Phillora. With his regiment, he broke repeatedly through the defences held by superior forces of armour and infantry. Despite being wounded and having his arm in a sling, he commanded his regiment fearlessly through ferocious battles. So did the first recipient of the Param Vir Chakra, Maj. Somnath Sharma, in 1947. And just like Maj. Sharma, he was posthumously awarded the Param Vir Chakra by a grateful nation, for his intrepid bravery.

"In the battle of Chawinda, Tarapore twice led the tanks of the regiment right in the middle of the enemy's killing ground, defying the enemy's violent efforts to prevent the outflanking of Chawinda. For his inspiring leadership, gallantry and determination, he was posthumously awarded the Param Vir Chakra, the country's highest award for valour." (Singh, 215)

The confidence of the Pakistan Army was shaken by the immeasurable bravery and tenacity of the Poona Horse. They conferred the title of *'Fakhr-e-Hind'* on this celebrated regiment. And it is the heroic officers of Poona Horse, especially the incomparable Lt. Col. Ardeshir Burzorji Tarapore, who most compelled the admiration of the enemy.

The 1965 war is memorable because of the glorious deeds of our armoured forces in defeating the better-armed Pakistanis. The odds in numbers were nine to five in favour of Pakistan. Yet, in Libbe, Phillora, Wazirwali, Jassoran and Butur Dograndi, Poona Horse and other units of the Indian Army achieved a resounding success. The battlefields became graveyards for Pakistani Patton tanks. About a hundred Pakistani tanks were destroyed or captured. Altaf Gauhar, Secretary of the Ministry of Information and Broadcasting of Pakistan, wrote in his foreword to Air Marshal M. Ashgar Khan's book *The First Round*: "Few people outside the armed forces realize how close Pakistan came to disaster in the 1965 war...." (Singh, 217)

Referring to the two recipients of the Param Vir Chakra in the 1965 war, Lt. Col. A.B. Tarapore and Company Quartermaster Abdul Hamid, Maj. Gen. Ian Cardozo writes, "It is the leadership and the courage of brave men such as these that sometimes change the course of history and the destiny of nations." (108)

Citation

Lieutenant Colonel A. B. Tarapore

Poona Horse (17 Horse) (IC 5565)

On 11 September 1965, the Poona Horse Regiment under the command of Lieutenant Colonel Ardeshir Burzorji Tarapore was assigned the task of delivering the main armoured thrust for capturing Phillora in the Sialkot Sector in Pakistan. As a preliminary to making a surprise attack on Phillora from the rear, the regiment was thrusting between Phillora and Chawinda when it was suddenly counter-attacked by the enemy's heavy armour from Wazirwali. Lieutenant Colonel A. B. Tarapore, who was then at the head of his regiment, defied the enemy's charge, held his ground and gallantly attacked Phillora with one of his squadrons supported by an infantry battalion. Though under continuous enemy tank and artillery fire, Lieutenant Colonel Tarapore remained unperturbed throughout this action, and when wounded refused to be evacuated.

On 14 September 1965, though still wounded, he again led his regiment to capture Wazirwali. Such was his grit and determination that, unmindful of his injury, he again gallantly led his regiment and captured Jassoran and Butur-Dograndi on 16 September. His own tank was hit several times, but despite the odds, he maintained his pivots in both these places and thereby allowed the supporting infantry to attack Chawinda from the rear.

Inspired by his leadership, the regiment fiercely attacked the enemy's heavy armour, destroying approximately 60 enemy tanks at the cost of only 9 tank casualties, and when Lieutenant Colonel A. B. Tarapore was mortally wounded, the regiment continued to defy the enemy.

The valour displayed by Lieutenant Colonel A. B. Tarapore in this heroic action which lasted six days was in keeping with the highest traditions of the Indian Army.

— Gazette of India Notification

No. 112–Press/65

The Ceasefire

On 20 September, our forces heard the rumour that the United Nations was negotiating a ceasefire. They were ordered to remain at battle stations for the night of 20-21 September. On 21 September, the Poona Horse was moved to Ingan for rest and refit. On the evening of 22 September, news arrived that a ceasefire would become effective from 3:30 a.m. on 23 September 1965. That night, Pakistani forces tried their best to regain their prestige and to recover as much of their lost territory as possible. Their shelling reached enormous proportions. But our 2nd Lancers, 4 Horse, 16 Cavalry and 62 Cavalry beat them back, inflicting heavy casualties. The last shell exploded at 3:32 a.m. and then there was silence.

The Hero and His Regiment

About the great regiment of the Poona Horse, Lt. Gen. K. K. Singh, Maha Vir Chakra (MVC), wrote, "Twice I have been privileged to go to war with the Poona Horse; as a soldier, I could not have been in a braver company; as a commander, I could not have expected more from the unit considering the huge odds against it." (Singh, 189) A compliment paid to a regiment by one of its own officers might be deemed biased, but even our adversaries, the Pakistanis, admired this regiment to the extent that they bestowed it with the title of *Fakhr-E-Hind*, 'The Pride of India'.

Its most inspiring leader, Lt. Col. Ardeshir Burzorji Tarapore, stayed true, until the end of his life, to his motto: "The country always comes first!"

Homage To Martyr Ardeshir

O great God of War!
Who watchest us from thy heaven afar.
Lord, are not these exploding shells thy laughter?
This devastation and · death, thy joy, 0 Master?

O great God of War!
Who reignest over us from thy heaven afar.
Today, I'll become a crimson pearl of oblation
Of victory and martyrdom a luminous ovation.
While still my heart beats and I have breath,
Into the Pak killing fields, into the arms of Death,
With cupola open, my tank I will ride,
Wooing victory, the shining and desirable bride.
My heart is aflame with battle's passion,
As tank after Patton tank I blast,
And Death's dark shadow on the enemy cast.
O God of Death, dark and red,
Accept my offering of a thousand enemy dead
Thy fiery embrace is the coveted reward of a martyr,
The pinnacle of glory for a soldier.

On India our enemies cast their 'eyes,

They took recourse to subterfuges and lies.

Glorious death may be my comrade and friend,

But these marauders to Hades I will send,

They who attacked my sacred Mother Land.

In the midst of bursting mortar shells,

My heart with the joy of battle swells.

I will not rest nor retreat

Their ranks I will pulverise and beat.

This is the moment, awaited by the brave,

This the raging battle that still I crave,

I will advance, cupola open, head held high,

Here I will proudly wager my life,

For thee to claim victory, O Mother India;

Thy child Ardeshir of Poona Horse will gladly die.

Indians grieve not for him, who is the nation's pride,

On a chariot of glory, with Death, his bride

Ardeshir, our ·hero, chose to ride.

— *Shyam Kumari*

Second Lieutenant Arun Khetarpal

"No tank will pull back even an inch!"

Second Lieutenant Arun Khetarpal was one of those rare people who never know fear. His mother, Maheshwari, who herself hails from a distinguished Tandon family of Hardoi in Uttar Pradesh, gave a glimpse into this aspect of her son's character, in an interview with Satya Prakash and Raka Agrawal in June 2005: "Arun grew up in a military ambience, in an atmosphere of freedom and fearlessness. We never stopped him from doing anything. We never instilled any fear in him by saying, 'Don't do this, don't do that, otherwise you will get hurt.' And I always encouraged him to be brave: 'Trust in God always. Never be a coward.' I often told him, 'Look at your father. He has fought so many battles, and he's such a high-ranking officer today.'"

Doubtless, it was words and thoughts like these that moulded Arun Khetarpal into the heroic soldier he became, willingly wagering his life on the battlefield to protect his country. The very name chosen for this youngster born in Pune on 14 October 1950 seems to have been prophetic of his fame, *Arun* being a synonym for 'sun' in Sanskrit and Hindi.

Arun had ample military role models in his own family. His family's roots were in the district of Sargodha of undivided India (in the present-day Punjab Province of Pakistan). His great-great-grandfather, a proud soldier of the Sikh Army, had fought in 1848 against the British Army at Chillianwala, and Arun's grandfather fought in World War I (1917–1919), before joining the Punjab Civil Service. After Partition, the family migrated to India. Arun's father, Brig. Madan Lal Khetarpal, AVSM, would serve in the Corps of Engineers till his retirement.

Arun with his Parents and younger brother

Arun's preparation for army life began early. Eight-year-old Arun would often play with the soldiers posted at his residence, listening with awe to their battle-tales. He shared an excellent rapport with them, even taking his meals at their *langar* (collective kitchen) sometimes. He later retained much the same friendly attitude towards his colleagues and subordinates, when he became an army officer.

There were early signs, not just of Arun's ability to relate to soldiers, but also of his strong instinct for duty and protectiveness. Having to study wherever his father was posted, Arun soon developed this caring instinct, especially towards his younger brother, Mukesh.

Arun's mother remembered an incident from when they were both students of St. Columbus School, Delhi. "One day after school, Arun and Mukesh were waiting for the car that would bring them home. When it failed to arrive, eight-year-old Arun shouldered Mukesh's bag, took him by the hand and walked 2½ miles to reach home, passing through the crowded streets of Delhi. We were surprised at his courage.

"On another occasion, when they were studying in Shillong, the school closed early on a particular day and Mukesh returned home with the servant. Arun did not know this; he kept searching for his brother for the next two hours, fearing that Mukesh may have been abducted by the rural Khasi tribesmen for a human sacrifice, a practice prevalent among those tribesmen at the time."

Arun always showed great respect for his elders. "When his grandfather came on a visit, Arun attended to him with love and respect," Maheshwari continues. "His grandfather would tell him heart-breaking stories of the Partition. When Arun received his first salary, he sent some money out of it to his grandfather with the words, '*Dadaji*, accept my humble offering.'

"Arun was a keen observer; he was courageous as well as friendly," his mother remembered. "He once saw his uncle's motorcycle. He did not even know how to turn on its headlight, but he actually taught himself to ride the bike that same day!"

In 1962, Arun joined the reputed Lawrence School of Sanawar as a boarder and studied there for the next five years, completing his Senior Cambridge. Mukherji, his house master, soon began entrusting the academically weaker students of 'Nilgiri House' to Arun for extra coaching.

Arun came home for the vacations after his matriculation examination. The family attended a party, and several people there asked the tall, strapping young man, "Are you an army officer? In which regiment are you?" Arun laughed. "No, I am just a student."

From childhood, Arun had but one aim – to do something great for the country. When his father, Brig. Madan Lal Khetarpal, received an AVSM from the President of India in 1969, nineteen-year-old Arun declared, "I will win a higher medal."

In school, Arun excelled in studies as well as games and other extra-curricular activities. He was in the school cricket team and played the clarinet in the band. In June 1967, he joined the National Defence Academy at Khadakvasla, Pune, and soon became a Squadron Cadet Captain there. He also proved himself adept at swimming, athletics, riding and golf. In June 1970, he moved to the Indian Military Academy (IMA), Dehradun, and was appointed a Senior Under Officer of Singharh Company. On 13 June 1971, he was commissioned from the IMA, after which he joined the Poona Horse Regiment.

Arun Khetrapal at NDA during training

Standing six feet two inches tall, Arun was a striking young man: strong, good-looking and capable. He threw himself wholeheartedly into whatever he did, and pushed himself to excel in every assignment he was given. Young officers in his regiment were customarily made to work their way up from below; they started as drivers, gunners, wireless operators, and then, having mastered these tasks, were promoted to the post of crew commander, finally rising to become a troop leader.

Arun took great pains over the cleanliness, upkeep and battle-worthiness of his tank. His friend Col. Brijendra Singh remembered: "What impressed me most about Arun was the urge in him to excel at whatever task he was entrusted with. When he took charge as a driver, he devoted himself totally to looking after the tank entrusted to him. Oblivious of what the other young officers happened to be doing, he would be immersed in maintaining his tank. I often saw him washing and cleaning his tank at the washing point, much after everyone else had broken off for the day. He was very fond of his men and would feel completely at home in their company, whether at work or at play. Off parade, Arun was full of life, with a delightful sense of humour." (Singh, 281)

This intimate knowledge of his tank would stand him in good stead a few months later. On that fateful day, 16 December 1971, when Arun wrote a glorious chapter of courage on the battlefield, he controlled and deployed his tank with such precise co-ordination that it almost seemed a part of his body, twinned with his mind and heart. Arun's comrade Col. Avtar Singh Ahlawat recounted several touching vignettes of his friend through these memories: "[After the mobilisation in October 1971] the training would start early in the morning and finish by lunch time, leaving the rest of the day to us to rehearse what we had been taught during the morning. As the main effort was directed towards improving gunnery, both Colonel Hanut and Major Ajai would come and sit on our tanks and check the firing of each crew. Though the acceptable time limit laid down for firing the three-round APDS technique from the Centurion tank was 60 seconds, and though we were completing the shoot in 40-50 seconds, yet the Commandant was never satisfied, for he wanted us to reduce the time still further. Towards this end, I would see Arun, his crew, and his troop practising on and on till, by sheer hard work, determination and dedication, he and his troop achieved the unbelievable timing of 25-30 seconds. Consequently, whenever the Commandant held a Field Miniature Range competition, which was almost every alternate day, it was a foregone conclusion that Arun's crew would come first."

Col. Ahlawat remembered another incident, which highlights Arun's determination and fearlessness. "Captain V. Malhotra, our squadron second-in-charge [who was affectionately called 'Mallu'], thought up a novel way of getting people to overcome their instinctive fear of getting hurt. He ordered all ranks of the Squadron to jump from the banks of the Ujh River onto its dry, stony bed, a sheer drop of well over 20 feet. The order of jumping was 4, 3, 2, 1, and SHQ troops. So it fell to Arun's lot to jump first, as it has been ingrained into us in the Regiment that the officers always led. The ground below was hard and slightly stony, and Arun sprained his ankle. However, when asked by Mallu if he was OK, he said: 'That was a beautiful feeling, Sir – like flying in the air.' He was limping, yet he went through the same exercise once again. Next morning, though his ankle was tied up in crepe bandages, he repeated the jumps, without flinching." (Singh, 283)

In October 1971, Arun and Brijendra were sent to Ahmednagar to attend the Young Officers' Course (YOC). Three days later, a general mobilisation was ordered and the YOC cancelled; every young officer (YO) was ordered to speedily rejoin his regiment.

Brijendra narrated an incident that exhibits Arun's leadership qualities, especially his presence of mind. As there was no direct train from Ahmednagar to Delhi, the YOs took a passenger train to Manmad and awaited the Punjab Mail there. The thirty officers in uniform waited, full of enthusiasm and ready to wrestle victory from the hands of the enemy; but when the Punjab Mail arrived, there was no place for them on it. Arun took up the responsibility of getting them on board: he made an impassioned plea to the conductor that it was absolutely necessary for them to reach their regiments soon, but the adamant conductor insisted that there was no place. Arun then led his group into the dining car. The railway staff wanted them to vacate it as it was past catering time. But now that they had a place, both for themselves and for their luggage, Arun refused to budge unless they were provided with a first-class compartment. Ultimately, Arun persuaded the railway staff to accommodate all of them, albeit in different compartments.

"However, before all of us could get into the compartments allotted to us, the train, which had been delayed now for over forty-five minutes, started moving," Col. Brijendra recounted. "Arun, who was helping me with my luggage, was still on the platform. In an attempt to board the moving train, my foot slipped, and I thought I would be crushed between the platform and the train. Just then, Arun, who was right behind me, literally lifted me up and held me there by clinging to the handrails next to the door of the compartment. His presence of mind and quick reaction saved me from a nasty accident as, had it not been for him, I would have been dragged between the platform and the train, with possibly fatal consequences." (Singh, 282)

Punjab Mail reached Delhi early the next morning, where the YOs had to change trains. There was time to spare before the next train was scheduled to leave; Arun informed his friends that he was going out and would be back in an hour.

"Where are you off to?" they enquired.

"Home – to collect my golf set and mess kit," he replied confidently. He was keen, he said, to play golf on the Lahore Golf Course after their victory (that he was so sure of), and his mess kit would be needed for a regimental dinner in Lahore. And so he took a taxi home, vaulted over the garden gate, climbed the verandah steps, and rang the bell.

"When I opened the door, I was surprised to see Arun standing there," Maheshwari Khetarpal told this author on the phone. "We thought he was at Ahmedabad for his YOC and knew nothing about the general mobilisation until Arun told us that he was going to the front."

She bade him farewell with a smile, exhorting him to fight bravely. "Your grandfather, father and uncle hold high positions in the Army and have been decorated with many medals. Do not come back like a coward – fight like the devil."

The year 1971 was a glorious one in the distinguished history of the Poona Horse regiment. In this extremely short war with Pakistan, lasting just 14 days, the tenacious and daredevil tank commanders of the Poona Horse rode their tanks like chariots of fire, virtually destroyed Pakistan's 8th Independent Armoured Brigade, and so badly decimated its elite regiment of the 13 Lancers that it ceased to exist as a fighting force. They were living up to their reputation – in the 1965 Indo-Pak war, PVC-recipient Lt. Col. A. B. Tarapore, also of the Poona Horse, and his troops had shown such exemplary courage, tenacity of purpose and ferocity in fighting that even the Pakistanis were awed and called this regiment *'Fakhr-E-Hind'* ('The Pride of India').

The 1971 Conflict

In 1970, elections took place in both East and West Pakistan. There was an intense power struggle at this time between the prominent political entities of the two parts: General Yahya Khan had replaced Field Marshal Ayub Khan as the president of Pakistan; and in East Pakistan (present-day Bangladesh), the Bengali populace had voted overwhelmingly for the Awami League. In spite of his party being in the majority, Awami League's Sheikh Mujibur Rahman was not given the post of Prime Minister and the West Pakistani leaders had him imprisoned instead.

The Bengalis revolted against this injustice. The Pakistan Army retaliated with brutal violence: three million Bengalis were butchered; ten million refugees fled to India and placed an unbearable burden on its resources. India tried to reason with Pakistan, but to no avail. Indian Prime Minister Indira Gandhi pleaded with world leaders, but America, under President Nixon, sided with the tyrant Yahya Khan. The only alternative for India was war with Pakistan; both sides began preparations.

Pakistan had already deployed three Army corps, two armoured divisions, eight infantry divisions, two artillery brigades and an infantry brigade on the border. To increase their offensive capacity, two additional infantry brigades were raised. Pakistan then armed and regrouped its armies and laid anti-tank minefields in three belts near the border. Both sides had deployed an almost equal number of troops and armour in the western sector.

On 8 October 1971, when the Poona Horse was carrying out its annual field firing at Naraingarh Ranges, it received an order to return to its permanent base in Sangrur. Its commandant, Lt. Col. Hanut Singh, was informed of the possibility of attack by Pakistan in the Gurdaspur-Dinanagar area and of Poona Horse being placed under the command of the CO of 323 Infantry Brigade, for containing this offensive.

A virtually phoney war occurred in October-November. There were numerous alarms and rumours of Pakistani attack, which kept Indian troops on their toes; they passed sleepless nights. By 14 November, the troops were all in their battle positions.

"A strange fact about the planning phase was that every time a specific plan was finalised for a particular area of operations, the enemy's obstacle system would come up there," Lt. Col. Hanut Singh later wrote. "Whether this was a mere coincidence, or whether it was due to a security leak, it was hard to say. For our part, reliable and reasonably accurate information of the Pakistani defensive layout, deployments and plans was received through some of the defecting Bengali officers." (240)

On 3 December 1971, the Pakistan Air Force carried out pre-emptive strikes against our airfields at Srinagar, Jammu, Pathankot, Adampur and Amritsar. Though the war had already commenced on the night of 3–4 December, with Pakistan attacking in Chhamb Sector, General Yahya Khan formally declared war on India only on the afternoon of 4 December 1971. Meanwhile, on an intuition that hostilities were about to break out, Lt. Col. Hanut Singh had ordered the dispersal, camouflage and concealment of his armoured squadrons. Due to this precaution, when the enemy planes arrived on the morning of 4 December to destroy Indian tanks, they could not locate a single one, despite making repeated passes over the area where the tanks were concentrated. Lt. Col. Hanut Singh's astute move had saved Indian tanks from potential destruction even before the battle began.

Col. Avtar Singh Ahlawat recalled: "On 6 December 1971, after hostilities had broken out, our Squadron was still on our own side of the international border and we were all raring to go, but we were being restrained for some reason or other. It was about ten o'clock in the morning when Arun decided that he must have a bath as we may not get another chance until we reached Lahore and that may take many days. But just as he was soaping himself, the Pak artillery decided to intervene by shelling our location. Our Squadron Commander, Major Man Singh, who was a veteran of the 1965 War, shouted at the top of his voice for everyone to take cover. But Arun continued to bathe unperturbed. Having finished, he walked back coolly through the shelling to his tank, thus showing to the men that shelling, if inaccurate, is quite ineffective.

"Another incident that took place on the same day was when our Squadron came under a heavy air attack, while it was on its way to Mukhwal. The Pak aircraft made three runs over our tank column and the camouflage net on Arun's tank caught fire after being hit by the aircraft's cannon.

"When it was finally over, Arun made the cryptic remark, 'The Pak Artillery was bad enough, but their Air Force is even worse.'" (Singh, 283-284)

The enemy had a thirty-foot observation tower at its border post of Galar Tanda, which overlooked the concentration area of Indian troops. One of the tanks of Poona Horse's B Squadron fired a shot which brought the platform of the tower down in flames. A troop of enemy tanks, hidden in the tall elephant grass below, panicked at this unexpected fire and pulled back, but the dense grass there prevented the Indian troops from chasing them.

On 6 December, the advance of the Indian tank regiment was held up at the minefield which the Pakistani troops had planted at Thakurdwara. In the evening, Jiti Choudhary, commanding the leading squadron, breached the minefield. He moved forward unopposed and established a firm base across the minefield. The advance of Indian tanks unnerved the Pakistanis so much that they abandoned three of their tanks at Thakurdwara, which were promptly blown up. Later, the tanks of 20 Lancers of Pakistan were strafed by the Indian Air Force, and they retreated behind the next minefield at Barkhaniyan. This raised the morale of Indian troops sky-high.

On 10 December 1971, Arun's squadron had advanced ten miles inside Pakistani territory.

"Dear Daddy, we are having a damn good time!" he exulted, in a letter to his father, Brig. Khetarpal. "Our regiment is at the top of the world. Soon we will finish the war." And he would certainly help do so but, sadly, at the cost of his life.

On 15 December, the Commander of the 47 Infantry Brigade briefed the Commandant of the Poona Horse on battle plans. The 18 Rajputana Rifles was grouped with Poona Horse and given the task of ensuring the security of the bridgehead being established by the 16 Madras across the Basantar River. Indian troops advanced: the first phase of the attack was successful, and the 16 Madras captured most of the Ghazipur reserved forest area. Fierce were the counter-attacks by the Pakistani troops; on 16 December, Lt. Col. Ghai, CO of the 16 Madras, reported that the opposition's tanks were building up for a major counter-attack, and unless India's armoured divisions reached there soon, it would not be possible for him to hold out any longer, and Brig. Bhardwaj, Commander of the 47 Infantry Brigade, was also becoming increasingly anxious about it. It was up to the engineers with minesweepers to breach the minefield and make a safe passage for the tanks of the 17 Poona Horse to help secure the bridgehead.

The engineers were only halfway through their task when the Pakistanis were reported to be advancing. The 17 Poona Horse then decided to advance through the minefield. Commandant Lt.

Col. Hanut Singh joined up with C Squadron, and even though the minefield was not yet fully cleared, he ordered Maj. Ajai Singh to take his squadron through it and into the bridgehead. The situation at the bridgehead was serious enough to merit such drastic action: the troops of 16 Madras were under severe attack, and their need for backup from the armoured divisions was critical at this point.

Whatever the cost, Poona Horse had to link up with the 16 Madras troops within a few minutes, or the bridgehead would be lost. The Commandant of Poona Horse decided that even if a tank blew up on a mine, the next tank was to bypass from the right and this was to be repeated till at least some tanks managed to get through. Only a commander with nerves of steel could have taken such a decision, and our troops needed to be equally courageous to see it through. Maj. Ajai led the squadron column, with Ravi Deol ahead of him as the navigating officer.

The gods must have been protecting the tank-troops on that pitch-dark night: every single tank managed to negotiate the minefield, of which approximately 600 metres were yet to be cleared, without being blown up – whereas, the next day, when a jeep and an armoured personnel carrier (APC) deviated slightly from the tank-track, they blew up on an enemy mine.

In the ensuing ferocious tank battle, unique in the history of our subcontinent, between Poona Horse and the 16 Armoured Brigade of Pakistan with its Patton tanks, many were the brilliant feats of mettle and bravery by officers, Junior Commissioned Officers (JCOs) and jawans, not only of the Poona Horse, but also of the infantry battalions of the 47 Infantry Brigade – the 16 Madras, the 18 Rajputana Rifles and the 13 Grenadiers.

As the fierce battle raged around him, 2nd Lt. Arun Khetarpal heard a transmission from Jarpal at the bridgehead. A fellow officer, Amarjit Bal of B Squadron, was asking for help, and Arun and his troops rushed to the rescue into the battlefield, guns blazing. They charged headlong towards the enemy position, but while crossing the Basantar River, they came under heavy fire from the recoilless guns of the Pakistan Army, entrenched in their well-dug gun emplacements. Time was of the essence; driving his tank over open and exposed terrain, Arun reached Jarpal at the bridgehead in the nick of time. The Pakistani tanks were withdrawing after the first assault on the squadron; the heady thrill of battle coursed through Arun's veins. Throwing all caution to the wind, he charged at the enemy strongholds with the sole, overpowering desire to annihilate them. His tank overran the enemy's vantage points and defence works.

Col. Avtar Singh Ahlawat recounted: "The events of 16 December 1971 stand out vividly in my memory. Our Squadron had inducted into the bridgehead in the early hours of the morning. Our tanks were employed in and around Saraj Chak. As nothing appeared to be happening, Mallu, Arun and self decided to search the village for Pak soldiers who may still be in hiding. Looking back, I now realise that we behaved in a rather childish manner, for we were going from one pill box and bunker to the other, throwing grenades first and entering the bunker, firing our pistols and sten guns, in the style of the war movies. We were quite oblivious to the situation and the impending danger looming over the Regiment. Our childlike play ended only when our Squadron Commander, Major Man Singh, gave us a mouthful and told us to get back into our tanks. Cursing our luck for not being able to get Pak POWs, we mounted our tanks.

"Not five minutes had elapsed, when we heard the commandant on the radio ordering Mallu to move with two troops to Jarpal and take up positions in line with our B Squadron. As Mallu, Arun and self started moving towards Jarpal, we were fired upon by RCL guns from dug-in emplacements." (Singh, 284)

Arun's tank commander, JCO (Junior Commissioned Officer) Risaldar Sagat Singh, was one of the finest in their battalion. He had been posted under Arun so that he could look after this youngster who had come straight from the Academy and, moreover, had not even completed his basic Young Officer's Course. During the wild charge by these tanks, Risaldar Sagat Singh caught a burst of machine-gun fire full in the face. Even as he was dying, he told his unnerved crewmen to look after Khetarpal Sahib, who was so young.

Ahlawat continued: "We charged these guns, and Arun's desire to get some POWs was fulfilled when he captured a couple of Pak Recoilless gun crews at pistol-point – in fact, there was no pistol, for in the excitement to capture the POWs, he had forgotten to take his pistol along when dismounting from the tank." (Singh, 284) He simply pointed his fingers at the enemy soldiers, who were so scared that they surrendered.

Chariots of Fire

Having driven their tanks right up to the enemy bunkers, the daredevil cavalry commanders of the Poona Horse A Squadron leapt out, got the Pakistani soldiers out of their bunkers, and had them trussed up and tied to the engine-decks of their tanks. On the return journey, the POWs were handed over to the 13 Grenadiers. One of the imprisoned soldiers remarked, "It proves that one should not fight with a superior force."

Capt. V. Malhotra, Ahlawat and Arun soon burst out of the grove south of Jarpal, just in time to see some Pakistani tanks pulling back after an initial attack. Carried away by the wild enthusiasm of their charge, they and their troops continued their headlong rush, gave chase to the withdrawing enemy armour, and destroyed a couple of their tanks. Their commandant reined them in with difficulty and ordered them to fall in line with the rest of the squadron. Some of the tanks found cover, but as the main Pakistani attack began almost immediately, the three commanded by Mallu, Avatar and Arun had no time to take cover and remained in the open. The Pakistani troops spotted them and began firing heavily. An entire Pakistani armoured regiment, the 13 Lancers, was launching this assault on Jarpal – a fast and furious tank battle developed.

The brunt of the attack was borne by Arun, Avatar and Mallu, as the Pakistanis were attempting a breakthrough in their sector. But, far from being dismayed, these young warriors and their troops began sporting with death and playing havoc with the attacking tanks. The 13 Lancers recoiled from the devastating fire that was mowing them down. About ten enemy tanks were destroyed, and the rest withdrew.

Though demoralised by the heavy casualties suffered by their tanks, the 13 Lancers of Pakistan were ordered to attack again. Maj. Naser, their leading Squadron Commander, told his troops that he and his fellow-officers would personally lead the attack. The major exhorted his men to be brave, as this was going to be a 'now or never action'.

This second attack by the tank-troops of the 13 Lancers was fierce. Led by their officers, they fought gallantly but suffered heavy losses. At this point, Avatar's tank was hit, wounding him severely. His driver pulled the tank under cover and Avatar was evacuated. Soon after, Capt. Mallu's tank gun developed a mechanical defect and became inoperative; Mallu came on air and asked permission to pull back. Sensing that any withdrawal by Indian troops at this stage might cause panic, the commandant ordered Mallu to stay where he was, even with a defective gun. He then sent out a net call, "All tanks will fight it out from where they are; no tank will move back an inch."

Filled with the heady enthusiasm of battle, a supernatural strength now seemed to enter Arun; he began to chase the withdrawing enemy tanks and destroyed one of them. Arun was now the sole tank commander fighting in that vital sector of the battle. His tank had been hit, but luckily the shot had ricocheted off his 'Famagusta' (named after a famous port in East Cyprus). Now, it was hit a second time and caught fire. Captain Mallu observed this and ordered Arun to abandon his tank; Amarjit sent a similar message.

Arun, however, had realized that the situation was critical; he was the sole survivor in that crucial sector and the only one in a position to prevent an enemy breakthrough. "Sir, my gun is still functioning and I will destroy the whole enemy lot," came his valiant reply. When Mallu insisted that Arun either abandon his tank or pull back, Arun switched his radio set off. All his concentration was now bent on destroying the enemy. His tank driver, Prayag Singh, pleaded that it would take only a few minutes to pull back, put out the fire and then rejoin the battle. Arun answered, "No, Prayag Singh. Didn't you hear the CO's transmission? No tank will pull back even an inch."

A fierce tank battle then took place, a sight to inspire the hearts of warriors. Tanks littered the area in every imaginable state –

overturned, burning, and broken. Smoke billowed from blazing armour. Scores of guns were firing shot after shot. The feeble cries of the dying went unheard in the din. The dead lay clutching their guns, some staring up with open, unseeing eyes, and others roasted alive in the gun-turrets of their tanks. The clash of tank against tank and the constant bursts from armour-piercing shells were deafening. Ten Pakistani tanks were hit and destroyed, of which Second Lieutenant Arun had personally accounted for four.

The commandant ordered Maj. Man Singh to take the place of the disabled tanks of Capt. Mallu and Ahlawat. But before the major and his troops could come to the aid of the beleaguered A Squadron, Arun realised that he would have to face the attack all alone. By now, most of the tanks of Maj. Naser's Pakistani squadron had been blown up, but four or five still survived, including Naser's own. Naser regrouped them and prepared to make a final rush in order to break through. As they advanced, Arun began to pick his targets and knocked them out one by one. It seemed, at one stage, that they might overwhelm him by sheer force of numbers, but Arun destroyed them all except Major Naser's tank. When it was only 75 metres from Arun's tank, both fired at each other simultaneously. Naser's shot penetrated through the turret porthole of Arun's tank: Arun was mortally wounded; his wireless operator, Nand Singh, was killed; and his gunner, Nathu Singh, was gravely wounded. The driver of Arun's tank, Prayag Singh, showed great presence of mind. With the battle raging all around, he evacuated Nathu Singh onto another tank from his squadron which had moved up alongside just then. Strafed in the leg by machine-gun fire while doing this, he carried on nonetheless, reversing his burning tank behind cover and putting out the fire. Prayag then examined Arun and found that he was still alive.

Arun asked for some water to drink. The morning being intensely cold, Prayag thought that cold water might do Arun harm. He began to make some tea on the electric stove of the tank. In the meantime, he called to Naib Risaldar Hamir Singh of the same squadron, whose tank had taken up its position nearby, to help move Arun.

Second Lieutenant Arun Khetarpal

Arun's soul left his body even as they were bringing him out of the tank. His was a brave death, a glorious death. With barely six months spent in service, Arun had sacrificed his young life for India's defence and glory. He showed supreme defiance of the enemy and made up for his lack of experience with his courage and determination. For this action, he would be posthumously awarded the country's highest decoration for valour, the Param Vir Chakra.

Second Lieutenant Arun died, but his valour helped save the day. Not one Pakistani tank could break through. At 11:20 a.m. on that eventful day, their attack petered out. At the end of the day's battle, a total of 48 Pakistani tanks were counted destroyed on the battlefield – 30 opposite the Jarpal Sector and 18 opposite the Ghazipur Reserve Forest Sector. The 13 Lancers, one of the oldest and proudest regiments of the Pakistan Army, had been destroyed, and the 31 Cavalry had received a crippling blow.

On 17 December, the guns fell silent and a ceasefire heralded the end of this fourteen-day war. Arun's family were rejoicing – the war was over, India had won and Arun would soon be home. They received a cruel shock instead: a telegram arrived on 20 December with the brief message that Arun had laid down his life for the country and that his body had been cremated on 17 December in Samba, near Jammu. His parents, unable to take even a last look at their son, were stunned and heartbroken.

When the author sent this chapter to Arun's father, Brig. Khetarpal, for verification, in January 2006, he wrote back that Arun had died at 10 a.m. on 16 December 1971, ten miles inside Pakistani territory. Escorted by a Havildar and three jawans, Arun's body had left the regiment at 9 p.m. the same day, inside a truck carrying the bodies of three other martyred soldiers, for cremation at Samba in India at 9 a.m. the next day, 17 December 1971. War was still going on, so no officer saw him off, no garlands were laid on his body, and no bugles were sounded to mark a nation's gratitude for his immortal bravery. His parents were informed by telegram, which reached them on 20 December. His ashes were brought to them five days later by Maj. Bal of his regiment. His parents never saw his dead body. But his unmatched bravery has earned this hero a place in the hearts of all patriotic Indians.

Maj. Gen. Ian Cardozo quotes from a letter written by Brig. Khetarpal, "General S. D. Verma, Poona Horse, wrote to me on 15 February 1972 after visiting the Regiment, then still in Pakistan: 'I have been to the spot where your son's tank was and where he was not prepared to abandon his comrades, both of infantry and armour. He died a soldier's death. I would have gladly given away ten years of my life to see him personally receive the award he deserved ten times over for his selfless conduct.'

"Arun wanted to be posted to Poona Horse; he lived like a Poona Horse officer, and he died like one. Lieutenant General Har Prasad wrote to me in February 1972: 'You had requested me to get Arun posted to Poona Horse, which I did. The boy got the regiment of his choice – but at what cost!' " (Cardozo, 130)

Brig. Madan Lal Khetarpal, 85 years old and wheelchair-bound, told Satya Prakash and Raka in a personal interview in June 2005, "We had hoped that our younger son, Mukesh, would join the Army, and Arun the IIT, but the reverse happened. We love the army life. The 17 Poona Horse celebrates 16 December as Basantar Day and invites us to the celebrations. On a visit to Ambala, we saw Arun's tank, 'Famagusta.' They have kept it spick and span."

Arun's mother, Maheshwari Khetarpal, said in the same interview, "A monument to Arun was raised at the place of his cremation in Samba. His statue is installed there. The supplier of marble for the statue gave his best-quality marble for this memorial and didn't charge anything. Samba became a place of pilgrimage. A cousin of Arun went to pay his respects at his memorial. The driver of his taxi refused to take any payment."

"During wars, and on the death anniversaries of war heroes, leaders and politicians pay glowing tributes to these heroes and honour their families, but that is all," Arun's mother said, in a television interview in 1974. "Have any of these men ever sent their children to the Army? Give me one example, if you can." When Arun's parents went to Ambala that year for the Basantar Day celebrations by Arun's regiment, the officers appreciated her frank, impassioned speech in this interview.

She, however, was distressed that the Government of India did not celebrate 16 December as Victory Day. "It is very surprising," she commented in the June 2005 interview. "Many requests have been made from the higher authorities of the Army that it should be so celebrated, but the government hasn't taken any notice. Now many non-governmental organisations are trying to persuade the Government of India to do something."

Her wish was soon to be fulfilled. On 16 November 2005, Lt. Gen. G. D. Singh, AVSM, Director General, Mechanised Forces, organised a function through the Ministry of Education. President Dr. APJ Abdul Kalam, as Supreme Commander of the Armed Forces, presided over the function. While delivering the Cavalry Memorial lecture in honour of Lt. Arun Khetarpal, the President paid him a glowing tribute: "I salute Arun's supreme self-sacrifice and know he will be a role model for all youth, particularly for officers and jawans serving in the armed forces." Later, the President personally administered to the gathered children a pledge to serve the country. He made the children repeat the following oath after him, "Courage to defend the nation, courage to innovate, courage to invent, courage to overcome suffering and to succeed are the traits that lead to the growth of human civilisation."

Arun's mother was invited to light the ceremonial lamp. More than a 1000 distinguished guests and 800 schoolchildren attended the function. Amongst them were the students of Lawrence School of Sanawar, Arun's alma mater. The President embraced Arun's mother and presented her with a shawl and a silver medal.

Many roads, colonies and parks have been named after Arun Khetarpal. The Indian Military Academy has named an auditorium after him, and every cadet passes out of the academy from there before being commissioned into the Army. A grateful nation awarded him the Param Vir Chakra posthumously. It was given to Arun's mother, Maheshwari Khetarpal, by President V. V. Giri during the

Republic Day parade ceremony on 26 January 1972. Arun was then the youngest recipient of the award.

Citation

Second Lieutenant Arun Khetarpal

Poona Horse (1C-25067)

On 16 December 1971, the Squadron Commander of 'B' Squadron, the Poona Horse, asked for reinforcement as the Pakistani armour, which was superior in strength, counter-attacked at Jarpal in the Shakargarh Sector. On hearing this transmission, Second Lieutenant Arun Khetarpal, who was in 'A' Squadron, voluntarily moved, along with his troops, to assist the other squadron. En route, while crossing the Basantar River, Second Lieutenant Arun Khetarpal and his troops came under fire from enemy strong points and RCL gun nests that were still holding out. Time was at a premium and as a critical situation was developing in the 'B' Squadron sector, Second Lieutenant Arun Khetarpal threw caution to the winds and started attacking the impending enemy strong points by literally charging them, overrunning the defence works with his tanks and capturing the enemy infantry and weapon crews at pistol point. In the course of one such daring attack, one tank commander of his troop was killed. Second Lieutenant Arun Khetarpal continued to attack relentlessly until all enemy opposition was overcome and he broke through towards the 'B' Squadron position, just in time to see the enemy tanks pulling back after their initial probing attack on this squadron. He was so carried away by the wild enthusiasm of battle and the impetus of his own headlong dash that he started chasing the withdrawing tanks and even managed to shoot and destroy one. Soon thereafter, the enemy reformed with a squadron of armour for a second attack and this time they selected the sector held by Second Lieutenant Arun Khetarpal and two other tanks as the point for their main effort. A fierce tank battle ensued: ten enemy tanks were hit and destroyed of which Second Lieutenant Arun Khetarpal personally destroyed four; just then, Second Lieutenant Arun Khetarpal was severely wounded. He was asked to abandon his tank but he realised that the enemy, though badly decimated, was continuing to advance in his sector of responsibility, and if he abandoned his tank, the enemy would break through; he gallantly fought on and destroyed another enemy tank. At this stage, his tank received a second hit which resulted in the death of this gallant officer.

Second Lieutenant Arun Khetarpal was dead, but he had, by his intrepid valour, saved the day; the enemy was denied the breakthrough it was so desperately seeking. Not one enemy tank got through.

Second Lieutenant Arun Khetarpal has shown the best qualities of leadership, tenacity of purpose and the will to close in with the enemy. This was an act of courage and self-sacrifice far beyond the call of duty.

—Gazette of India Notification,

No. 7-Press/72

Arun Khetrapal's mother receiving PVC from the President

The Tribute of an Enemy Soldier

It is natural that a warrior be appreciated by his nation, but greater is he whom even his enemies praise. For years, Arun's father, Brig. M. L. Khetarpal, had occasionally heard that a Pakistan Army officer wanted to contact him. Decades passed, but no such contact was made. In his old age, Brig. M. L. Khetarpal wanted to visit his birthplace, Sargodha, now in Pakistan. He got a visa and, in 2001, at the age of 81, finalised his trip plans. He was to be the guest of Brig. Khawja Mohamad Naser at Lahore, who would arrange for his visit to Sargodha.

Brig. Khetarpal knew nothing of the role his host had played in the battle of Basantar. Brig. Naser was most hospitable and courteous. His entire family welcomed the visitor; and after his trip to Sargodha, Brig. M. L. Khetarpal stayed for three days as their cherished guest.

On the last day of his visit, Brig. Naser drew him aside: "I have something to tell you. It concerns your son. Arun Khetarpal is your national hero, well known now as one of the youngest recipients of the Param Vir Chakra – but on that fateful day, at the Battle of Bade Pind (known to the Indian Army as the Battle of Basantar), we were soldiers unknown to each other, fighting for the safety and honour of our respective countries. I regret to have to tell you that your son died at my hands.

"Arun's courage on the battlefield was exemplary. He moved his tank with fearless courage and daring, completely unconcerned about his own safety. Tank casualties on both sides were very heavy, and finally, it was just the two of us who faced each other. We both fired simultaneously – it was destined that I was to live and he had to die. It was only later that I came to know who he was and how young he was. I salute your son for what he was and what he did at such a young age; and meeting you, I salute you too, because I understand how he grew into such a fine young man."

Later, Brig. Naser wrote, on the back of a photograph taken during the visit, before sending it to Delhi:

With warmest regards, and utmost sincerity,

To Brigadier Khetarpal, father of Shaheed Second Lieutenant Arun Khetarpal, PVC –

who stood like an insurmountable rock between the victory and failure of the counter-attack by the 'SPEARHEADS' 13 Lancers on 16 December 1971, in the 'Battle of Bara Pind', as we call it, and the 'Battle of Basanter', as 17 Poona Horse remembers it.

Khawja Mohamad Naser, 13 Lancers

02 March, 2001, Lahore

How bitter must the realisation have been for Brig. Khetarpal that he had accepted the hospitality of the one who had killed his son.

And how poignant this battle and these sacrifices seem when we remember that, before the Partition, India's Poona Horse and Pakistan's 13 Lancers, who fought against each other in the Battle of Basantar, had been part of one unit of one Army!

Arun A Sun

Glorious was his bravery indeed,
Super-human his valorous deed.
A raging fire, a searing flame,
He blasted tank after enemy tank
As if in a dare-devil game.
Words are inadequate to describe
That battle of battles,
On Basantar's bank,
That fiery strife,
Where, as a wager sublime
Arun the valiant,
Laid down his life.

There was a rumour of death
In the enemy's ranks,
As this young god blasted
One after another
Their mighty Patton tanks.
None could stop his swift advance,
The 13 Lancers had not a chance.
Sure was his aim, steady his hand,
As ten miles inside the enemy land,
In his burning tank Fama Gusta
He advanced, and with his blood,
Washed and sanctified,
The land that was once India,
The land that will again be India.

Durga's indomitable strength,
Coursed through Arun's heart
To steady his nerves,
To steel his heart
When like a bolt of thunder
He cleaved their tanks asunder,
They lay burning, overturned
With turrets askew, guns silenced.
The enemy commanders
Eyes dialated with terror,
They were stuck
With awe and wonder.

Such was the glorious action
So total the 13 Lancers destruction
So matchless Arun's bravery,
Such his battle-perfection
That the god's
Watching from space
Rained flowers
On his mortal remains.

On that morn
Of 16th December,
On a chariot of fire,
Rode to his death
This arrow of God,
This live wire.

On India's sky
Was born a new sun,
Centuries will sing
Of the bravery of Arun.

Hon. Captain Bana Singh

"Whatever I do, I will do it with full attention, enthusiasm and passion."

In the fourth decade of the 20th century, in the town of Sialkot (now in Pakistan) lived a famous wrestler called Bana Singh. Amar Singh, a landowner in Kadyal village of Ranbir Singh Pura district (J&K), admired him so much that he vowed: "If I have a son, I will name him Bana Singh after this man."

And so he did, when a son was born to him and his wife, Bholi Kaur, on 6 January 1949. Nobody knew then that this child would one day win a special place on the map of India for this otherwise unknown village.

Early Life

The eldest of five sons, Bana has three sisters as well. His family is deeply religious; two of his brothers have become *raagis*, singers of the Gurugranth Sahib (the holy scripture of the Sikhs) in gurdwaras in Britain and Canada. Bana's parents laid great stress on honesty and character, so it came naturally to Bana to be forthright and to do his utmost, whatever the situation.

Amar Singh's elder brother, Subedar Kartar Singh, was in the army, a figure of awe to the simple villagers of Kadyal. "Son, I have passed my life in the cultivation of our land," Amar Singh would say to Bana. "But look at your uncle. How nice it is when he comes on leave! How majestically he sits – how well he eats! I am a mere farmer – but if you follow in the footsteps of your uncle, the well-being of our family will improve vastly." Many other relatives had also served the country with distinction; serving in the Army was considered superior to most other professions. It was thus natural that Bana's thoughts turned towards an Army career.

It had always been his aspiration to achieve greatness in some way. Whenever he met soldiers and officers, home on leave, and heard their stories of guarding the frontiers of the nation, he grew impatient to join the Army and follow in their footsteps.

Bana had another uncle, formerly in the service of the British Indian Army and now living in retirement in a village several miles from Kadyal. Bana, always respectful to elders, found inspiration from him too. His uncle would regale the village boys with his many thrilling tales of army days.

Bana's early education was in the Kadyal school; after passing Class Eight, he was admitted to R. S. Pura High School in the nearby village of Badyal Brahmna, where he enjoyed playing kabaddi matches with the village lads. One of his teachers, Nishan Singh, gave 14-year-old Bana a mantra: "In play or in work, whatever you do, do it wholeheartedly, with enthusiasm, and then success is sure." It was a motto that the teenager took to heart.

At 16, Bana passed matriculation; there ended his formal education. He then worked in the Military Engineering Service for three years. His heart, however, remained focused on his desire to become a soldier.

Bana's aspiration was fulfilled at long last when he was selected for the Army, joining the 8 Jammu & Kashmir Light Infantry on his twentieth birthday, 6 January 1969. He took his first training course in Srinagar. Eager as he was to learn and to lend a helping hand to anyone, it is no wonder that Bana was liked by officers as well as peers in his close-knit unit and sub-unit.

Battle of Chhamb

On 3 September 1971, Pakistan attacked India, who fought back on both the eastern and the western fronts. Bana's battalion, the 8 J&K Light Infantry, was posted at Dewa Post in the Chhamb sector.

Bana Singh narrated the events of the battle to this author: "Our Army was thinly spread out. Only one battalion was posted to safeguard each 20-km area. There was constant firing in Chhamb sector. Our 8 J&K-LI battalion had mounted a medium machine gun (MMG) under a big banyan tree in the area of Dewa Post. When it was fired, the enemy was able to locate it by the light of its shell-burst and they blasted its barrel. The fire power of my battalion was thus much reduced.

"To the right of the battalion was a well with a water pump, and on one side of the pump was a *nala* (small drain). The Pakistanis began to attack from the sides of this *nala*, trying to advance strategically by pushing a herd of goats and sheep in front; they believed that the mines laid by the Indian Army would kill the animals first, thus helping them have fewer casualties. But the plan did not succeed, and many died while crossing the minefield. After a non-stop barrage of shells from our troops, the Pakistanis positioned a wireless operator under a mango tree roughly fifty feet from us. He climbed the tree and relayed information to the enemy about our position – but his radio frequency could be heard on our wireless. Our battalion could thus pinpoint his position and we shot him. But the constant and heavy shelling by the Pakistani artillery soon made our position untenable; we were forced to start withdrawing.

"Our Lance Naik Amarnath of the Sunderbans had been shot in the abdomen. The brave soldier pushed in his disembowelled intestines and tied a towel around his waist. 'I am not going to live,' he told us. 'But I will hold the Pakistanis back at least for some time while you withdraw.' Amarnath was racked with unbearable pain, yet he singlehandedly delayed the Pakistani advance by half an hour. Our battalion was able to take another position in the meantime. But we soon had to withdraw from there too, due to heavy enemy shelling.

"We retreated half a kilometre from Dewa Post and climbed to Point 1886, where we had two posts, Post 707 and Laliyali. The enemy attacked and captured Post 707. When the CO, Maj. Sapan Kumar Mandal, heard the news, he prepared to lead a commando platoon of our battalion to retake the post. Before our departure, our colonel, Jasbir Pal Singh Randhawa, addressed us: 'Today will show who is true to his mother's milk.'

"We were electrified by these challenging words. Maj. Sapan Kumar Mandal, CO of our D Company, alighted from his jeep and led us from the front. When an officer walks two steps with his troops, the soldiers walk fifty – with an officer leading from the front, the morale, courage and enthusiasm of his soldiers increase manifold. This is the quality of a true leader.

"There was a track by which one-ton and three-ton trucks of the Indian military came up with equipment and supplies for our troops. The Pakistanis began to climb from the side of this track in a single file towards where our battalion had taken a position. They were shouting their battle cry: 'Ya Ali, Ya Ali!' My CO ordered artillery fire. We mowed them down. During the ensuing fierce fighting, though we suffered some losses, we recaptured Post 707. Bodies of hundreds of Pakistani soldiers killed by our bullets and shells rotted in the minefield and the stench persisted for two or three months. But who was going to remove them from the minefield! The Pakistanis did not seem to care for or honour their dead comrades, while we Indians would risk our lives to retrieve the bodies of our friends killed in these operations."

8 J&K-LI was jubilant after their hard-won victory in this short war. "The bravery of our battalion was highly appreciated; we received the Vir Chakra and the Sena Medal," Bana recalled. "The awards were given to the battalion as a whole for their combined effort."

The Prophecy

Sardar Sant Singh, Bana's relative, lived in Kadyal after retirement from the Indian Police Service. One summer, three years after joining the Army, Bana visited him while on leave. Deeply moved by the love and respect shown by this youngster, Sardar Sant Singh blessed him: "My son, one day you will win a prize and honour which no one has received."

Bana mused, "I have served only three years in the Army. What will I get? Maybe I will become a Havildar or a JCO at the most."

Decades later, when Bana Singh received the Param Vir Chakra, he remembered his uncle's prophecy. "There is such power in the blessings of elders. When blessings rise from the heart of one who is simple and quiet, they become true. I have no way to repay my uncle for his blessings," Bana confided to this author in an interview.

After the 1971 war, Bana's parents arranged his marriage with 18-year-old Ravinder Kaur of Kirpind village; the two were wedded on 18 March 1972.

Bana's is a joint family. When he was posted to far-off places, his wife lived with his parents. Two sons and two daughters were born to the couple in due course; his children studied in the same schools as he had.

Bana's first posting had been in Poonch. After the 1971 war, he was posted variously to Sunderbani (near Akhnoor in J&K), the Gurez Sector of J&K (1973-76), Jodhpur (1976-78), Sikkim (1978-1981), Meerut (1981) and Jalandhar (1982). In 1986, he was posted to Kheru in Jammu and Kashmir. On 13 April 1987, his battalion was sent from Kheru to Siachen.

In 1972, Bana Singh was made a Lance Naik; in 1978, he became Havildar; and in 1985, he was promoted to the rank of a Junior Commissioned Officer (JCO). He had thus attained the highest that he had aspired for.

Siachen, the World's Highest Battlefield

'Siachen' is Tibetan for 'bed of roses'. The one who gave this name to the place must have had an ironic sense of humour – not a blade of grass grows in that breathtakingly beautiful wilderness of roaring avalanches and towering snow peaks. Located in the Karakoram Range of the Himalayas, it is a glacier, an immense wall of moving ice, approximately 80 km long, at 21,153 feet above sea level. Almost at the northernmost tip of India, it shares a border with Pakistan and is very close to China. It can truthfully be described as a deadly domain. When an avalanche hurtles through the glacier, the tons of snow sweep off everything in their path, even huge boulders. And sometimes, terrifyingly fierce blizzards hit the area, with wind velocity rising to over 60 km per hour.

It was here that Bana Singh and his regiment were posted, in 1987. The terrain at Siachen is cruel: oxygen is scarce, and temperatures are below -35°C on the good days, often going down to -70 during the windy winters. The relentless cold chills even the bone marrow; icicles form on the nose, even toothpaste freezes and – what is a much more serious problem for the soldiers – weapons freeze at night.

The effects on the body of such severe cold, combined with the lack of oxygen, can be anything from memory loss, high-altitude pulmonary oedema and high-altitude cerebral oedema to frostbite. Special clothes need to be worn, but as the face remains uncovered, its skin blackens, dries up and peels off like that of a fruit. It is so difficult to remove the multiple layers of thick clothing with cold-numbed fingers to attend to nature's call that the soldiers try to eat as little as possible. They eat mainly biscuits with nuts, enriched with extra protein and vitamins. Each step requires a special effort due to the cold and the lack of oxygen at these high altitudes. Lack of oxygen leaves the soldiers feeling exhausted after even a little exertion.

A more daunting enemy the soldiers face at Siachen is the presence of treacherous crevasses hidden under fresh snow. This light layer of snow on top cannot bear the weight of several people. Soldiers can suddenly fall into a crevasse which may be hundreds of feet deep, with temperatures as low as -75°C. Rescue is extremely difficult and rare, so our officers and jawans join themselves together by ropes tied at the waist whenever they march over such terrain. They have instructions that if a comrade falls into a crevasse, no more than four or five minutes may be spent in trying to pull him out. If unsuccessful within that period, they must cut the rope and continue on their mission. How hard it must be to abandon a comrade so!

At Siachen, most of the action takes place at night, when even lighting a matchstick can bring on a landslide or an avalanche. India has to spend crores of rupees every day to safeguard this small area of 25 square kilometres.

To reach the glacier top where the Indian Army has its defences, one has to walk for about ten days, acclimatizing at five different altitudes, through a treacherous, avalanche-prone area interspersed with hidden crevasses. The snow-clad, towering peaks of Siachen are awe-inspiring; it is hard to imagine even living in such excruciatingly painful conditions, leave alone fighting on this highest battlefield of the world. More Indian soldiers have died there due to climatic conditions than by enemy fire. One small mistake or thoughtless move can invite death or disability. Metallic objects like guns or shells, if picked up without wearing gloves, stick to the skin and have to be surgically removed. Hallucinations and depression are constant companions of the soldiers posted at Siachen. The jawans have to maintain constant vigilance as they have eye-to-eye contact with the enemy at many of these spots.

It is a matter of pride for the Indian Army that the severity of these conditions does not deter the soldiers; large numbers continue to volunteer for a Siachen posting, year after year. But since 2008-2009, Indian troops have taken extraordinary precautions, so much so that only one soldier died that year due to the climate. The Army authorities have decreed that a jawan is allowed to stay at this post for no more than 90 days, due to medical reasons, and is not permitted to have a second tenure there for the rest of his service.

Maj. Gen. Ian Cardozo, who has served in Siachen, describes this unique and beautiful place: "Siachen is a world apart ... It is undoubtedly beautiful beyond words, in the pristine and primaeval majesty of snow and rock and ice that cap the roof of the world.

"Time has carefully marked its passing in the serrations that countless centuries have etched on ancient rocks that vary in every imaginable shade of brown and black, orange and indigo, and within whose depths are concealed the fossils of living fish and plants and other aquatic organisms that were pushed up from beneath the sea in the awesome cataclysm that created the Himalayas millions of years ago. The snow and ice that cover these mountains – the icing of the cake, as it were – sparkle in scintillating hues of green and blue and white that make it breathtakingly beautiful. 'Breathtaking' is apt because at that formidable height, there is not enough oxygen to even breathe." (Cardozo 195-196)

The History of the Siachen Conflict

After the 1947-48 war, a ceasefire line was accepted by India and Pakistan in July 1949. "In the Karachi agreement of 1949, representatives of both nations drew the 'Ceasefire Line' across maps of Jammu and Kashmir from Manawar in the south, to Khor in the north and thence 'North to the glaciers' through NJ 9842. Presumably, when they came up to this glaciated wilderness of snow and ice, they stopped at grid point NJ 9842 on the presumption that neither side would be interested in contesting an area where not a blade of grass grows and even breathing is a problem." (Cardozo, 196)

The demarcation was clearly done on the principle that if a territory was no-man's-land and not occupied by either of the two armies, it would be deemed a part of India. "Pakistan, however, complicated the issue subsequently: first, by illegally ceding some 5180 square kilometres of Indian territory to China in the area where the boundaries of India, Pakistan and China meet, thereby altering the geo-strategic importance of this area; and second, by permitting and assisting a series of foreign mountaineering and scientific expeditions in the area, thus raising the issue of 'rights' in an area that did not belong to her. Being aware of the implications of the cartographic ambiguity of 1962, the devious nature of certain powers, and the turn events could take, the Indian Army became concerned at Pakistani activities in the area. Sometime in 1983, the Indian Army got wind of Pakistani plans to move physically into the area and, in April 1984, took pre-emptive action and occupied the Saltoro Ridge which marks the western boundary of the glacier." (Cardozo, 196-197)

In 1987, Pakistan established a post on the highest feature overlooking the Indian forces posted near the Bilafond La pass on the Saltoro ridge. Indian radio operators intercepted an order from the Pakistani government to its commander: "You will place the Pakistani flag on the crown of the Indian peninsula."

The Pakistanis sent a crack commando team for this job. So proud were they of conquering this peak that they named it Quaid Post, after the founder of Pakistan, 'Quaid-e-Azam' Mohammad Ali Jinnah. From those dominating heights, they began to shoot at the helicopters supplying rations and weapons to Indian troops posted nearby. India had to pay a high price, in terms of casualties.

In April 1987, India made a decision to retake the Quaid Post and chase away the Pakistanis from there at any cost. For this most difficult task, the Army decided to send 8 J&K Light Infantry, who did not flinch from this seemingly impossible mission.

Bana Singh recounted the story of the mission to this author, in a personal interview in February 2007: "When our battalion reached Sonam Post, the Pakistanis believed it to be an assault party and began to fire indiscriminately at our posts. Two soldiers of our battalion and two of another lost their lives. Our brigade commander, Brig. Chandan Singh Nogyal, was also present there and he realised the gravity of the situation. Because of the constant fire on our positions and helicopters, we were unable to supply rations to our posts; Quaid Post had become a constant thorn in India's side.

"On 29 May 1987, the CO sent a secret patrol of 8 J&K-LI under the command of Second Lieutenant Rajiv Pande for reconnaissance, with the object of finding a route to the Quaid Post and, if possible, to discover how many Pakistanis were stationed there. With him were JCO Hemraj Sharma and some jawans. Unlike the Pakistani side, there was a steep wall of ice, 1500 feet high, on the Indian side. Nobody knew of a route to reach the top, but brave 2nd Lt. Rajiv Pande and his soldiers inched up the perilous wall of ice. The ascent was at an angle of ninety degrees. When our soldiers were thirty metres from the top, the Pakistanis saw them and opened fire. Lt. Rajiv Pande, an only son, and several others in his team were killed, but their sacrifice was not in vain – two of them escaped and came back with the information about the route. Also, they had succeeded in laying a rope for part of the way up, which would help their comrades in the next assault. This rope had *jhumars* attached to it – a *jhumar* is a swing-like loop by which the soldier can remain suspended even if he has to let go of the rope and thus he can rest for some moments during the climb.

"All of us were livid at the killing of Lt. Rajiv Pande and his men. We wanted to avenge their deaths. Brig. C. S. Nogyal called all the officers for a meeting. 'I want that post,' he told my CO, Col. A. P. Roy. 'Even if 800 soldiers have to sacrifice their lives, I want that post.'

"My CO suggested my name as the right man for this mission, as I had done a mountaineering course. A team of 62 men were selected. For nearly a month, we prepared for the assault on Quaid Post, which was at a height of more than 21,000 feet above sea level. We discussed the obstacles which could come in our way and how we would tackle them. We were given the chance to opt out from this seemingly suicidal mission, but none of us did. Our helicopters did 400 sorties to carry our 62-member assault party, along with all our arms, luggage and rations, from Kamal Post to Sonam Post."

Although Bana had been trained in high-altitude warfare in Gulmarg, fighting in the harsh climatic conditions of Siachen was altogether different. It was going to be a tough assignment.

"On 23 June, the enemy were distracted by some celebrations," Bana Singh recalled. "We decided to take advantage of it, climb from Sonal Post and attack by direct fire. We resolved to dislodge the enemy at any cost, even if we had to die in the service of the country. A task force under Maj. Virendar Singh launched this new attack to dislodge the Pakistanis. It was code-named Operation Rajiv, in honour of late Lt. Rajiv Pande. But the weather was not favourable, and our soldiers could not locate the rope tied earlier by the ill-fated team of Lt. Rajiv Pande. The plan to overthrow the Pakistanis had to be postponed until a new rope could be tied to help our soldiers climb up the ice wall.

"At those frozen heights, to tie a rope in the ice is not an easy thing," Bana Singh explained. "Pitons (iron spikes about four feet long) have to be hammered into the ice, and three or four thick ropes have to be tied to them so that they can take the weight of several soldiers at a time. 'Bana sahib, go and tie that rope,' our CO ordered me. The words of Brig. C. S. Nogyal rang in my ears – 'Even if 800 men have to sacrifice their lives, I want that post.'

"At 8 p.m. on 24 June, I took two soldiers with me and succeeded in tying the rope, up to 500 metres below the top. After marking the place from where we were to climb, I came down and informed Maj. Virendar Singh that the rope was in place. The Major organised us for the assault in four groups: Subedar Harnam Singh was to lead the attack with ten soldiers; Subedar Sansar Chand, accompanied by ten more, was to be next; the Major would lead the next set of ten soldiers, wireless operators, and so on. I was to be the last, following with ten soldiers.

"'If anybody shows his back, he will deserve a bullet,' said the Major. Subedar Harnam Singh advanced with his group and neared the enemy. Unfortunately, the Pakistanis, alerted to their advance, started a barrage of bullets. Two of our jawans were killed, and the rest had to retreat."

Bana Singh continues: "Dawn was breaking. At 4 a.m. on 25 June, Maj. Virendar turned to Subedar Sansar Chand. 'You will have to complete the task now.'

"Three hours passed after Subedar Sansar Chand and his group reached the top – with no message from them. We tried contacting them in our code, but there was no response.

"Maj. Virendar now turned to me. 'Bana, take four soldiers, go up and see what the problem is.' I crawled up to Subedar Chand's group and asked them in code the cause of their silence.

"'Our communication sets are not working,' came their reply. And they needed more soldiers to help them attack the Pakistanis holed up in the bunker. I crawled back and informed the Major about the malfunctioning communication system.

"'Sir, I fought in 1971 in the Chhamb sector. If communications fail, it is a sign of death for the soldiers,' I said. 'They cannot make out the difference between our troops and the enemy's, in this zero visibility.' I took another set from the Major and crawled up again to give it to Subedar Chand's men. Meanwhile, our soldiers sat tight because ammunition was limited and we had to use it sparingly.

"When I came down, Maj. Virendar took his group and went up to provide support to the group above. Nearly 45 minutes later, there was still no action.

"I crawled up to the Major. 'Sir, what happened?'

" 'Subedar Sansar has developed a lung problem,' he replied. 'He has to be taken down. You will have to be the one to help him.'

"By then, it was evening; I brought Sansar Chand down the cliff with the help of two jawans."

June 25-26: The Longest Night

"It was now my turn to lead the attack." Bana recounted. "There was such heavy snowfall that, after struggling upwards for eight hours from 8 p.m. to 4 a.m., we could climb only 100 metres. For a moment, I lost courage, and then, for the first and only time, I heard the voice of our tenth guru, Govind Singh *ji*. 'Bana Singh,' he said, 'I was only testing you.'

"In a moment, my dejection vanished and I was filled with an indescribable peace. I was ready to live or die according to the will of the Lord. From that time onwards, I lost all fear of death. I understood that success is achieved only by the help and grace of God and that the higher powers will always help sincere and fearless people.

"The enemy too were sitting tight. It is very difficult to carry ammunition to those heights; both sides had to be careful about saving it. The cold winds were like a knife, but we did not feel it for death stared us in the face. The enemy had the advantage as they were already settled at a greater height, and secondly, their weapons were superior to ours. Then we decided to attack from the front in broad daylight. We took the most dangerous route, barely a few feet wide. One wrong step and we would fall 1500 feet into enemy territory and, if still alive, into enemy hands. Luckily, due to the heavy snowfall, visibility was low for the enemy too. We decided on who would go first and who second. I was to lead. I told my team that if anybody tried to turn back, I would shoot him. In the military, there are only two options: 'Do or die.' I can say with pride that all those of my comrades who died in this action had bullets in their chests, not in the back."

When day had dawned, Bana asked the Major on the phone, "Sir, what are our orders?"

"We will unleash an artillery barrage on the enemy to immobilize them," he replied. "In the meanwhile, you and your men must crawl to the enemy bunker."

"We followed his orders," Bana recalled. "When we reached near the bunker, we radioed the Major to cease firing. I was hoping that, due to the sudden stop in the barrage of fire, the startled enemy soldiers would stand up, revealing their location.

"And that is exactly what happened. We threw grenades at them. Some of the Pakistanis retreated wounded, some hid, and others ran away. Some soldiers of the Pakistan Shaheen Company of 3 Commando Battalion of the Special Service Group (SSG) were still left outside their bunker. We attacked them like a fury and they were soon decimated by bayonets. I threw grenades into their bunker and closed the door from outside. We heard desperate cries from inside, then all was quiet. When the last voice died, we went in cautiously. In all, the bodies of seven Pakistani SSG commandos were recovered; the rest had fled.

"Maj. Virendar arrived and inspected the whole area to find out if there was a possibility of a fresh enemy attack. A light machine gun (LMG) was now fixed to cover the route from which the Pakistanis had climbed to the top, and three soldiers manned the LMG. Also, soldiers were posted at all the strategic places from where the enemy could come up.

"On that day of 26 June, we hoisted India's Tricolour on top of the post. Pakistani RTOs informed their headquarters that the Indians had captured the Quaid Post. For a long time, there was intense shelling from the enemy side. One of our sepoys, Omraj, was hit by a shell fragment – his shoulder got dislocated and we had to bandage it. Then a shell-splinter hit our Major sahib. Luckily, it only grazed him; had it entered his body, the result could have been serious. We informed Brig. C. S. Nogyal about the Major's injury and were instructed to send him back. A helicopter carried him to Kumar Post. Our wounded colleague Omraj, however, expired at the Sonam Post itself, due to excessive bleeding.

"We had thus successfully completed our mission, despite the heavy costs. To this day, the Tricolour flies there proudly."

Early morning on 27 June, Brig. C. S. Nogyal reached the top, inspected the area and marked the places from where Pakistani soldiers could possibly attack. He also inspected the weapons, papers and other effects left behind by the Pakistanis.

"Bana Singh *ji*," he said, "nobody could have done what you've accomplished, on these heights. Henceforth, this post will be called 'Bana Post' after you." Then he returned to Headquarters, and the injured were evacuated.

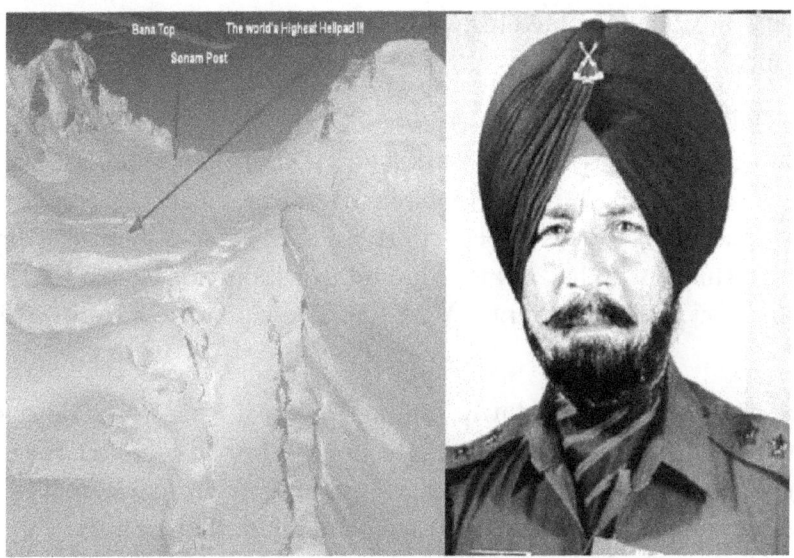

Bana Post named after him (Pic-Social Media)

Bana Singh remained on top along with some soldiers for a few days, but chilblains forced him to descend, and he was admitted to Chandigarh hospital. Upon recovery, he returned to his unit at base camp in Siachen. They handed over their weapons and special clothing to another unit and returned to Srinagar in December 1987.

The Surprise

"On 15 January 1988, a captain came to our unit and said that the Army HQ officers at Delhi had asked for my photograph and biodata," Bana recounted. "Nobody had any inkling about why they required this information. On 21 January, our unit received a message that I, along with some other soldiers, must reach Udhampur immediately."

In Udhampur, Col. Ahluwalia gave Bana his instructions: "You have to reach Delhi, accompanied by your wife, today itself." A military jeep took Bana to his village, Kadyal, situated 60 kilometres from Udhampur.

His family, startled to see him so unexpectedly, asked, "Why have you come?"

"Get ready," he informed his wife, Ravinder. "We have to go to Delhi at once."

At Delhi airport, a Major received them. He addressed Bana as 'Naib Subedar Bana Singh, *Param Vir Chakra–Vijeta*.' Stunned and confused, Bana asked him to explain what he meant. By this time, they had walked out of the airport, and they met PVC Col. Dhan Singh Thapa, who had come to attend the Republic Day parade that year. "You are now a Param Vir Chakra–recipient just like me," he said.

The grand reality was slowly sinking in, but it would take time for Bana Singh to fully comprehend the honour he had received. He and his wife were lodged at a five-star hotel in Delhi. On 23 January, it was announced that Naib Subedar Bana Singh had won the Param Vir Chakra. On 26 January 1988, Bana Singh received the Param Vir Chakra from the hands of President R. Venkataraman.

It is interesting to note that, in June 1987, when India's flag was put on Quaid Post, the Pakistani SSG group involved in that fight had been under the command of Brig. Musharraf. He and Benazir Bhutto, who was then the Pakistani Prime Minister, were furious at the loss of Quaid Post; in retaliation, they attacked the Bilafond La Pass on the Saltoro range in September 1987. It resulted in a misadventure, however, which is said to have cost Pakistan about a 1000 of its elite troopers. It is also believed that, in 1998, when Musharraf became Chief of Army Staff of Pakistan, he attacked Kargil to take revenge for the defeat of 1987. And he lost badly, again. He then made a proposal that both India and Pakistan should withdraw from Siachen and end this confrontation. Indian Army authorities, who had sacrificed so much to retain Siachen, were understandably upset by this proposal, not least because there would always be the danger of Pakistan recapturing Siachen, as the access is much easier from the Pakistani side.

Luckily, the proposal seems to have been shelved.

Citation

Naib Subedar Bana Singh

8 JAK LI (JC 155825)

Naib Subedar Bana Singh volunteered to be a member of a task force constituted in June 1987 to clear an intrusion by an adversary in the Siachen Glacier area at an altitude of 21,000 feet. The post was virtually an impregnable glacier fortress with ice walls, 1500 feet high, on both sides. Naib Subedar Bana Singh led his men through an extremely difficult and hazardous route. He inspired them by his indomitable courage and leadership. The brave Naib Subedar and his men crawled and closed in on the adversary. Moving from trench to trench, lobbing hand grenades, and charging with the bayonet, he cleared the post of all intruders.

Naib Subedar Bana Singh displayed the most conspicuous gallantry and leadership under the most adverse conditions.

—Gazette of India Notification
No. 9 – Press/88

The Ways of the World and Ways of the Army

Bana Singh was naturally elated upon being honoured with the Param Vir Chakra. "What happened later was funny, though," he remarked. "Once I received the award, many government officers and ministers promised to give scholarships to my children, jobs to my family members, and many more things besides: 'I will help your sons to study engineering (or MBBS),' and so on. But these proved to be only empty promises. Later, whenever we approached them, these people replied, 'It was another minister or officer who promised, not I.' and they did nothing for us."

On 15 January 1996, an Army Day parade was held at Mumbai. General Cariappa personally greeted Naib Subedar Bana Singh, whose regiment had come from Nicobar to participate in the parade. During their conversation, Bana Singh informed the General that he was to retire soon.

A great admirer of PVC Bana Singh's bravery and mettle, the General recalled Bana's file when he returned to his office, and decided to recommend Bana for an out-of-turn promotion. Bana Singh could thus serve the Army for four more years as Subedar Major of his battalion. He was posted at the J&K-LI Regimental Centre in Srinagar, and also served as an instructor in IMA. By the time he retired in October 2000, he had been promoted to (Subedar Major) Honorary Captain.

During 'Operation Rhino' in Assam in the 1990s, the 8 J&K-LI, the proud battalion to which Bana Singh belonged, had already earned such a reputation that the inspecting authorities would say, "8 J&K-LI is an ideal platoon – where is the need to inspect it when it has won so many awards and even a Param Vir Chakra?"

"Such praise was like a shot in the arm for us and raised the morale of our troops and officers," Bana Singh admits.

In the Indian Army, each soldier stands for the rest of his unit. Many a time in the Indo-Pak wars, the Pakistanis did not even claim the bodies of their dead and left them to rot. But so well-knit are the Indian regiments that the jawans would lay down their lives, not only to save their friends, but even to recover their bodies when they fell in battle.

Bana narrated one such experience: "Once, I was posted at Gurez, which is situated 100 miles from Srinagar. For jawans carrying rations from one post to another in this avalanche-prone area, the orders were to move only at night and never after sunrise, because the chances of avalanches are greater during the day.

"Two of our jawans were asked to deliver some rations from their post to another before going on leave. Their passes had been signed, and in their eagerness to go on leave, they left a little before sunrise for delivering the rations, without informing anybody. There is a highly avalanche-prone area in Gurez, where even a little sunlight may bring down a terrible avalanche which can sweep away even big trees. Our two jawans were buried by such a sudden avalanche.

"When the head count began, the two jawans, Ramesh and the other (a wrestler), were found to be missing. The CO was informed and he asked us to search for them. There was no chance of their being alive, but we could at least retrieve their bodies. The danger of another avalanche burying all of us was very real as it was day. But a great bond of love and loyalty exists amongst us soldiers. We live away from our near and dear ones, and consider our comrades to be our family. We ignored the possibility of being swept away by fresh avalanches, and toiled, without any food, for at least ten hours before finding the bodies. It was a heart-breaking sight – trapped in the avalanche, where no sense of direction exists, one of our friends had broken the ice with his head for ten feet, but, alas, in the wrong direction: he had gone further and further down. We rested only after bringing out their dead bodies."

After an eventful and meritorious service of thirty-two years in the Indian Army, PVC Bana Singh retired on 31 October 2000. One of his sons, Rajinder Singh, followed in the footsteps of his illustrious father and entered the Army; his older son, Gurdeep, after working in South Korea for some years, has returned to look after family affairs. Bana Singh's two daughters, Surinder Kaur and Rajinder Kaur, are married to two soldiers respectively, Harnek Singh and Balwinder Singh, both Havildars now. His three sisters, Manjit Kaur, Bhajan Kaur and Ranjit Kaur, are also married to soldiers. Manjit Kaur's husband has recently retired as a captain. Most of Bana Singh's family is thus devoted to guarding the nation.

On 25 October 2006, the chief minister of Punjab, Amarinder Singh, a royal scion and himself a former Captain who had served in the 1965 Indo-Pak war, heard that a PVC-recipient by the name of Bana Singh lived in a village of Jammu and Kashmir. This admirer of bravery sent a proposal at once: if Bana agreed to settle in Punjab, he would be given 25 acres of land of his choice, anywhere in Punjab, 25 lakh rupees in cash, and a pension of Rs. 12,500 per month. It was a truly magnanimous offer, especially when compared to the meagre monthly pension of Rs. 160 given to Bana by the J&K government. Bana, however, refused the offer: "I will not leave my village."

So impressed was Amrinder Singh by Bana's disinterestedness that he sent an invitation: "Will you at least come have tea with me?" This, Bana accepted. Amrinder Singh presented him with a silver sword and a cheque for 10 lakh rupees when they met.

In February 2007, this author invited PVC Bana Singh to Pondicherry. "Madam, I am ready to even walk to Pondicherry, as you've invited me with such love," he said, moved. Several grand functions were held in his honour, and PVC Bana Singh was overwhelmed by the love, respect and admiration showered upon him at Villupuram and Pondicherry.

PVC Bana Singh felicitation programme on 24-03-2007, at Rajiv Gandhi Stadium Pondicherry, in which nearly 25,000 students and teachers participated.
(L to R) Sri Ragesh Chandra Director Education Pondicherry, Shyam Kumari, Mrs Bana Singh, PVC Bana Singh, Maj. Gen. K. K. Tewari, Prof. Kittu Reddy of Sri Aurobindo International Center of Education, Dr. Ramadas, Joint Director Education Pondicherry, Mrs Aruna, Director 'The Little Angels English School'.

"For 19 years, I have been living in a corner, unknown to anybody," he said in a voice choked with emotion, before he left. "Today you have given me such honour that there is nothing more I can want now. I wish to jump into the sea to end my life at this high moment!" But it is as well that Bana Singh chose to live because, inspired by the example set at Pondicherry, many such felicitations and awards were to follow.

Col. Ashok Chaudhery, an erstwhile officer of 102 Infantry Brigade, to which 8 J&K LI belongs as well, of the 28 Infantry Division, had also served at Siachen from February 1987 to May 1989 under Maj. Gen. Suresh Thadani. He gave a talk on the occasion of the Bana Singh felicitation programme at Sri Aurobindo International Centre of Education, showing rare slides of that awesome snow-bound peak, Bana Top, where the Tricolour of India flies proudly today.

Cause of Retired Military Personnel

Bana's heart goes out to fellow soldiers, who are generally retired at the age of 37, as that is considered the limit of their battle-worthiness. Most of them are unable to find civilian employment at that age, thus facing great difficulties in raising their young families. On 29 December 2009, he met with the young chief minister of Jammu & Kashmir, Sheikh Omar Abdullah, and put forward some concrete proposals for the re-employment of these retired but young soldiers, which will help them as well as the J&K state. He pointed out that the government was sinking several new tube wells across the state, each costing 30 lakh rupees, but there was nobody qualified to run them; and there was a similar problem with government vehicles – not enough qualified drivers. Therefore, he asked, why not re-employ these retired but well-trained military personnel? They could also be employed as electricity metre-readers and given a small commission for each such assignment.

Omar Abdullah heard Bana's suggestions patiently and, finding his proposals practical, promised to do something for the retired servicemen. Impressed by the PVC-recipient, he gave instructions to his security guards that Bana Singh should in future be allowed in to see him, even without prior appointment.

"In Britain," said Bana, "the government looks after its retired soldiers, especially those who have won the Victoria Cross or shown special gallantry, while, in India, the leaders care only for their power. We have guarded Siachen by paying a terrible price, both in lives lost and in the money spent. Now we hear that the government is considering the proposal of ex-President Musharraf who says, 'Withdraw from Kashmir, withdraw from Siachen.' The fact that our leaders can even think such suggestions worthy of consideration wounds the pride and honour of our Armed Forces."

He also comments on the harsh realities faced by the common Indian soldier: "The life of a soldier is different. Before mobile phones came, we used to write letters or send money orders to our families, which would sometimes take fifteen days to reach them. It was so difficult to wait for their reply. A life in the Army is not for the faint-hearted. A soldier has to live away from one's family, and often in harsh terrain – jungles, mountains and deserts. For the sake of his duty, and for the honour of our motherland, a soldier accepts all these hardships and teaches himself to be happy anywhere he is posted."

PVC Bana Singh with the President

HON. CAPTAIN BANA SINGH

On the Snows of Siachen Glacier

On the razor-edged ice,

Hand upon hand, he inched forward;

His eyes again and yet again

Closed of themselves

As the Fury winds

Knocked out his breath

And tore the skin

From his face,

Exposed for a moment

When he opened his visor

To wipe his eyes.

Driven snowflakes,

Sparkling diamonds,

Fleecy or brittle,

Large or little,

In a myriad brilliant shapes

Blurred the eyes.

But what was the use

Of vision

When one could not see

Beyond a foot or two?

Tied in a harness,

Trussed up like a bird

The soldier hung

From the rope which was

Tied to clamps

Driven in a sheer slope.

All around

The merciless gods of snows

Sat tight, leasing terror,

Through hail, snow, crevasse

And roaring avalanche.

"Soldier! what if your foot slipped?"

Asked his heart.

"What if it slipped!" answered he;

Resigned to fate,

When his turn came

He would quietly die.

But what will be,

If it will be,

When it will be

He knew not,

"But let it be

Soon, O cruel God!"

He prayed as

Vehemently he drove

A tiny flag in the ice

Near the mouth of

The treacherous crevasse
Where the second soldier
His friend lay buried.
Only the day before
In the night,
On the march,
His friend, his buddy,
More to him than son and wife,
Had told him
Of his first born
And as they laughed
The ice broke.
The treacherous ice
Sucked him and two others;
Down, down
The gaping mouth
Of the dark hell
Inside the crevasse,
Elbows stretched out
Instinctively
To save the head
From the jagged sides.

Yet benign gods
Fought the design

Of evil ones,

For the rope held

As they found a tiny toe-hold

On an invisible ridge.

The radio still worked

And they called the base

For help.

Under the ominous moon,

Staking their lives,

Slowly their comrades arrived.

Playing with their lives

In that icy hell

To rescue they descended,

Moving in slow motion,

For speed was impossible

On those rarefied heights.

It took an hour

For hauling up the first one,

Of the patrol of three.

He, the first soldier,

Was in the middle.

By the time

He was pulled out

The decree of death

Was proclaimed

Hon. Captain Bana Singh

On the walkie-talkie
For his friend,
The third soldier,
Whose son was born
On the new moon day
A week ago,
He who now moaned
From some lower
Invisible depth.
But alas!
The fall had sheared
His harness.

The night, the precious night
Was fading and the sun
Was the adversary, for in daylight
The enemy could see
And annihilate rescuer
And rescued.
When they signalled
With the rope
No answer came
And the radio
Broke in staccato,
"Return, order, return at once,

Enemy activity sighted,
Abort further attempt to rescue."
The commander had kept his voice
Purposely bland, pushing back
The raging storm within,
A storm more fierce
Than that outside,
Condemning
A comrade, still alive,
To an icy grave
In the cavernous crevasse.

Oh! their boots on the way back
Weighed a ton,
Each step away, a torture,
For they could hear
A faint moan
From the heart
Of the dark mountain.
Oh! to abandon,
To leave behind,
Ask this not,
Ask if you must
For willing sacrifice.
"No! it is a command,

Hon. Captain Bana Singh

You must return;
It is many versus one."
How cruel can be numbers!
O woe to the dead,
And thrice woe to the living.
"No," checking
This dark chain of thought,
The soldier chided himself,
The one who still lived.

One must not lament the martyrs,
For honour demands the sacrifice,
And what greater fate
Could a warrior pray for?
Forget the many small heaps of stones
Marking the scattered graves
All over the valley,
The tiny flags fluttering
In the vale of Siachen.
Siachen! glacier cold and harsh!
Relentless art,
Yet the spirit of men
Is indomitable, is dauntless.
The Furies may come astride,
The eerie screech

Of your roaring avalanches

May bury in mushy snow,

May maim with frost,

May blind and bedevil

The mind pushed to limit

Again and yet again,

Pushed to the brink,

With their cruel cold.

Monstrous sentinel cliffs

May annihilate and overpower,

Yet thou also reflect

The dark face of Death –

Death that is but a face

Of life eternal.

O Glacier, thou hurtled

Tons of ice to bury sentinels,

No friendly fire,

No friendly bivouac

Allowed.

The lone sentry

Pushed back, unshed

The lone tear,

And drove

Like a demon

The pitons, the crampons,

So that nothing might

Dislodge and trap

His comrades.

A furry animal,

The uncanny dog

Of Ladakh,

The mascot of the battalion

Suddenly pressing flat its ears,

Whined and darted away.

And when a relief party was leaving

The fibreglass hut,

The cold Goddess of Snows

Rode an avalanche,

Always hungry

For more and yet more

To claim him.

O, when will they end

This futile confrontation –

These two halves of one nation?

"O Mother of the Worlds,

Lay Thy hands of peace

On the burial ground

Of the high Siachen,"

Prayed the dying soldier.

"This is not a burial ground,
But the cradle of the brave.
Valour is always born
From fighting
Impossible odds,
A new tale of
Human endeavour
Is being limned here
By India's hero-sons."
Saying this Durga gathered
In her golden bosom
The smiling soul
Of the buried warrior.

–Shyam Kumari

Captain Vikram Batra

"I'll either come back after raising the Indian flag in victory or return wrapped in it."

When Captain Vikram Batra came home on leave before the Kargil war, he visited his favourite restaurant, Neugal Cafe. "War has begun," said an acquaintance. "Who knows when you will be asked to go? You'd better be careful."

"Don't worry," Vikram replied staunchly. "I'll either come back after raising the Indian flag in victory or return wrapped in it."

As it so happened, Vikram, whose very name indicates an abundance of bravery, fulfilled both his assertions. He raised India's tricolour on Point 5140 at 17,000 feet. Later, when he fell fighting for the country, at Point 4875, his body was brought home wrapped in the Indian national flag.

In the shadow of the Dhauladhar Mountains, Himachal Pradesh, nestles an almost unknown town called Palampur. In its city square stands a statue of the first recipient of the Param Vir Chakra, Maj. Som Nath Sharma, who sacrificed his life in 1947 while saving Srinagar from the marauding Pakistan Army and its tribal allies. Before he sacrificed his life, Maj. Som Nath Sharma spoke on the wireless set to his CO, Brigadier Sen. His last words have been etched on the hearts of all Indian soldiers and patriots ever since: "Sir, I will fight to the last man and the last round."

Facing Som's statue is a bronze one of Capt. Vikram Batra of the 13 Jammu and Kashmir Rifles. The 24-year-old from this little town won the Param Vir Chakra, the highest Indian wartime gallantry award, for his outstanding bravery and leadership in the Kargil war.

Vikram's father, Girdhari Lal Batra, is the retired principal of a college in Palampur, and his mother, Kamal Kanta Batra, a former school teacher. Already blessed with two daughters, the couple were overjoyed at the birth of twin sons in September 1974. They were nicknamed 'Luv' and 'Kush', the names of the twin hero sons of Lord Ram, but were formally called Vikram and Vishal.

For the first few years, Kamal Kanta educated her sons at home, instead of sending them to nursery school. From the age of 5, Vikram had his schooling at the Dayanand Anglo-Vedic Public School and, later, the Central School at Palampur.

Courage seemed to define Vikram at a young age. "One morning, when Vikram was 16, one of my colleagues at the school in Palampur told me that she had seen my son in the hospital," Kamal Kanta revealed to this author over the telephone. "I panicked and rushed there. But when I saw him hale and hearty, I asked him what he was doing in the hospital. He smiled and told me about how he had saved a young girl who had fallen out of his moving school bus that morning. The bus door had not been properly secured, and as the bus took a sharp turn on the hill road, the door swung open and the girl fell out. Vikram had lost no time in reacting – he jumped out immediately and took the injured girl to the hospital."

Every night, Vikram would ask his father to tell him a story at bedtime. Spiritually inclined and a patriot as well, Girdhari Lal would tell him tales about the centuries of slavery India had suffered under Muslim and British rule, about great revolutionaries and freedom fighters like Chandrashekhar 'Azad' and Sardar Bhagat Singh, and about the great warrior-king, Guru Govind Singh. Such stories of valour, patriotism and self-sacrifice were strongly imprinted in the impressionable mind of young Vikram.

The boy excelled as much in sports as in academics – he won most of the sports prizes each year. At 15, he had gained a green belt in karate and was a good skater, though it was at table tennis that he most excelled and was selected to represent Himachal Pradesh in the national school-level competitions.

Blessed with a happy temperament, he was also considerate and respectful – no wonder Vikram was the darling of his teachers as well as classmates. He was adjudged the best cadet of the NCC (Air Wing) of the DAV College, Chandigarh.

Joining the Army

"In 1994, my son took part in the Republic Day parade in Delhi as an NCC cadet, and when he came back, he told us that he would love to join the Army," Girdhari Lal told this author. "His maternal grandfather had been in the Army, and so were several other relatives. Earlier, he had been selected for the merchant navy and almost joined it. He was supposed to join a ship in Hong Kong – his uniform was ready and his tickets booked.

"But something made Vikram change his mind. He told me he was not after money – he wanted to do something extraordinary that would bring fame to his country. He got commissioned as a lieutenant on December 6, 1997 and, within one and a half years; he had won the highest award for wartime bravery. I am proud of my son – he was ambitious, willing to do anything to achieve his goals. He was a bit of a spendthrift as well. But he was also altruistic: at 18, he decided to bequeath his eyes to an eye bank. He carried this card always with him. He was extremely friendly and pleasant; he could get along with anyone. I always told him he should be number one in whatever profession he chose, and he achieved this goal. He was indeed the best in his profession."

In July 1996, Vikram entered the Indian Military Academy. After passing out in December 1997, he joined the Army as a lieutenant in 13 Jammu & Kashmir Rifles, posted at Sopore in Jammu and Kashmir. After about three months there, he was sent to receive his officer's training at the infantry school in Mhou for two months.

"You should do your best," wrote his father. "This training will help mould your character as an officer." Vikram achieved Alpha grade in this training. Later, he was sent to get commando training at Belgaon for two months. There too, he achieved instructor's grade.

The last time he came home was during the Holi festival of 1999. His mother pampered him with his favourite pakoras, home-made potato chips and mango pickles, even packing some for him to take back. The holidays were soon over. Vikram's friends and his parents saw him off at the bus stand.

The finest hour of his young life, the hour of his triumph and sacrifice, was nearing. His unit had received orders to move to Shahjahanpur in Uttar Pradesh. But war broke out in the meantime, so his unit was posted to Kargil instead, and Vikram was asked to join it there. On 1 June 1999, 13 J&K Rifles proceeded to the Kargil sector.

Kamal Kanta recalled, in a telephonic interview with the author, that her heart sank for a moment when Vikram called to say his unit was being sent to Kargil. "The last war between India and Pakistan had been fought before the birth of Vikram. He was just 24 and had been in the Army for only 18 months. What if something were to happen to him?" But she quickly pushed the thought away. "If all mothers began to think that their children should not join the Army, then who would protect this vast nation?"

Vikram reassured his parents by calling them at least once in 10 days from Kargil. He inquired about his elder sisters, Neetu and Seema, and his twin, whom he lovingly called 'Kushli'. His mother was relieved when he told her, "Ma, I'm absolutely fine. Don't you worry." Those would be his last words to her.

Vikram Batra (Pic: Social Media)

Victorious Battles

On 12 June 1999, Vikram's battalion, 13 J&K Rifles, was ordered to move to Drass as reserve for forces fighting at a feature called 'Hump', an extension of Tololing. On 16 June, Captain Vikram – he was promoted to the rank of Captain on the Kargil battlefield – wrote to his twin brother, Vishal, from Drass: "As you have been reading in the papers and listening on the news daily, things have become very hot here. I am sitting at a height of 15,500 feet and fighting the war with Pakis. Life is at total risk. Anything can happen here, everyday we're facing hell, lots of bullets and [artillery] shells. Today is a very sad day for our battalion as we have lost one officer. Dear Kushu, take care of mom and dad. As I have written, anything can happen here."

'Hump' and 'Rocky Knob' were captured on 17 June 1999 after two nights of fierce fighting by 13 J&K Rifles. Eight enemy soldiers were

Vikram Batra (Pic: Social Media)

killed and nine wounded. The Pakistani soldiers fled, leaving behind three Universal Machine Guns which Vikram and his comrades used against them.

After this victory, 13 J&K Rifles was asked to capture Point 5140, the highest peak on the Tololing ridge, at 17,000 feet, a strategic location of the Drass region. Pakistani troops entrenched on that peak had brought down one of India's helicopters in that area. No helicopter could land safely on Tololing Top, which made the capture of Point 5140 of paramount importance. It was the first crucial step in clearing the Pakistanis from the Tololing sector and paving the way for a total Indian victory. The task was given to B and D Companies of 13 J&K Rifles. On 19 June, D Company, commanded by Capt. Vikram Batra, and B, by Capt. S. S. Jamwal, moved quietly onto the slopes of the 'Hump' and hid themselves. Both captains made a detailed reconnaissance of the snow-clad area leading to Point 5140. Their battalion commander, Lt. Col. Y. K. Joshi, briefed them in detail.

"*Yeh dil mange* more!" announced Vikram, when asked what D Company's success signal in this operation would be. The popular Pepsi advertisement catchphrase meant 'My heart wants more', but the words, when aired later on TV, caught the nation's imagination in a new way – and became the slogan for the Kargil war itself. Capt. Jamwal chose "Oh, yeah, yeah, yeah!" as his company's signal.

As dawn lights up mountaintops first, Capt. Vikram knew that he had only that one night to finish his task. Pakistani troops had taken positions in bunkers at a height of 17,000 feet. From their vantage point, they could see the advance of Indian troops and target them as they climbed the steep incline. When daylight faded from the mountaintops on the evening of 19 June, the B and D Companies began to move towards Point 5140 under cover of artillery fire. Aware of the enemy's advantage, Capt. Vikram decided to attack from the rear and thus take the Pakistanis by surprise; he ordered his men to climb the treacherous, almost vertical rock-face stealthily. Arduous was the ascent and Vikram's men crawled silently and carefully. A single wrong step could result in their hurtling down the mountain to certain death on the rocky ridge below.

An expert commando himself, Capt. Vikram did not intend to lose any of his soldiers if he could help it. He had already experienced such a loss: during his first posting in terrorist-infested Sopore in Jammu and Kashmir, a bullet had hit the man behind him.

"*Didi*, it was meant for me, but I lost my man," the deeply upset Vikram had confided to his sister, in a phone conversation. To understand this attitude, one needs to know the famous motto of the Indian Military Academy in Dehradun: "The safety, honour and welfare of your country come first, always and every time. The honour, welfare and comfort of the men you command come next. Your own ease, comfort and safety come last, always and every time." This motto had been etched deep in Vikram's consciousness; it moulded his feelings, thoughts and actions, both on and off the battlefield.

Climbing the 17,000-foot-high mountain towards Point 5140 in total darkness was extremely arduous; the soldiers had to halt frequently to regain their breath. Time and again, they had to slow down or stop altogether when the area was illumined by the enemy's artillery para flares. Disregarding the added dangers of enemy artillery fire, the B and D Companies continued to advance carefully up the rough ascent towards Point 5140. The silence of those snow-clad hills was constantly broken by the hellish din of guns and bullets, the whines of the aircraft above, and the booming of the anti-aircraft artillery below.

Capt. Vikram's code name was *Shershah* (Lion King), so apt and catchy a title that even the Pakistani troops came to know of it. Breaking in on the radio-net of D Company that night, they challenged him: "Why have you come, O Shershah? Not one of you will return alive!"

Capt. Vikram was not one to take a challenge lying down: "Within one hour, we'll see who will remain on the top!"

That night, there was no stopping the Indian jawans. The two companies from 13 J&K Rifles were not far from their target. At 3:15 a.m., the companies neared Point 5140, which had 2 bunkers on top and 5 on the eastern slope. B Company, led by Capt. S. S. Jamwal, reached the top bunkers and attacked them. Vikram looked at his watch. It was 3:25 a.m. The sun would rise at 4:30. They had only an hour to achieve their target.

The first victory was Capt. Jamwal's – there was jubilation at Command Headquarters on hearing his "Oh yeah, yeah, yeah!" over the wireless. In the meantime, D Company fired three rockets on the eastern bunkers. Capt. Vikram then took the lead in physical combat and, charging into the nearest bunker, lobbed in a hand grenade. He moved to the next bunker without stopping to see the damage done to the first. *"Durga mata ki jai!"* he yelled as he attacked the remaining three bunkers on the eastern side.

Inspired by the charge of their young officer, the troops attacked with renewed vigour. Vikram and Jamwal had cleared all seven bunkers in very little time. In the fierce fighting, 8 Pakistani soldiers were killed and the others fled, many falling to their death from 17,000 feet. The 13 J&K Rifles had won a decisive victory, but the most impressive fact was that not one of Vikram's men had been killed in these exchanges. The Indian troops had captured a large quantity of arms, ammunition, and even an anti-aircraft gun from those bunkers; they had won another hard-fought battle and held high the glorious tricolour on Point 5140. At 4:35 a.m., Capt. Vikram Batra broadcast his victory signal – *"Yeh dil mange* more" – and a huge cheer went up at the brigade headquarters.

"How many casualties?" asked the commander, expecting heavy losses. He could not believe his ears when Lt. Col. Joshi replied, "By the grace of God, not a single soldier died in the operation." The Chief of Army Staff, Gen. Ved Prakash Malik, personally congratulated Capt. Vikram on the phone later.

Srinjoy Chowdhury of *The Statesman* met Vikram in the Kargil battlefield. "Vikram was awash in adrenaline, with much of the 'high' of the recent capture," he wrote. "… the fact that his company had not lost a single man during the battle gave it a Commando-comic-like 'the Invincibles have done it again'-air. He would do outrageously brave things and you would wonder what makes a young man do what he did."

"Our chaps were highly motivated and our commanding officer had put so much spirit in us, there was no looking back," Vikram told Srinjoy. "We were waiting to go up. We knew that we would have them nice and proper."

Srinjoy wrote, "No one would say this in the early days of the war when the 'mantra' was 'containment'. Batra's Delta Company *would* go up, even though the weather was turning ugly, the rocks slippery with frozen rain and, as they climbed, a powdery snow."

"Our soldiers started shouting, 'We have to do it. We'll take our revenge,' " said Vikram. "The Pakistani regulars were firing continuously: artillery from across the LOC and machine-guns and automatic rifles from the bunkers. Then they fired illumination rounds and there were moments of virtual daylight. It was night but everything was lit up. We were 50 metres from the objective and right ahead was a patch of snow. When they fired illumination rounds, we lay there, pretending to be dead. They were firing machine guns and rockets. We kept advancing and, once we reached the point, we yelled

'*Jai Durga*' – our war cry – and ran towards them. There were 80 to 100 of us, and we were firing as we went, and those chaps panicked. We were charging and charging, and they were running here and there. We were following them and we were firing. I saw four bodies fall in a gorge. We could not retrieve them. We knew there were other chaps there, hiding behind the rocks. We sanitized the area, secured a firm base and fired our automatics and made our plans. We would attack the last two bunkers – we called them Bunkers 9 and 10 – we suspected there would be two or three Pakistanis there. Again we charged and managed to kill two chaps. We searched the entire area after that, but there were no Pakistani soldiers alive.

"It was then that we sent our signal '*Yeh dil mange* more' to the commanding officer. We could not believe we had done it. We could not believe it – we had done it without losing a single chap. It was a big achievement. The gradient was a big problem. We were climbing from about 15,000 feet to 17,000 feet and it was very, very steep. After every five steps, we had to stop just to catch our breath. We were climbing over big boulders. At one point we were not sure if we would reach or not. If we were stuck on the slopes at dawn, we would have been in great difficulties. We would have been perfect targets for the Pakistanis on top."

"How did it feel to charge at the enemy and fire at soldiers running away?" asked Srinjoy.

"It was us or them," was Vikram's staunch reply. "If we hadn't reached, we would have been sitting ducks. It was all by the grace of God. Luck was with us. God was with us" (*Despatches from Kargil*, 195-197).

It was one of India's toughest campaigns in mountain warfare. To reach Point 5140, eight mountainous 'humps' had to be crossed. The Pakistanis had effectively deployed machine guns on these peaks and had also called for artillery backup from Pakistan-Occupied Kashmir. Indian fighters, however, achieved victory without sustaining any casualty. Lt. Col. Joshi later said, "The victory of Point 5140 would make a textbook on mountain warfare for the manner in which this perfect operation was executed."

Vikram's men swore by his name. Photographs of him and his men astride the captured Pakistani gun at the base camp were splashed across the front pages of all major national newspapers; his youthful slogan *"Yeh dil mange* more" became the redefining motto for the patriotic spirit of the Kargil fighters.

Once Point 5140 was captured, Barkha Dutt of NDTV asked Capt. Batra how he felt about his victory. Millions of viewers heard the daredevil captain's answer: *"Yeh dil mange* more." And ever since, those words have become suffused with the shades of fierce patriotism and the crimson of self-sacrifice. Later that year, the chairman of Pepsi wrote to Vikram's father acknowledging that his son had immortalised their advertisement slogan. This 'Lion of Kargil' showcased a new breed of soldier: he represented the 'never-say-die' spirit of the brave, young heroes who fought and died selflessly in this war being fought under daunting conditions.

In Maj. Gen. Ian Cardozo's words: "The Kargil War was a war where young officers of the Army were in their 'element'. In no previous war had young officers dominated the scene as did these young gladiators in Kargil. Amongst them were some who deserved better and some whose deeds were not recorded at all and therefore not recognised. However, from amongst them all, the one who captured the imagination of the public most through the media was young Vikram Batra. His bold courage and the daredevil risks he took in mission after mission filled the public with wonder and awe. He seemed to be invincible, but every time he sallied forth to meet new challenges and dangers, people prayed for his safe return." (*Param Vir: Our Heroes in Battle*, 157-158)

On the morning of 20 June, a wave of happiness spread over Drass town, now completely inhabited by the Army, the police, and the CRPF jawans. Girdhari Lal can never forget the phone call he received that morning – Vikram's animated voice crackled through the satellite phone: "Daddy, I've captured." He spoke so fast in his excitement that his words were not very clear. For a moment, his father thought that Vikram had been captured, but his reason told him that had that really happened, he would not have been allowed to talk to his parents on a satellite phone.

"Speak clearly," he said, and Vikram announced more slowly, "Oh Daddy, I've captured the enemy's post. I'm OK, I'm OK!"

Bursting with pride, his father replied: "*Bete*, I am proud of you. May God bless you to carry on your task there."

"It was the happiest moment of my life," Girdhari Lal said, in an interview with this author. "I had named my son 'Vikram' because the name spelled character and strength, and he had lived up to it."

Over the next few days, he and his wife saw their son several times on television. With his camouflage jacket and beard, he looked different – but he always seemed to be brimming with confidence, always smiling. When Vikram's mother heard that he had captured his first peak, she felt as elated as if it were her own victory. "I have lived all my life in the lap of the Dhauladhar Mountains in Palampur," she said. "Each day, I saw the mountains and thought them invincible. Now my son told me he had conquered a perilous peak as high as the Dhauladhar, maybe even higher."

With the capture of Point 5140, the tide of battle turned in the Drass sector; helicopters could land at Tololing Top. After about four days, B Company's rest at Ghumari was cut short and, on 30 June 1999, 13 J&K Rifles was sent to prepare for operations to win Point 4875 in the Mushkoh valley under the command of 79 Mountain Brigade.

Last Battle

This assignment was a near impossibility. It is difficult even to imagine the hellish weather and terrain conditions prevailing on those heights. But winning this point was absolutely necessary for India, as the Pakistani artillery entrenched there had in its gunsights the whole stretch of National Highway 1A from Drass to Matayan. They could pick out any vehicle on the road for about 40 kilometres. Many of the Indian truck drivers who dared, nonetheless, to move on this stretch were blasted by the Pakistani artillery. Helicopters could not land at Drass, targeted as they were, constantly, by the Pakistani troops from Point 4875. Even then, the daredevil Indian Air Force pilots did fly their helicopters very low, along the Pandrass ridge, but it was risky.

Over the next few days, after returning home from college, Girdhari Lal would watch the evening news for a glimpse of his son. A television correspondent interviewed Vikram at the base camp: "You are going for another crucial operation – what are your thoughts at this moment?"

"Our government is doing well about the supply of our food material and other things as far as possible in this tough war-field at very high altitude," Vikram replied. His superiors revealed later that they had appreciated this mature answer from the young officer.

"I hope that the families of the deceased soldiers will be looked after well by the government and society," Vikram added, and turned his face away from the camera. Hundreds of miles away, Girdhari Lal read the expression on his son's face and thought, with a sinking heart, "Oh God, he doubts his return." He could see no more – there were tears in his eyes. His wife asked why he had broken down all of a sudden, but he could not tell her.

On 1 July 1999, Lt. Col. V. K. Joshi and the commander of A Company, Maj. S. Vijay Bhaskar, climbed to a high vantage point for an aerial view of the operation area. Based on their report, the commander prepared a battle plan at the headquarters of 79 Mountain Brigade. On 2 July 1999, the battalion was airlifted to 1,500 metres below Point 4875, to an area which offered some cover. Indian porters bravely carried up to this area, on foot, all the ammunition and heavy weapons for the battalion.

Vikram wrote to his parents on 2 July 1999, before leaving for this mission: "I am fine here by the grace of the Almighty. I had come down to Drass from top for 5-6 days, for rest and recuperation, but again moving up today for another offensive action. So all set to go.

"I had undertaken a very big operation earlier also, in which I got 100% success and it was the biggest success in this sector. I had also received congratulatory calls from Army Chief and other senior commanders from all over. Was also interviewed online from media.

"Don't know when I will be moving down again. So whenever I will get a chance, I will call you up. So do pray for the success of my next operation."

On 4 July, Company Commander Maj. Gurpreet Singh showed the operation groups their objectives. At 6 p.m., the Bofors guns commenced their bombardment. Sitting quietly amidst all the noise, Vikram wrote his last letter to his twin: "Dear Kushu – I am sitting at a very high altitude and ready for my task. I might go up today in the evening. Two [companies] are already up and are engaged in very heavy exchange. They are very near to the objective (about which I can't write to you). As you have asked about the situation here, [I can tell you that] the situation is improving ... don't know how much time it will take, but our Army is doing a fantastic job here."

At 8:30 p.m. on 4 July, Vikram's group started the tortuous climb, in pitch dark, their eventual objective being to strengthen the flank of the Indian troops fighting the invaders at 17,000 feet. The thick fog made the advance even more precarious at that 80-degree gradient.

When they were 200 metres below the top, the Pakistani troops started heavy fire. Through the interception of the Indian radio frequencies, they had got wind of Vikram's presence. They taunted him again over the wireless: "Shershah, this time, nobody will be left alive to carry your body."

Undaunted, Capt. Batra flashed back: "You just take care of yourself!"

The Pakistanis continued their heavy shelling. Vikram and his troops began to retaliate with their automatic guns. But they were pinned down by the heavy enemy fire, and this was reported to their company commander. On 5 July, Lt. Col. Joshi personally fired, from the fire-base, two Faggot Missiles at the enemy bunkers on Point 4875. They were direct hits, and they could see the enemy fleeing.

Vikram attacked with his troops at once and captured Point 4875, but the enemy continued deadly, accurate fire from a position north of it. The battle continued the whole day. Indian troops succeeded in beating back two counter-attacks, but how long could they hold out without reinforcements?

On 6 July, they spotted a strong contingent of Pakistani troops on a long and narrow ledge on the northern slope above Point 4875; it became clear that this post had to be conquered.

On 7 July, Capt. Vikram volunteered to head a party to help attack this ledge. "I will go up, sir," he offered, eyes bloodshot with fatigue. It was an extremely cold day; Vikram had fever and sat wrapped in a blanket. Seeing his condition, his CO hesitated, but Vikram insisted. Hearing their hero's offer, many of his soldiers volunteered to accompany him. Vikram and these jawans prayed to Goddess Durga, and then the group began their gruelling ascent.

Suddenly, Vikram's expression changed: the signs of fatigue and fever vanished, and he became a man fired by a mission. The base relayed a message to the hard-pressed troops at the top that 'Shershah' was coming with his men to help them and asked them to somehow hold their ground till he came and took charge.

A new courage coursed through the exhausted troops at the top, and they cheered – Vikram had already become a hero for them as well, and many were the stories of his bravery that were passed on from soldier to soldier. The Pakistanis, intercepting the Indian wireless message, also came to know of the imminent arrival of 'Shershah'. They knew and feared Vikram, the first man atop Point 5140.

The chill wind of Mushkoh *nala* penetrated the bones of Indian soldiers. It was pitch dark and foggy, so visibility was very low. And the climb was near vertical. To make matters worse, it began to snow.

But Vikram climbed like a snow leopard, coaxing and encouraging his exhausted troops to press on. As they neared the objective, he heard the rat-a-tat of the machine gun which had pinned down the Indian troops. He moved towards it, hiding behind one rock and running to the shelter of the next till he was close enough, when he lobbed a hand grenade at the gun position and destroyed it.

Then he whispered to his troops: "Follow me, boys." They advanced to the next position, as the enemy guns had to be silenced before daylight crimsoned the peaks. At the altitude of 16,087 feet, the air was so thin that it was difficult even to breathe. The soldiers were panting, yet they went inexorably forward, fuelled, as it were, by some supernatural strength.

Two more guns had to be stopped before dawn. It seemed an impossible task. Day dawned. By the time Vikram reached near the guns with his troops, it was broad daylight. Vikram must have known even while volunteering for this assignment that it might cost him his life, but such was his enthusiasm that no thought for his safety bothered him then or now. Patriotic fervour coursing through his veins, he moved ahead, firing constantly with his AK-47. He closed in on the enemy. It was a fight at such close quarters that he could not even use his rifle. He pulled out his bayonet and charged. Grappling with a Pakistani, he floored him with a punch on the nose and plunged his bayonet into the fallen soldier. Another attacked him from behind. Vikram threw him off his back and pierced him with his bayonet. It was ferocious hand-to-hand combat, with seven enemy soldiers killed.

Unnerved by the fury of the attack, the remaining Pakistanis retreated. Vikram and his jawans had gained the upper hand. Pursuing their advantage, the enthusiastic troops attacked the last machine gun position on the ledge. Like the lion he was nicknamed after, Vikram plunged boldly inside the fortification. Most of the Pakistanis had fled from the fury of his attack, but two soldiers were still feeding the machine gun and a third was firing it, spraying death on the Indian soldiers. A JCO of the Pakistan Army was directing them. Vikram leaped inside and single-handedly killed all four of them.

Despite being wounded, Vikram, along with another young officer, Anuj Nayyar, fought off the enemy's counter-attack ferociously. They cleared the enemy bunkers, egged their men forward, engaged in hand-to-hand combat and forced the Pakistani retreat. The mission was almost over, when Vikram ran out of the bunker to rescue another officer, Lt. Naveen, whose legs had been severely injured in an explosion. Vikram's subedar had begged him not to go, volunteering to go in his place.

But Vikram would have none of it: "You have a wife and children. Step aside." He lunged forward to save the young lieutenant. Even as he dragged Lt. Naveen towards cover, the gravely wounded officer pleaded with Vikram to let him continue the fight. It was then that a bullet pierced Vikram's chest. He had saved Lt. Naveen's life at the cost of his own. Enraged by his death, the soldiers of 13 J&K Rifles pursued the enemy relentlessly.

"Nobody was bothered about the bullets flying in any direction," a soldier later revealed to Gaurav Sawant, Special Correspondent with *The Indian Express*. "There was only one thing on everybody's mind: to avenge Captain Batra's killing. We followed the fleeing soldiers. They were running away. Such was their fear that some of them fell to their deaths while fleeing." (*Dateline Kargil*, 188) Once they had routed the enemy, the soldiers returned and sat surrounding the body of their beloved 'Shershah'. It was hard for them to believe that their brave captain, the live dynamo who had been energising, inspiring, and coaxing them just a few minutes ago, was now no more.

"Vikram Batra had succeeded in clearing the ledge, securing the peak, and also securing the movement of the 17 Jat troops pinned down by effective Pakistani firing. Under the guidance of Colonel Dinesh Badola, Jawans of the Second Battalion of the Naga Regiment advanced silently at night to capture the Twin Bump Peak. Mounting a ruthless attack, the Nagas dislodged the Pakistani soldiers. Once Nagas took Twin Bump, Pakistani forward troops did not get reinforcements, weapons and ammunition. They were choked and left with no option but to retreat." (Sawant, 188) Taking the ledge near Point 4875 had thus been the crucial turning point in ending this war.

Srinjoy Chowdhury writes, "Vikram *would* volunteer for the most difficult task, climbing up a sheer rock-face to take the enemy in the rear [at Point 5140]. And how thin the margins between death and glory are! This time, there was no return to adulation, no TV cameras, just a few tears and a letter home. A hidden machine-gun opened up; he crawled up and silenced it with a volley of grenades. When three enemy soldiers rushed out, he killed them all, but was seriously wounded in the fire fight. He refused to be evacuated; he would regroup his men and charge towards the final defences, dying in the effort. They didn't give him the Param Vir Chakra for nothing." (198)

By morning on 7 July 1999, India had won Point 4875, but lost Vikram Batra. Those of the unit who survived the battle later reported that Capt. Batra had died with the words, *"Jai mata di!"* on his lips. With the conquest of Point 4875, our lifeline to Ladakh was secured – our vehicles could now safely move on the Leh-Matayan Highway.

Today, Point 4875 has been renamed 'Captain Batra Top'. Vikram's comrade, Anuj Nayyar, also died while clearing the fourth bunker. Anuj was awarded the Maha Vir Chakra, the second highest award for bravery. For Capt. Vikram Batra's sustained display of most conspicuous bravery and leadership of the highest order in the face of the enemy, he was posthumously awarded India's highest decoration for gallantry in battle, the Param Vir Chakra.

Citation

Captain Vikram Batra (Posthumous)

13 Jammu and Kashmir Rifles (IC 57556)

During 'Operation Vijay' on 20 June 1999, Captain Vikram Batra, Commander, Delta Company, was tasked to attack Point 5140. Captain Batra with his company skirted around the feature from the east and, maintaining surprise, reached within assaulting distance of the enemy. Captain Batra reorganised his column and motivated his men to physically assault the enemy position. Leading from the front, he, in a daredevil assault, pounced on the enemy and killed four of them in a hand-to-hand fight. On 7 July 1999, in another operation in the area of Pt. 4875, his company was tasked to clear a narrow feature with sharp cuttings on either side and heavily fortified enemy defences that covered the only approach to it. For speedy operation, Captain Batra assaulted the enemy positions along narrow ridge and engaged the enemy in a fierce hand-to-hand fight and killed five enemy soldiers at point-blank range. Despite sustaining grave injuries, he crawled towards the enemy and hurled grenades, clearing the position with utter disregard to his personal safety. Leading from the front, he rallied his men and pressed on the attack and achieved a near impossible military task in the face of heavy enemy fire. The officer, however, succumbed to his injuries. Inspired by his daredevil act, his troops fell upon the enemy with vengeance, annihilated them and captured Point 4875.

Captain Vikram Batra thus displayed the most conspicuous personal bravery and leadership of the highest order in the face of the enemy and made the supreme sacrifice in the highest traditions of the Indian Army.

Gazette of India Notification

NO. 16 – Press/2000

Shades of Memory

Capt. Vikram's family received the news the same day. When Kamal Kanta returned from teaching at school, her neighbours told her that two military officers had come when no one was at home. Vikram's mother cried out in fear; she knew that military officers came only to announce bad news. She prayed with all her heart before she dialled her husband's number. When Girdhari Lal reached home and saw the officers, he guessed there was bad news. He told the two colonels to wait, went inside and bowed his head in the *pooja* room first. When he came out, one officer stepped nearer and took his hand. "Batra *Saheb*, Vikram is no more." Batra collapsed to the ground.

The next day, his son's body was brought home and cremated with full military honours. Nearly 20,000 people participated in the impressive cremation ceremony; many dignitaries were present. Chief of Army Staff Gen. Ved Malik visited the Batra home, where he told Vikram's father, "Had this kid returned from Kargil, he would be sitting in my seat in 15 years."

"The day his body was brought home – it was excruciating," recalled Kamal Kanta, in a telephonic interview with this author. "Parents cannot bear to see the dead body of their young son. Our Vikram had captured three peaks, he had taken the nation by storm, but suddenly he was no more. Yet when God gives you a mortal blow, he gives you the strength to cope with the grief. Guru Govind Singh sacrificed four sons for the country. Maybe there was some reason that God gave me twins – one had been marked for the country and one for me. I feel proud of my son. I feel honoured that I gave birth to a son like him who did not flinch from his duty when the hour arrived and gladly sacrificed his life. He has sanctified my womb and enhanced my motherhood."

Vishal, Vikram's twin, had hoped that one day his brother would rise to the rank of a brigadier or even higher, and then his friends would be greatly impressed when he would walk by his side. Now he has lost count of the number of times his twin has made him proud. Once, when he signed his name in a hotel register in Scotland, an Indian standing nearby read the name and asked, "Do you know Vikram Batra?" Vishal, a banker, wrote in a letter to this author, "Is there any better reward than that people know his name even in far-off Scotland?"

Vishal remembers his visit to the Indian Military Academy fifty days before Vikram's passing-out parade. Vikram, with his passion for perfection, had beautifully decorated his cubicle with lovely collages. Their last meeting was on 9 March 1999 when Vikram, after finishing his commando's training, telephoned Vishal and asked him to pick him up from Hazrat Nizamuddin Railway Station, Delhi. Vishal drove him to his flat. The twins chatted animatedly. There was so much to say, yet so much was left unsaid because Vikram had to leave right away to meet their parents at Palampur. At the bus stand, the brothers embraced, and Vishal had no inkling then that it was their last embrace, their last meeting. Vishal says, "That last embrace is going to be with me throughout my life. His physical presence haunts me. Now we have to live with his beautiful memories. Every morning, standing in front of his photograph, I salute him for all his heroic deeds and the sacrifices he made for this nation."

A natural charmer, Vikram was very popular among his friends and teachers during his college years in Chandigarh. And it was there that he found the girl whom, had he lived through the war, he would have married. When he joined the Army, Vikram asked Vishal to meet his friend as often as possible. Five days before Vikram's death, Vishal was in Chandigarh on account of work and contacted her. She came to see him at the station. When Vishal alighted, she called out his name and said, "This time, make sure to get us married."

"Sure," replied Vishal.

When the news of Vikram's martyrdom came, Vishal did not have the courage to speak to her. During the cremation, she stood to one side with her parents and wept quietly. Decades after the death of the only man she ever loved, she remains single. Vikram's parents have repeatedly urged her to change her mind about marriage, but in vain. The cards and the teddy bear that Vikram had presented to her adorn her shelf. She is a teacher now and has sworn never to marry.

Vikram's parents live alone in a house where Vikram never lived but which bears his name on the nameplate in front. When sorrowful memories overwhelm them, they look at his pictures and remember his words, his laughter.

"Ours is a lifelong grief at losing him," they wrote to the author. "But our son gave his life for the glory of this country. He made us proud in his death." Hanging in the centre of a wall, in a wooden frame lined with gold, is the PVC citation. 'Param Vir Chakra' is written in glowing, inspiring letters on it. A picture of Girdhari Lal receiving the PVC award from the late K. R. Narayanan, the erstwhile President of India, also hangs on the wall. That their son's sacrifice was recognised by a grateful nation reassures the parents.

Capt. Vikram Batra's cap and the tricolour in which his body had been wrapped were given to his mother before the cremation. She has wrapped the flag reverently in transparent plastic and placed it on a table, in front of Param Vir Vikram's photograph.

Recently, the Indian Oil Corporation paid tribute to Vikram in one of their advertisements, 'Sometimes an ordinary Indian can make a Rs. 120,000-crore company feel humble. For every step we take, there's an inspired Indian leading the way.' Placed alongside was a black-and-white etching of Capt. Vikram Batra. A framed picture of the text hangs in the petrol pump awarded in Vikram's honour to his parents. The advertising agency also sent the etching (below), which Girdhari Lal Batra has preserved carefully.

Homage to Captain Vikram Batra

"Vikram, Vikram," the Kargil ranges called,
"Vikram, Vikram," whispered the soldiers
Of 13 Jammu and Kashmir Regiment
As they negotiated the sheer slopes,
With bated breath they clambered
Over the sleet-covered rocks,
Rocks hard and silent since ages,
On whom no human feet had ever left,
Such immortal foot-prints of courage.

For the Pakistanis there was left no hope:
With "Vikram", the raging volcano
Of matchless valour, none could cope.
Destined was he to become a part of the lore
That would sing the glory of his hero-soul.
On India's T V screens a hundred images flashed,
In which the bravery of Vikram was projected.
" 'Shershah', why have you come?" the Pakis taunted,
"To annihilate you I come," our Shershah retorted.
To escape from Vikram's fiery onslaught,
To escape from that thundering avalanche,

The enemy drew back and many fell.

On the rocks they lay spread-eagled,

With unseeing eyes, battered, broken and dead,

Thus "Hump", and "Rocky Knob" Vikram s men overran.

Then he was tasked to fly the Tricolour

On well-defended Point 5140 Peak, a difficult feat,

Vikram climbed from behind, he hacked and pulverised,

"Yeh Dil Mange More" declared India's pride,

Indians cheered upon hearing his victory cry.

On the captured Pakistani machine-gun he sat astride.

India's Tricolour was unfurled on that peak with pride.

"More" and "More" Vikram asked for, ever more he tried

Then "More" was he given, asked to conquer peak 4875,

Where four Pakis with his bare hands he crushed,

The impossible was done, victory almost won,

When to save a wounded comrade, he leaped

From the safety of a bunker, a bullet cleaved

The heart of this lion-king, the Shershah, the wonder,

A nation's hope in that time of great danger.

Of his brave mother Kamal Kanta he was the pride,

Of his father Girdhari Lal he was the star child.

Of him, Mother India will forever be proud,

Him the Gods of India will forever bless,

On seventh July, in the year nineteen-ninety-nine

Vikram, of 13 Jammu and Kashmir, laid down his life

Captain Manoj Kumar Pandey

*"If death strikes before I prove my blood,
I swear I will kill death."*

On the night of 6 July 1999, in the Gomati Nagar colony of Lucknow, the capital of Uttar Pradesh, hundreds of people worked in near silence, sweeping and covering with flowers the six-kilometre stretch of road that led from Gomati Nagar to the cremation ground of Vaikuntdham. People tried not to step on the delicate blooms, and more and more were being brought in by trucks. The powerful and pleasing fragrance of the flowers was everywhere. Soon, it became clear that all the flowers of Lucknow would not suffice to cover the entire route of the cortege; one stretch of the road would remain uncovered.

An urgent message was sent to the organisers; Subroto Roy of the Sahara Group sent an aeroplane to Calcutta in all haste. It returned a few hours later with a fresh load of flowers that were rushed to the people decorating the road. The volunteers gave no thought to food or sleep, focussing all their energies on completing their sacred task alone.

The road was being decorated thus, not for some king or prime minister, president or great religious leader. It was being covered with flowers for the last journey of a 24-year-old youth, Manoj Kumar Pandey, who had lived, for almost all of his life, in an ordinary house in Gomati Nagar. Among the bravest of the brave sons of India, this young man had sacrificed his life to win the crown of victory for India in the Kargil war and was awarded a Param Vir Chakra for his exemplary valour.

The next morning, a detachment of soldiers from Manoj's Gorkha regiment marched in formation in front of the garland-festooned gun carriage bringing Manoj's body to his home. "Long live Manoj Kumar! Victory to Manoj Kumar!" a million throats cried out.

At 9:30 a.m. on that 7 July, his body was brought to his house, where Manoj's parents, Brijmohini and Gopichand, his brothers, Manmohan and Mohit, and sister, Pratibha, were waiting. An hour was given to the family to take leave of him. Gopichand opened the casket and looked at his beloved son; the family tried to stamp his image on their hearts. But they did not have much time – lakhs of people were waiting to take leave of their Manoj, a martyr who belonged to the whole nation.

Punctuality is a hallmark of the military. Exactly at 10:30 a.m., the casket was closed and, wrapped in India's tricolour, placed on the military carriage again. The cortege made its way to Shaheed Chowk. It was placed there on a platform decorated with garlands, to give the assembled people a chance to pay their homage. Lakhs of people had been eagerly waiting for a last glimpse of the brave son who had made Lucknow proud. Only a few lucky ones got to see the coffin; the rest had to pay their homage from a distance and be satisfied with a glimpse of the cortege. Many of those coming to pay their last respects to their young hero had found no space on the near bank of the river Gomati, from where the cortege was to pass, and so stood patiently for hours on the other bank.

At 2:30 p.m., as per schedule, the gun carriage began moving towards the cremation ground, with the Gorkha Rifles marching in front again, but so large were the crowds that all they could do was inch forward. At 3:45 p.m., the cortege reached the cremation ground, where the Governor, the Chief Minister and other dignitaries respectfully took down the casket and placed it on the flower-decked bier. A guard of honour was presented.

By 4:30 p.m., his mortal remains were consigned to the fire.

The Early Years

Born on June 25, 1975, in Roodha village, Sitapur district, Uttar Pradesh, Manoj showed signs of intelligence as early as at about two; his parents fostered it by telling him tales of the great freedom fighters and encouraging him to follow high ideals.

Gopichand, a far-sighted man, decided to move to Lucknow, to give his children a better education. He took up a simple job, but their finances were not too good.

Once, when Manoj was only three years old, he visited his maternal uncle. "Manoj, do you only play or do you also study?" asked the uncle.

Manoj answered, with superb self-confidence, "I know everything." Then he counted up to hundred, in one breath.

Stunned, his uncle said, "In future, don't count like this before anyone, Manoj. Or somebody's evil eye will fall upon you."

His precocious brilliance ensured Manoj's admission to the Green Field School of Nirala Nagar in Lucknow, where he studied up to the fifth standard. Later, he transferred to Lakshmi Bai Memorial School in Rahim Nagar, about five kilometres from his home. The family could not afford to send him by rickshaw or bus; Manoj would therefore walk to and from school, about eleven kilometers every day.

"How will such a small child walk so far with a heavy school bag?" his mother would worry, and Manoj would laugh away her fears: "Ma, why do you worry? For me, it is all play."

Manoj was an unusual child, full of extraordinary self-confidence. Once, when his father wanted to engage a tutor for him, he refused to have one. "Father," he said, "I don't need a teacher. I will study by myself." Right up to the twelfth standard, he stood first in his class. His loving nature, determination and exceptional ability for hard work ensured that he won the hearts of his teachers as well as fellow students.

Manoj loved skipping. He would skip rope forwards and backwards, as well as to left and right. During the monsoons, his mother would turn an earthen drinking-water pot upside down on the roof, and Manoj would skip on it. His mother was often apprehensive about the noise disturbing the people downstairs, but Manoj was an expert – nobody ever heard the sound of his feet, and the pot never broke. He skipped so gracefully that it seemed as though he never touched the ground, though sweat poured from his body. All that anyone ever heard was the swishing sound of the rope. His love for skipping continued until the end.

Theirs was a simple life. "It's better to have a small house, so the family can live together and do things together," Manoj would say. "If the house is too big, then the family members will be isolated." Money did not hold any attraction for him. "After all, man needs only *dal-roti*. Where is the need for more money?"

Once, the school authorities took the students of Manoj's class on a trip to Haridwar. His mother wanted to give him 100 rupees for incidental expenses. Manoj refused, and when she insisted, accepted only 24 rupees. Upon his return, he gave 2 rupees to his mother. She assumed that he had spent the rest buying sweets or some such thing. It was only a few weeks later, when the family began receiving the magazine *Akhand Jyoti*, that they realised that he had spent the 22 rupees not on himself but on the magazine subscription!

After completing his seventh standard, Manoj received a boarding scholarship, which entitled him to join any of the famous residential schools of India, like the renowned Doon School in Dehradun or Mayo College in Ajmer.

"*Bhaiya*,[1] join the Sainik School in Lucknow," advised his mother. "We do not have much money, so if you go to Dehradun, Ajmer or Gwalior, we will not be able to visit you." Manoj accepted his mother's choice. As his last school had been a Hindi-medium one, the Principal of the Sainik School did not believe him capable of coping with the level of English in the eighth standard and admitted him into the seventh instead. Manoj wept at this demotion, but his mother consoled him and he finally agreed to join the seventh standard. At the end of the year, when Manoj stood first in the class, the Principal called his parents and apologized: "I made a great mistake by placing Manoj in the seventh standard instead of the eighth. He has achieved what we never expected." So popular was Manoj with both teachers and friends that he was twice selected as School Captain. Anybody with whom this friendly boy talked for even ten minutes would come to believe, quite firmly, that Manoj loved him best.

His concentration in anything he did was absolute. "Why do people say that this is difficult, that is difficult?" he would wonder. "If you really want to do something, then nothing is difficult." In the evenings, when other children of his age would talk, play, and while away their time in other ways, Manoj would sleep. But he would study from midnight to 3 a.m., prompting his classmates to wonder, "Manoj goes to bed so early, then how does he top the class?"

Manoj took the greatest care of his things. When he was eight, he would often pick out his own tunes on a simple flute his mother had bought him when he was about three. He took such good care of it that the flute looks like new, even to this day. At fifteen, when he

---

[1] In a quaint family tradition, mothers in this clan never called their eldest sons by name. Manoj's mother always called him *bhaiya*, the Hindi word for 'brother', an appellation that constantly reminded him of his responsibilities as the eldest among her children.

received his boarding scholarship, he used some of the money to buy slippers for his mother and sister. Respect for elders and love for youngsters were ingrained in his nature; no complaint was ever received against him from relatives, classmates or school authorities.

As School Captain, Manoj was sometimes asked to select a film to be shown to his fellow students, and he would invariably choose an old, idealistic movie. Except for some patriotic ones, he never saw films, nor did he watch television. From the age of 13 until he passed his Intermediate Examination (equivalent to the present-day Class XII Board exam), he studied in the Sainik School of Lucknow, where he received many prizes for studies as well as sports. On one such occasion, he received the medal from the Governor of Uttar Pradesh himself.

After his Intermediate Examination, he was selected by the Roorkee Engineering University as well as by the National Defence Academy. "Anyone can become an engineer," Manoj told his parents. "I will study in the National Defence Academy and win the Param Vir Chakra." His already ardent love for the motherland had been reinforced by his years at the Sainik School. For three years, he studied at the National Defence Academy, Khadakvasla, in Poona. While there, he also received a graduate degree from JNU. Thereafter, he was trained for one year in the officers' course of the Indian Military Academy at Dehradun.

Manoj was commissioned into the Army in June 1997. When his parents came for his passing-out parade, they learned that he was posted as a Lieutenant in the 11 Gorkha Rifles, which was fighting a bloody battle with terrorists in Kashmir.

"I told you not to go to war," said his mother. To which he answered, "Then why did you always tell me stories of Chandra Shekhar 'Azad' and Sardar Bhagat Singh, Ma? And if I am not to go to war, what is the use of my studying in the National Defence Academy and joining the Army? Ma, please don't weaken me."

With tears in her eyes, his mother said, "After all, we did teach Manoj that this body is mortal – today or tomorrow, one year or ten years hence, it has to go."

"*Bhaiya*, you are an officer," his mother said, one day. "In war, aren't the soldiers in front and the officer behind?"

"Ma, would you send me in front if there is danger?" asked her son. "The jawans of my battalion are my children. How can I remain behind while they face death?"

His mother was troubled about another aspect of war: "Will you have to kill men?"

"Ma, wouldn't I kill someone who tried to kill you?" Manoj explained patiently. "In the same way, how can we spare someone who attacks *Bharatmata*? If we do not kill him, he will kill us."

Lt. Manoj's battalion faced a fierce encounter with terrorists in Kashmir, on the day after he joined it. His company commander, Lt. P. N. Dutta, laid down his life for the country; for this brave deed, he and his battalion were awarded the Ashok Chakra, India's highest award for bravery in military peacetime operations. This encounter and the self-sacrifice of his immediate senior left an indelible imprint on Manoj.

Once, Manoj was leading a patrol that got unusually delayed on one of its missions; this led to a lot of concern. When the patrol returned two days later, his commanding officer asked Manoj the reason for the delay.

"We were not able to get any militants," replied Manoj. "We went further till we found some, and we could not come back in time because the terrain was very difficult to negotiate."

On his very first assignment, Manoj killed three terrorists. So enthusiastic was he to serve the country that one of his COs, Col. Shekhar Upadhyaya, made a comment that 'anchors' were required to control Manoj Pandey. The toughest jobs were taken up by him willingly and completed to perfection. Amongst his colleagues and subordinates, his name soon became a byword for enthusiasm and courage.

Those who knew Manoj were quick to notice three unique features about him: first, his truthfulness, second, the piercing and dazzling light in his eyes, and third, his thundering voice. Manoj never lied; his mother recalled that there was such a fierce glow in his eyes that it was sometimes difficult to look into them. His father confides that he has never heard such a powerful voice in his life. Manoj roared like a lion, as many Pakistani soldiers would discover to their shock, in the Battle of Batalik.

Siachen Glacier

From Kashmir, Manoj's battalion was posted to the Siachen Glacier, the highest battlefield in the world. No unit of the Army can remain in this area for more than a few months at a time, due to the intense cold.

Manoj was away completing the course for young officers when his battalion was ordered to Siachen. Disappointed that he could not join his battalion at once, he wrote to his CO, requesting the officer to keep the 'Bana Post' for him if the battalion was posted to the Northern Glacier, or the 'Pahalwan Post' if it was sent to the Central Glacier. These are the toughest posts in the area. Manoj would, eventually, spend the longest tenure to date by anyone in the Army at the 'Pahalwan Post', at a height of 19,700 feet.

The second-in-command of Manoj's battalion, Lt. Col. A. Asthana, in an article in *The Indian Express* dated 10 September 1999, remembered: "In the glacier, we admired Manoj's ingenuity. There was this ice wall, 2,300 feet high, and we had to carry our equipment and supplies up. Manoj improvised a double-pulley and it made life so much easier. We held a post in the central glacier – it was called Pahalwan Post. It was the highest post there, and bitterly cold. The stint there was usually for forty-five days and, believe me, every day counts. You don't want to be there an extra day; you want to run as soon as your stint is over. Manoj stuck it out for sixty days, and not only that, he worked out a new route that helped us to evacuate casualties by day without drawing enemy fire." (quoted by Srinjoy Chowdhury, *Despatches from Kargil*, 146) Impressed by his endurance and grit, his officers recommended his name for the Shaurya Chakra, the third-highest peacetime gallantry award of the country.

In March 1999, after completing their tenure at Siachen, Manoj's battalion was sent for rest and recuperation to Leh-Ladakh. Shobhita Asthana's reminiscences of Manoj reveal a new aspect of his personality. "The memory of the Pied Piper haunts me," she writes. "A young officer, full of life, dancing ahead of the village children, wild with joy, running after him. The Piper would suddenly stop, turn around and shower sweets. The children would catch them and then again sprint after the Piper. The Piper of Tamisgamn, as we would later call him.

"After humouring the kids, he came to the platform and won the respect of the entire village with his humble words. At the mike, with the whole village in the backdrop, standing tall ... that is how our camera caught him. Now that's the photograph my children hold next to their hearts as they narrate stories of Pandey Uncle, their

Pied Piper, who became the target of enemy bullets and is known to the country as the Batalik hero, Captain[2] Manoj Pandey.

"In the spring of March 1999, your presence of mind and sense of humour never failed to amuse us. At dinner time we would hear the tales of the glacier, tales which were frightening and hair-raising, tales of brave adventures, rough climate, tough terrain, tales of hidden crevasses and steep climbs, of sickness and laughter – little did we know that there were tougher times ahead ... Most vividly we remember the welfare mela you organised single-handedly ... small children performing their traditional dance, and for the hungry, there were fancy eats. You had thought of them all. The mela was a great success ... brave Gorkha officer, we all salute you."

After the rigours of Siachen, Manoj's battalion was looking forward to its peace tenure at Poona. On those tough heights, each soldier had lost nearly five kilos. They were bone-weary. The advance party of the battalion reached Poona and handed over their winter clothing and some of their equipment as well as weapons. Many went on leave, including the second-in-command; the CO took premature retirement. In consequence, the battalion was being commanded by the officiating second-in-command.

It was at this time that the Kargil war broke out. The depleted and weary battalion, lacking its CO as well as a lot of its manpower and equipment, received the order to go and fight at Kargil. It was an almost impossible task, but the soldiers of the 1 Battalion of the 11 Gorkha Rifles rose to the occasion, answering the call with indomitable courage, fortitude and enthusiasm. Their sole aim was victory, and if the price of saving the country was death, then it would be gladly welcomed.

---

2 Manoj had displayed such startling bravery in his first posting in Kashmir that he had been selected for promotion to the rank of Captain – it was approved, but before the promotion could be gazetted, he had laid down his life in Batalik.

Pakistan's Double Perfidy

The Kargil war was the third attempt by Pakistan to grab Kashmir from India. They broke an unwritten agreement that both sides would withdraw from their Army bunkers in Kargil during winter and re-occupy them only in the spring. The Pakistan Army stealthily occupied the Kargil heights during the winter of 1999 – and the irony was that they encroached upon Indian territory and entrenched themselves in the bunkers built by the Indian Army.

Eternal vigilance should be the watchword for guarding a country's freedom, but, despite three wars with Pakistan, Indians had not anticipated this move. This illegal occupation of Indian territory was doubly treacherous on the part of Pakistan as, during this period, the Indian Prime Minister had gone on a bus trip to Lahore and signed a peace pact with Pakistan's Prime Minister, Nawaz Sharif. Having lulled India into the belief that it wanted peace, Pakistan simultaneously pushed its troops into Kargil.

It had meticulously planned and made preparations for this attack, and the following evidence is enough to prove it. The intensely cold temperatures of Kargil require the soldiers posted there to wear special clothes and boots, but Indian soldiers did not have enough of them. Only one firm, a French one, makes this type of boots, and when India tried to order them at the beginning of the Kargil War, the company declared it had no stock left. On further enquiries, it was found that Pakistan had bought all its stock in February 1999. (Vinayak Parab, quoted by Heeralal Yadav, *Salam Sainik*, 26-27)

Pakistan had established 40 camps in Pak-occupied Kashmir to train terrorists, which helped them make the false claim later that the attack was launched by Kashmiri militants. But the troops that attacked Kargil, though comprising some Afghans and Jihadis, consisted mainly of soldiers of the Northern Light Infantry of the Pakistan Army.

Pakistan never could, it seems, reconcile itself to the loss of East Pakistan, the creation of Bangladesh in 1971, and the shameful surrender of its 93,000 fully armed soldiers. Similarly, in June

1987, the Indian Armed Forces wrested back the Quaid Post from Pakistan's Special Commando Group, enraging its commander, Brig. Musharraf, and Pakistani Prime Minister Benazir Bhutto. It did not help that their retaliatory attack on the Saltoro Range in September 1987 was a dismal failure as well, costing them about 1000 elite troopers. History was to repeat itself in 1998, when Musharraf, as the Pakistani Chief of Army Staff, planned the attack on Kargil to take revenge for the defeats of 1971 and 1987, but to no avail – Pakistan was to be defeated and badly humiliated once again.

The original plan for the Kargil invasion was drawn up in 1987, when Gen. Zia-Ul-Haq controlled Pakistan, but was not implemented at that time as the foreign minister, Lt. Gen. Yakub Khan, pointed out its military, political and diplomatic defects. It was taken up again in 1997 during the tenure of Pervez Musharraf as the General Officer of the corps that was supposed to implement the scheme. When Pakistani Prime Minister Nawaz Sharif appointed Pervez Musharraf as the Army Chief in October 1998, the scheme was put into effect.

During winter, the Kargil area, consisting of the Mushkoh Valley, Drass, Kaksar and Batalik, receives heavy snowfall, with frequent avalanches and blizzards endangering survival. Taking advantage of such weather as well as an easier access to these heights from their side, Pakistan Army penetrated 4 to 8 kilometres across the Line of Control into Indian territory in these sectors. Nearly 2,000 Pakistani troops occupied the Indian military bunkers, with the full support of artillery, mortar, anti-aircraft missiles and other heavy weapons.

Not many Indians have heard the name of Tashi Namgyal, but then, not many in India know the names of their military heroes, even of the 21 recipients of the Param Vir Chakra. Tashi Namgyal, a farmer of Garkhun village of Kargil Tehsil, was the first to spot the intruders, in April 1999, and informed the Indian authorities about their presence. Later, he guided the Indian Army to the hills occupied by the intruders.[3] (T. Samphel, member, National Commission for

---

3 As a reward, the Army authorities deployed on the spot gave him a cash award of Rs. 50,000 and he also received commendation letters from the GOC of 8 Mountain Division, Headquarters, 192 Mountain Brigade, and from the CO

Scheduled Tribes, "Unsung Hero of the Kargil War," *Border Affairs*, January-March 2010, 27)

India paid a dear price for its lack of vigilance and its naive trust in a country that had never kept its word, that broke treaties at will and seemed to mock the Geneva Convention. The Pakistanis were jubilant, once they occupied the Kargil heights. Parts of their wireless transmissions, overheard by Indian soldiers, revealed that they expected to teach India a lesson and win Kashmir to avenge the loss of East Pakistan. Their confidence stemmed from the fact that their gunners could, from the heights they were occupying, blast any vehicle off the Srinagar-Leh National Highway. Their aim was to cut Ladakh off from Kashmir as well as to isolate Kargil, thus severing India's lifeline to Siachen.

More proof of their intense aggression was to follow. Upon receiving news of the incursion, India sent a patrol, on 15 May 1999, to ascertain its truth. The Pakistanis ambushed this patrol on the Indian side of the LOC, tortured the patrol leader, Lt. Saurav Kalia, and his five soldiers for weeks, and returned their mutilated, broken and battered bodies near Indian Post 43 on 9 June 1999. The Pakistanis had pulled out the fingernails and gouged out the eyes, pierced the ears with red-hot rods, cut out the noses and genitals of these soldiers, and then shot them. Even seasoned, battle-hardened soldiers found the sight unbearable. (Lt. Col. Rajkumar Pattu, *Indian Prisoners of War in Pakistan*, 307-308)

On 5 July 1999, Brian Cloughley reported this incident in *Canberra Times*: "Half-dozen soldiers ... were tortured and put to death after capture ... The victims resembled pulped and messy colanders of meat, with eyes and teeth shattered, and bits of flesh torn away by the lacerating impact of point-blank bullets ... the eyes had been destroyed ... 'gouged out'. " (Pattu, 338) The bodies were returned after 22 days, during which time India had done nothing to save them; regrets do not make amends for that criminal neglect.

---

of First Battalion of the Bihar Regiment, in recognition of his courageous, outstanding and meritorious service.

In a telling contrast to Pakistan's behaviour, Indians treated the 93,000 Pakistani prisoners of the 1971 War with kindness, providing them with comforts like mosquito-nets, which were not given even to Indian soldiers in some postings.

This inhuman action sealed the fate of the Kargil misadventure for Pakistan. For India, it was now a fight to the finish.[4]

Kargil

This war with Pakistan was fought on the slopes and jagged peaks of Kargil, at altitudes of up to 17,000 feet, where it snowed even in June. Worse still, the near-vertical slopes had to be scaled at night, in absolute silence, while carrying heavy backpacks, with fog reducing the visibility, and with hardly a toehold available on the slippery rocks where Indian soldiers had to fix ropes with pitons and crampons. Some threw away their last food packets to lighten the weight. And if, in the meantime, the Pakistani troops who were holed up on the heights saw them coming, there would be a rain of mortars, grenades, bullets and boulders upon them. Their comrades

---

4 Saurav Kalia's father, Dr. N. K. Kalia, wrote, on 27 July 1999, to the Northern Command Chief, Lt. Gen. H. M. Khanna, "We felt immensely proud of the way [Saurav] showed his mettle, undergoing the most brutal and barbaric treatment along with five brave soldiers ... That was the real battle he faced. The enemy gave up ultimately and shot him dead ... Sacrificing oneself for the nation is an honour every soldier would love to do, but no parent, army or nation can accept what happened to these brave sons of India. I am afraid every parent [will] think twice before sending their wards to the Armed Forces if we all fall short in our duty of safeguarding the prisoners of war and let them meet the fate of Lt. Saurav Kalia." Shamefully, the parents of Saurav Kalia came to know about his fate from newspapers, not from the Army. Dr. N. K. Kalia wrote to Indian President K. R. Narayanan, "I am given to understand that Army ethics says that, in the event of missing, injured or casualty, the next of kin is informed within 6-8 hours of any eventuality. We came to know about his missing status from *The Indian Express*. It is all the more painful that the Army preferred to break the news to the Press instead of the parents, flouting all norms" (<http://www.indiaworld.co.in/home/skalia>). Dr. Kalia has tried untiringly to goad the Government of India into challenging Pakistan to get the guilty punished under the Geneva Convention. Lakhs of Indians have signed the petition. But nothing has happened so far.

would fall dead by their side, but there would be no time to linger or even to throw a backward glance at them.

At such moments, a cold fury would possess the hearts of the surviving soldiers. They would advance with redoubled determination to annihilate the ruthless killers, feeling no pain and not even aware of the bullets which pierced them or the splinters that shredded their flesh. Millions of Indians watched this war on their TV sets everyday, inspired and electrified by the valour of their Army.

On those freezing heights, each step required effort; even breathing became a difficult task due to the lack of oxygen. Temperatures in the minus thirties and the steep gradient of the climb meant frequent stops to rest and recover every few steps. In that killer cold which was their greatest enemy (after the Pakistani soldiers), the troops needed special clothing, shoes and goggles. Though they wore layers of thermal garments, special gloves and socks, and insulated shoes, the soldiers were still at the mercy of winds that could pierce through these layers of cloth and freeze their blood. Nonetheless, they climbed and fought every inch of the hard way up, sporting willingly with death. The Indian infantrymen may not have had proper clothes for surviving on those killing heights – their shoes were inadequate and their rucksacks too bulky to be carried on those treacherous slopes – but of superhuman courage they had plenty.

A surviving Pakistani soldier later gave a statement about his Kargil war experiences in *Time* (USA), 10 July 1999: They, the Pakistani soldiers, were entrenched in a concrete bunker on a mountaintop. Suddenly, the Indian soldiers started to climb up. At first, one or two, and then more than a hundred. They appeared within range of the gunsights of the Pakistanis, who took careful aim and fired, trying not to waste their ammunition. The Pakistanis shot the Indians dead till their arms ached from constant shooting. But according to this soldier, the 'mad' Indians continued to advance and die.

The same issue of *Time* magazine also reported on the differing psychological conditions of soldiers in the rival armies. Before the battle, Indian soldiers had spoken to their families over the telephone, their words full of hope and courage. There was no trace of discouragement, none of despair. Pakistani soldiers, however, were in a different state of mind. When they had called their homes before the war, they cursed their officers for sending them to certain death. They wept and told their families that they had been pushed into the arms of death by their officers and that it would not be possible for them to return alive.

But it was not merely the brave infantrymen who were responsible for the Indian victory. In this war, where no quarter was asked for or given, the gunners of the Indian Army did their best to provide cover for the jawans climbing those treacherous, almost vertical slopes against heavy odds. Indian Air Force planes wheeled in the sky, trying to blast the intruders from their bunkers. And in the end, India did win this war – but at a terrible cost. 25 officers and 436 jawans were killed, and 54 officers and 629 jawans were wounded, some of them disabled for life.

It was a heroic battle. The Indian infantry attacked with a ferocity which took the Pakistanis by surprise and destroyed their belief in their victory. The Indian gunners fired till the barrels of their guns grew red-hot; the Air Force pilots risked their lives repeatedly, trying to blast the enemy strongholds; and the Indian navy blockaded the Pakistani ports so effectively that, in July 1999, only two weeks of petrol supply remained in Pakistan. Indian TV took the battle to the numerous homes of India. The entire country rallied behind the troops; this unprecedentedly augmented support raised the morale of the Army.

The Pakistani government tried to claim that the men fighting up there were Kashmiri 'freedom fighters', but the documents left behind by the invaders and the fallen bodies of dead soldiers of the Northern Light Infantry of Pakistan proved to the world that the operation was launched by the Pakistan Army and not by the so-called freedom fighters of Kashmir. Defeat stared Pakistan in the face. Their seemingly invincible strongholds were destroyed by Indian troops; 45 Pakistani officers and 700 soldiers were killed. Ultimately, Nawaz Sharif went on 3 July to Washington and pleaded with President Bill Clinton to broker a ceasefire and save Pakistan from further humiliation.

In that short war of two months, hundreds of deeds of matchless courage and fortitude occurred, both recorded and otherwise. Four from amongst those bravest of the brave won the Param Vir Chakra. Two of them were officers and two were jawans. Two lived to tell the tale and two gladly laid down their lives for India. One of these four dauntless warriors was Capt. Manoj Kumar Pandey.

He came home on leave one last time, before leaving for Kargil. "Make some parathas for me, won't you, Ma?" Manoj asked his mother. "I want to go to Naimisharanya." He left on foot around 5 a.m. for this pilgrimage to a shrine situated about 90 km from Lucknow, and returned by the next afternoon, an extraordinary feat of speed and endurance.

Just before leaving for Kargil, Manoj's mother recounted, he had poured *sharbat* in three glasses. One he gave to a friend who had come to see him, the second to his mother. When he picked up his own glass, it fell to the ground and broke. It was an ill omen, his mother felt.

A Saga of Valour, Sacrifice and Victory

From 4 May to 2 July, Manoj and his unit fought the enemy in Operation Vijay. Srinjoy Chowdhury writes: "The depleted and weary Gorkha Rifles Battalion was sent to Batalik. There was no precise information about the enemy strength, positions, [or] weapons ... Those were early days, of fresh troops, yet to be acclimatized, blundering into enemy traps. More and more enemy posts were being spotted ... the Gorkhas weren't really prepared but they were pushed in. In those difficult early days in Batalik, the Gorkhas were immediately ordered up the mountains. A 16 Grenadiers patrol was ambushed and cut into pieces. Capt. Manoj Pandey had his orders. He was to bring them back. It was 9 May. Lieutenant Colonel A. Asthana remembers, 'We didn't have any clue about where we were going. The enemy positions weren't on the map, and as we started moving up on 8 May, we began [encountering] the enemy. There were four dead Grenadiers lying there, under the nose of the enemy. Manoj got them back. He was everywhere – in Kukarthang and then in Jubar in mid-May, and till then nobody knew that the enemy had occupied the area. Manoj was the first to [have had any] contact with the enemy in Jubar, and in fact, when 1 Bihar Battalion was moving up, the commanding officer had only Manoj with him [to command and guide them]. "I am throwing you into impossible situations again and again because I have no choice. I don't have too many officers," a senior officer explained to him after [the fight for] Point 5203. "Sir, it is my good fortune. I am not complaining about the cold or the enemy fire. All I want is more ammunition," Manoj replied. We didn't have the warm clothing for the operation, but again, he managed well and remained there till 24 June.' " (*Despatches from Kargil*, 146-149)

Manoj killed a great many enemy soldiers, and witnessed the martyrdom of several of his close associates. Each sacrifice of an Indian soldier increased his courage. "Dear Ma, Pakistanis have penetrated into India up to seven kilometres," he wrote, in June 1999. "It will take a month to chase them out. Ma, give your blessings for our success."

"*Bhaiya*, never look back," replied his mother. "My blessings and the blessings of the whole country are with you." In bygone days, fearless Rajput ladies would send their sons to war, into the very jaws of certain death, in just this way, with a smile and a blessing, a tradition that is still intact in the hearts of many Indian mothers.

When his battalion took part in 'Operation Vijay', Capt. Manoj always volunteered for the most difficult tasks. He was the first to reach the forward posts. As the previous CO of 1/11 Gorkha Rifles had taken premature retirement, Col. Lalit Rai of the Rashtriya Rifles was asked if he would like to take charge of the 1/11 Gorkha battalion, in the thick of the battle, and this brave officer agreed. A helicopter brought him to the battle zone, where there was fierce fighting.

Col. Lalit Rai wrote a vivid account of this battle on his website: "In the Batalik sector, the terrain was really tough and unforgiving, compounded with the most inhospitable weather. After due deliberation and reconnaissance, everyone, right up to the highest commander, had more or less assessed that if the formidable and dominating enemy position at Khalubar were to be captured, the complete area would become untenable for the enemy. But the problem was that Khalubar was located at an altitude of 17,500 feet above sea level, with the enemy sitting well entrenched, with lethal and sophisticated weapons, in a dominating position; it was also located deep in the heart of the enemy defences … the attack would have to be made uphill under accurate and intense enemy fire."

Col. Lalit Rai led the attack from the front, taking Capt. Manoj Pandey and his Bravo company with him. It took them 14 hours of extremely torturous and dangerous marching to reach the objective, carrying heavy loads of arms, ammunition, rations, winter clothing and other special equipment needed for negotiating the steep, snow-covered slopes. Col. Rai continued: "Throughout the move, we came under heavy enemy small-arms fire and artillery shelling. The intensity and the accuracy of the enemy's fire grew even as we laboriously plodded our way up through snow and sharp, jagged rocks, at steep inclines. The temperature was 29 degrees below freezing point, a really marrow-chilling temperature which numbs your whole body and deadens the senses.

"We had started the attack with a few hundred people. We had closed to about 600 yards of the enemy position, where the enemy fire became very intense and effective and it seemed impossible to proceed further against this curtain of lead and fire from the tracer bullets. You could see the bullets and rockets hurtling towards us with fearsome intensity and sound. My heart still shudders when I remember the heart-wrenching screams and cries of my boys who fell under this wilting fire from the enemy's heavy machine gun as also from his air defence gun. The sight of my boys, battered, torn, and ripped apart by machine-gun fire, bleeding profusely, still haunts me, and I often wake up sweating. It was a real test for me, egging [them] on towards almost certain death from effective and intensive enemy fire, to close in and finish the enemy off before he finished us.

"We pushed ahead despite heavy casualties, with the 30 to 40 soldiers I could muster. The others were either injured or pinned down by heavy enemy fire. Maximum casualties were being caused by fire coming from Khalubar Top, while another was from a flank, which we later named 'Bunker Area'. I decided to capture the top with 40 men and sent Captain Manoj Pandey to capture and silence Bunker Area with approximately 30 men."

Manoj had written to a friend from the Kargil battlefield: "I assure you and my countrymen that whatever the price we have to pay, we will chase away the intruders. Many of our soldiers have attained martyrdom, but I am still alive, maybe to attain some higher aim." In his last letter from the battlefield, he wrote, "If I return from the battlefield, I will have an extraordinary experience to tell, which can never be forgotten."

Battle for the Bunkers

Capt. Manoj Kumar Pandey was commander of 5 Platoon during the advance to Khalubar. He struggled relentlessly up the jagged, 80-degree rock slopes. As his platoon approached Khalubar, it came under heavy fire from the surrounding heights, including Area Bunker GR 193910. Manoj was given the task of clearing the bunkers. He manoeuvered his platoon to a position of advantage and sent Havildar Bhim Bahadur's section to assault the two bunkers on the right, while he himself proceeded to clear the four bunkers on the left. Engaging in assault on the first bunker, he killed the two soldiers inside. He sprang to attack the second and destroyed it, killing two more Pakistani soldiers. Enemy fire struck him while he assaulted the third bunker, injuring his shoulder and legs. *"Na chhornu, na chhornu!"* ("Don't spare them, don't leave them!"), he shouted out in his formidable voice in Gorkhali – and the Gorkhas obeyed the command of their fiery leader, killing every enemy soldier within reach. Capt. Manoj Kumar Pandey led his men from the front in the finest tradition of the Indian Army. He inspired them by acting gallantly and courageously, in spite of being grievously injured. Manoj ignored his injuries, leapt on the fourth bunker and destroyed it with a grenade. Sadly, at the same time, he was hit on the forehead by a fatal machine gun burst.

Thanks to this valiant fight by Manoj and his team, 6 well-defended enemy bunkers were captured and 11 enemy soldiers lay dead. A huge cache of arms and ammunition, including one air-defense gun, was recovered. As his citation explains, he thus provided the crucial base for the companies to successfully capture Khalubar.

"It is not Manoj alone, but all the jawans who were brave, otherwise how could they fight a battle on heights of almost 18,000 feet?" said his mother. "All of them fought together bravely, only then could victory be won. Pakistanis were sitting on the heights in bunkers made of stones, not exposed to the cold winds. They had sacksful of cashewnuts, almonds and pistachio; they had enough food to last a whole year. They were in a position to shoot from the heights. Yet we won. So the credit for victory goes to all of our soldiers."

Capt. Manoj Kumar Pandey received the first Param Vir Chakra of the Kargil war. General Ved Malik, who was then the Chief of Army Staff, told Manoj's father: "Pandey *ji*, the credit for our Kargil victory goes mainly to Captain Manoj Pandey. Many more of our young men would have died, otherwise. Shortly after the destruction of the Khalubar Post, the battle stopped."

Manoj and his mother had been very close. They often spent hours together in *satsang* and *kirtan*. Such was the empathy between them that whenever Manoj fell ill at boarding school, she had known it instinctively. "What happened on that date?" she would ask, when he came home for a visit, and invariably, it would turn out that he had been unwell on that day.

"*Bhaiya*, now you should marry," she would say, whenever Manoj came home from the Army on a visit.

"Where's the hurry?" was his constant reply.

Once, his loving mother dreamt of a beautiful wedding ceremony for Manoj. "In your marriage procession, we must have a military band and the *shahnai*."

"Ma, the whole of Gomati Nagar will participate in my marriage," Manoj replied, as though looking into the future.

Sometimes his mother would plan far ahead. "*Bhaiya*, your father and I do not know English – how will we teach your children? Where will you educate them?"

As if his instinct had warned him of his untimely end, Manoj answered, "Never mind, Ma. Let's just talk of today, shall we?"

Manoj often asked his mother to meet his friends. But she would protest shyly: "*Bhaiyaji*, your friends are great people. How can I meet them?"

"Ma, you will have to learn how to meet people in high positions," said her son.

"Now I understand why he asked me to meet people," his mother recalled. "Since his death, nearly five lakh people have visited us – some of whom hold very high positions."

Manoj visited her dreams every night after his death, offering solace and courage to his mother, whose tears would not stop: "Why do you weep, Ma? Did I sacrifice my life for this?"

"Now we feel he is always somewhere near us," his mother said. "He was a great soul who had come for a great purpose and returned after fulfilling it."

In an interview with R. B. Singh, Manoj's father, Gopichand, and mother, Mohini, said, "We are proud of our son's bravery, but we have become half-dead after his death" (*The Sunday Express*, 2 June 2002). His father has been afflicted with high blood pressure and diabetes after Manoj's death. "We have to fight a decisive war with Pakistan," he said. "How long will we suffer from this proxy war? If our Intelligence Bureau had done its work properly, then we need not have fought the Kargil war – our son and hundreds of others need not have died." The family has received ten lakh rupees from the UP government and eight lakh rupees from the military. The central government has also given them a gas agency. But Manoj's father said,

"We were happier when we earned two hundred rupees per day from our hosiery shop while Manoj was alive. His brothers, Manmohan and Mohit, and his sister, Pratibha, have still not recovered from the shock of his death. It has snuffed out their smiles."

Manoj's family has bought a house where his sister lives. His parents and brothers live in the old one, which is full of memories of Manoj. In the new house is a room decorated with mementos of Manoj: his uniform, his medals and certificates, his books, and the flute he played in childhood.

Citation

Lt. Manoj Kumar Pandey, Param Vir Chakra (Posthumous)

1/11 Gorkha Rifles (IC-56959W)

Lieutenant Manoj Kumar Pandey took part in a series of boldly led attacks during 'Operation Vijay', forcing back the intruders with heavy losses in Batalik, including the capture of Jubar Top. On the night of 2/3 July 1999, during the advance to Khalubar, as his platoon approached its final objective, it came under heavy and intense enemy fire from the surrounding heights. Lieutenant Pandey was tasked to clear the interfering enemy positions, to prevent his battalion from getting daylighted, being in a vulnerable position. He quickly moved his platoon to an advantageous position under intense enemy fire, sent one section to clear the enemy positions from the right and himself proceeded to clear the enemy positions from the left. Fearlessly assaulting the first enemy position, he killed two enemy personnel and destroyed the second position by killing two more. He was injured on the shoulder and legs while clearing the third position. Undaunted and without caring for his grievous injuries, he continued to lead the assault on the fourth position, urging his men on, and destroyed the same with a grenade, even as he got a fatal burst on his forehead. This singular daredevil act of Lieutenant Pandey provided the critical firm base for the companies which finally led to the capture of Khalubar. The officer, however, succumbed to his injuries.

Lieutenant Manoj Kumar Pandey thus displayed most conspicuous bravery, indomitable courage, outstanding leadership and devotion to duty, and made the supreme sacrifice in the highest traditions of the Indian army.

Gazette of India Notificatiob

No. 16 – Press/2000

In Memoriam

The Lucknow Development Board has developed the Vishal and Vivek Khand Crossings of Gomati Nagar in memory of Captain Manoj Kumar Pandey and has named it 'Amar Shaheed Manoj Pandey Chowk'. They have installed there a bronze statue of Manoj, 14 feet high and weighing 3 tons. The park near Manoj's home has been dedicated to his memory. The Lucknow Development Board has also created a beautiful, 100-acre park named Kargil Pushkarni in memory of the Kargil martyrs.

Bronze Statue of Manoj Pande in Lucknow. His parents seen in the picture

His Father receiving PVC from the President

Captain Manoj Kumar Pandey

Manoj, Where Are You?

O Hero , with you we want to speak,
From you guidance we want to seek.
O, tell us what was your motive
And what made you so emotive?
Kargil's winds whisper of your passionate rage,
The mountains of your indomitable courage,
We hear from high peaks of your eagle soar,
Still they echo your thunderous, lion roar,
As you sprinted from bunker to bunker,
Like the flashing trident of Lord Shankar,
From your eyes a flame blazed
As with your bayonet you impaled
The enemy, leaving many of them dead
Unseeing they lay, with their eyes glazed.
With bare hands you pulverized some,
As with God of death, you became one.
What made you thus, to do the impossible?
What made you so utterly invincible?
In your footsteps we will like to walk,
Just one thing more we want to ask,
What made you so fearless, so brave?

O Warrior! to be like you, we do crave.

On those heights of Batalik and Dras,

Where grows not a blade of grass,

Where heavens embrace a mountain top,

Where winds roar and all tracks stop,

There like you we will like to go,

In your image we will like to grow.

Like you for Mother India our lives sacrifice,

Like you in every Indian's heart to survive.

O Mother India's hero-son!

Forever, you shine like a sun.

Grenadier Yogender Singh Yadav

"If I haven't died even after all this, then I cannot die."

In Aurangabad Ahir, a village in Bulandshahar district of Uttar Pradesh, lived Karan Singh Yadav, ex-serviceman of the Kumaon Regiment of the Indian Army. His tales were much in demand amongst his family and other villagers – anecdotes from his own battle experiences as well as the exploits of great Indian warriors and freedom fighters. Having fought in the 1965 and 1971 Indo-Pakistan wars, many indeed were the stories he could tell.

One eager member of this audience was his second son, Yogender Singh Yadav, who would listen to him with wide eyes and bated breath. Hearing of the thrilling sacrifices and martyrdom of young heroes like Sardar Bhagat Singh gave him goose pimples. He dreamt of fighting for the country, like Rani Lakshmi Bai of Jhansi, or of doing something spectacular, like Netaji Subhash Chandra Bose raising the I.N.A. during the Second World War. Mughal ruler Babar, who had established an empire by the age of 16, was also among young Yogender's heroes. So strong was his desire to emulate them that he felt impatient for his turn to grow up and accomplish noble deeds in the service of the country. As it turned out, he did not have long to wait.

Born on 10 May 1980 into a family that, aptly enough, had the Hindi word for lion – 'Singh' – in its name, Yogender showed early signs of the unquenchable spirit and grit that would do his family proud one day. Though he was the naughtiest of Karan Singh's three sons, his spiritedness prompted predictions of great accomplishments. At 5, Yogender was admitted to the Government Primary School of his village, where he studied up to Class 5. He was then admitted to Srikrishna Inter College in Sonata village, where he studied up to Class 12. Each weekday, he walked to Sonata, 3 km from Aurangabad Ahir, and back.

Yogender's was a completely rural upbringing; he would often spend his spare time working in the family fields. He decided to follow in the footsteps of his older brother, Jitender Singh Yadav, a Sepoy in an Artillery regiment of the Indian Army. Yogender was truly a son of the soil; he had never travelled far from his village. To him, Meerut and Delhi seemed far away. In fact, it was only when he went to enrol in the Army that he visited Meerut, just 50 miles from his village. In 1996, at sixteen and a half, he was recruited into the Grenadiers Regiment of the Indian Army.

Army Life

The 18 Grenadiers were a mixed lot, with Rajputs, Khemkani Muslims, Dogras, Ahirs and Jats. In the olden days, being tall and hefty was basic requirement for every new recruit to this regiment, as heavy grenades had to be thrown over a long distance. Now the grenades are much lighter, and the Grenadiers are not so uniformly tall and well-built any more, but there is no shortage of courage nonetheless, as exemplified by their battle cry, *'Sarvada Shaktishali'* (Always Strong). (Srinjoy Chowdhury, *Despatches from Kargil*, 56)

Yogender underwent rigorous Army training for the Ghatak or Commando unit of the Grenadiers. Well-trained in rock climbing, these men are expected to re-assemble their dismantled howitzers, from six pieces, within three minutes. Along with the dismantled howitzers, they are also expected to carry enough food and ammunition for 10 days.

Even during this period, Yogender proved to be above average. "The aim of training in the Army is to increase endurance and other physical capabilities of the recruits," he commented about his military training days, in an interview with this author. "They made us do such difficult things that we became accustomed to pain. They increased our physical fitness to such an extent that when we were required to do something tough later, especially in war, we did not panic; if we were wounded, we did not groan. Great stress was laid upon developing our firing skills as well. During my entire training, I practised firing regularly and acquired considerable proficiency. I was trained at Jabalpur, where I joined a team named Young Blood TRG, and my firing demonstrations were considered very good by my officers."

The Grenadiers were posted in Srinagar when Yogender went home on leave – his family had arranged his marriage with 20-year-old Reena of Sadbhar village. Ten days after their wedding in May 1999, while he was still on leave, events took a serious turn. "When somebody beats up your brother, your mother wakes you and tells you to go help him. That was how I was awakened as well," Yogender said. "One night, I had a dream – that some people were running away with our national flag, the tricolour, and we were chasing them. They fired and killed my comrades. In the morning, I told my mother about it. She replied, 'You are in the Army, after all, and live in Srinagar. You dream about such things because of what you see every day.'" Yogender's instincts, however, whispered that something was about to happen. "I told my wife, Reena, about it," he said. " 'I know what it means – now that I've joined the Army, there will be war. That is fate.' "

When confirmed news of war reached him, Yogender cut his leave short and took a train to Jammu. At the Army Transit Camp, he was informed that his battalion had gone to the battle.

"Where?" he asked.

"Kargil."

Battle and Victory at Tololing and Hump

By the time Yogender joined his battalion on 22 May, it had reached the Tololing area. "When we got there, we found thick fog surrounding the whole area," he remembered. "The Pakistanis could see us but weren't certain of our route upwards. So they withdrew to the top, where they had underground bunkers, and started firing at us from there. Our unit was given the task of capturing Tololing Hilltop, and, on the day of my joining, suffered its first casualty. Then, Naib Subedar Lal Chand and Subedar Randhir attacked with their respective groups on 25 and 26 May, but none came back.

"Since I rejoined my unit late, I didn't get a chance to fight in the battle of Tololing. I was instead given the task of supplying ammunition to our troops. I went with the ammunition in the morning and returned at three the next morning; then, after a few hours of rest, I started carrying loads of ammunition again. This gruelling and back-breaking work went on for more than three weeks." Yogender's officers appreciated his tremendous stamina and perseverance in climbing with heavy loads the treacherously steep, snow-covered and slippery slopes almost constantly, for 22 days.

"I gathered strength from this thought: if I didn't supply ammunition to my comrades on the heights, how would they protect us? They were relying on us. Their lives depended on us and our lives upon them. If we didn't support each other, neither would be able to fight. 20 of us set out carrying ammunition. In the end, only 3 or 4 survived. One complained of chest pains, another of leg pain, but I said that I felt no pain. Whenever one of the soldiers was hit by a bullet, I'd think that he must feel terrible pain, but when I was shot later in the Battle of Tiger Hill, I felt none. A man becomes mad at such times.

He thinks only of what he has to do and not of what's happening to him. For 22 days, this was how we fought in Tololing."

Hard was the duty expected of these soldiers: to steel their hearts and continue with the task on hand even while their officers and comrades lay dead or dying right beside them. They could not stop, not even to help a fallen comrade. But the sacrifice of their friends further steeled the resolve of these warriors; a fierce courage entered them, and their spirit became indomitable. Not when each breath rasped and seared their lungs, not when they went hungry for two or three days, not even when they watched friends being blown to pieces in front of their eyes did they allow their zeal and resolve to wane.

The Pakistanis took careful aim and shot Indian soldiers inching their way up, one by one, till their arms ached from the constant firing. They called the troops 'the mad Indians' – but this was no madness; it was extraordinary courage and willing self-sacrifice. "Theirs but to do and die," as Lord Alfred Tennyson wrote in his memorable poem "The Charge of the Light Brigade."

A military victory is undeniably a collective triumph, but the extraordinary deeds of some stood head and shoulders above others. In that short war of two months, 2 officers and 2 soldiers would earn the Param Vir Chakra, the highest award for wartime gallantry in the Indian Armed Forces. 19-year-old Yogender Singh Yadav was one of them.

"We lived in Tololing for 22 days in all," Yogender continued. "In that period, we lost 2 officers, 2 JCOs and 22 jawans because, initially, we didn't get any artillery support. History tells us that, to achieve an important goal, we have to first lose something dear. But the memories of our friends are with us, and will remain so throughout our lives. At first, we didn't know that we were fighting the Pakistan Army; the general impression was that these were fanatic Jihadi intruders. The villagers told us that they used to come down to buy supplies. But when the Indian Army reached there, the intruders withdrew to bunkers made at the height of 500 metres. Then, on 28 May, our troops asked for helicopter support to bombard the enemy machine-gun nests on top, which were not letting us advance. When a helicopter was downed that day by an enemy missile, then the Indian Government knew for sure that these were not some fanatic Jihadis but the regulars of the Pakistan Army – it was only they who had missiles, not the so-called Kashmiri freedom fighters. From then on, we were supported by our artillery and Air Force.

"On that same night, a group of six soldiers, under the command of Maj. Rajesh Adhikari, went to attack Tololing Hilltop. Almost reaching the enemy's position, they fought bravely but were killed. We had recovered the bodies of all our soldiers so far except the group led by Maj. Adhikari, since they lay very close to the enemy's position. When we tried to retrieve their bodies, the Pakistanis abused us, shouting: 'Give us your Tiger [the code name given to Lt. Balwan] and we will allow you to take down the bodies.' The higher authorities asked our colonel, Khushhal Chand Thakur, to bring down his unit, since they were thinking of deploying another. But the valiant Colonel refused to give up. We prepared to attack again. On 2 June 1999, another group, led by Second-in-Command R. Vishwanathan, attacked Tololing Hilltop. But all were killed in fierce fighting.

"Then, 2 Rajputana Rifles was deployed to help us, and their CO, Col. Ravindran, demanded artillery backup. By that time, our Air Force had done an aerial survey and taken photographs of the enemy positions. On 12 June, 2 Rajputana Rifles attacked Tololing Top and found that all except two of the Pakistani soldiers holed up there had died. Our officers wanted us to capture the two alive but, while pretending to surrender, those two soldiers killed several of ours. Enraged, the remaining jawans killed them and put the tricolour on Tololing Top."

Yogender recalled: "Our unit was next given the task of capturing the feature called Hump. While we were making preparations for the attack, the enemy rained artillery shells on us, injuring and killing several soldiers. More than a hundred of our jawans were kept busy carrying the dead and the wounded down the mountain. In spite of this setback, our soldiers attacked the hill called Hump and succeeded in conquering it. Then 13 Jammu & Kashmir Rifles was deployed to conquer further mountaintops." After their resounding victory at Tololing and Hump, 18 Grenadiers was sent down to base camp at Gumari, for rest and recuperation.

Battle for Tiger Hill

On 26 June, their brigade CO gave orders to the Grenadiers to start preparations for their next mission – Tiger Hill. Reconnaissance was assigned to Lt. Col. D. V. S. Panghal, the second-in-command of 18 Grenadiers, along with company commanders and selected JCOs and NCOs. By 30 June, this important task was complete, the requisite information about the Pakistani troops was obtained, and the final orders from the COs about the tasking of the companies were issued.

A clay model was made of the Tiger Hill complex, based on the information and photographs obtained by Indian Army helicopters and Air Force planes. Jawans were briefed about the geographical features of Tiger Hill; the role of each unit in the attack plan was clearly defined. As a tradition, prayers were offered at a temple ceremony to acquire the blessings of the Almighty.

"Once we'd planted the victory flag on Tololing Hill of Drass sector, Maj. Gen. Mohinder Puri of 8 Mountain Division entrusted 18 Grenadiers with the onerous task of conquering Tiger Hill," Yogender remembered. "He was so impressed by the bravery we had shown at Tololing that he was giving us a similar opportunity now. Burning with the desire to avenge the death of our comrades, we too were glad for this chance. A commando unit of 18 Grenadiers was organised under the leadership of Lt. Balwan Singh. We were to be the first to attack the feature.

"Tiger Hill is the highest peak in the Drass sector. Snowfall takes place even in the month of June, it is so cold in that area. The Pakistan Army had occupied the top, with reserves of arms and ammunition and ample rations, which clearly shows how long they must have been preparing for this war."

The peaks of the Tiger Hill complex of the Drass sector are at the forbidding height of about 16,000 feet. From there, the Pakistani artillery made any movement by Indians on the Srinagar-Leh Indian National Highway (1A) suicidal. All military and civilian vehicles moving on this highway were sitting ducks for the Pakistani gunners. Nonetheless, Indian truck-drivers tried to drive their vehicles on this highway time and again, with disastrous results. It was thus imperative that the Pakistani troops should be dislodged from Tiger Hill.

The capture of Tiger Hill would turn out to be the crucial turning-point in the Kargil war, once again pulverizing Pakistan's dreams of annexing Kashmir. It must be remembered that, in contrast to the ill-prepared and ill-equipped Indian Army, Pakistan had plenty of everything: grenade launchers, Kalashnikov assault rifles, machine guns, mortars, rocket launchers, high-powered wireless sets, night-vision devices, suitable clothes and loads of spare ammunition and food, while the first food the Indian soldiers ate in this 36-hour campaign was the dates left behind by the retreating enemy.

"Before the battle, our brigade commander briefed our unit," Yogender recounted. "Then our colonel, Khushhal Chand Thakur, briefed us about Tiger Hill. Col. Thakur, CO of the 18 Grenadiers, was a man of tremendous energy and a living inspiration to our battalion. He made a plan for our attack on the eastern side of Tiger Hill, in which A-company had to attack from the left side and the Ghatak Platoon of the unit had to attack from the right. C Company and D Company were to give support to the Ghataks, and B Company was kept in reserve."

The Indian soldiers had an extremely difficult task ahead: they had to climb at an eighty-degree gradient, using ropes, while carrying a backpack weighing about 25 kilos. "Ours was so difficult a route it was almost impossible to climb, and the enemy could never have predicted the possibility of such an attack. We prepared and practised intensively for 10 days," Yogender remembered. It was estimated that the attack would go on for three days at least. As it was not possible for the Grenadiers to win this battle alone, 8 Sikh Battalion was asked to attack from the western side, the Gorkhas from the south, and the Grenadiers from the east. The latter were divided into two groups: one was asked to help the 8 Sikhs and the other to attack from the eastern side.

By the night of 30 June, battle preparations were completed and all was in readiness. On 1 July, the Indian Air Force fighter planes attacked the hidden enemy in a lightning strike. Indian howitzers rained shell after deadly shell upon them.

During the first phase of the attack on Tiger Hill, Yogender Singh Yadav's Ghatak Platoon was given the task of conquering the 'Three Bunkers' complex. But to reach it, the Ghataks had to climb, in the dark, up a vertical, snow-covered slope, to 16,000 feet. 19-year-old Yogender volunteered to lead the group: "I was a scout of the Ghatak Platoon and showing them the way to Kargil Top. I didn't have the advantages of age or experience, but I was well-trained and had the blessings of elders.

"Our attack party consisted of 2 officers, 1 JCO and 23 jawans from the 18 Grenadiers, including me. Our lieutenant, Balwan, was leading the platoon. The slope we had to climb was too steep, much too steep. We had to use ropes. I kept thinking: We've been given the task of finishing the enemy and we have to succeed. And I prayed to Shankar *bhagwan*. I'm grateful to my officers that they appreciated my courage and made me the leader of the scout group although I was the youngest in age and service.

"We began the climb on the evening of 2 July. After climbing the whole night, we reached the spot where 8 Sikh was deployed. Each of us carried rations for 72 hours. On 3 July, during the day, we hid under overhanging rocks in utmost silence. There were three Pakistani-held bunkers on top that we had to clear, but we waited for the night because, during the day, there was every possibility of our being detected and killed by enemy fire. We began our hard ascent that night, and D Company was with us. After a gruelling climb in darkness, we reached a mountaintop and thought it was Tiger Top. But then we saw another peak ahead. The commander of D Company, Capt. Sachin Nimbalkar, told our Lt. Balwan, 'We will breakfast on the next hilltop.' But by the time we reached it, we saw yet another one ahead. We established our MMG fire-base there, and Capt. Sachin Nimbalkar advanced from there with his jawans. They had gone forward some distance, when they were trapped by enemy fire. We tried to help them but were not successful. Then we informed our CO about the gravity of the situation. It was getting dark, and our artillery began its bombardment, but even with that support, we could bring out Capt. Sachin and his jawans only at 11 p.m. All of them were safe except one, whose hand had been injured by a bullet."

The final attack commenced on 3 July 1999 at 8:30 p.m. It was multi-directional, with emphasis on surprise. The first column of Delta Company, led by Capt. S. A. Nimbalkar, advanced cautiously, making use of the adverse weather and Indian fire support. Time was of prime importance. The artillery kept up an incessant bombardment to keep the enemy guessing and to cover the advance of the infantry. But continuous retaliatory enemy fire was taking its toll on the jawans as they climbed.

By 1:30 a.m. on 4 July 1999, Maj. R. S. Rathore, with his 'Alpha' Company, had the first taste of success when they captured the area named 'Tongue'. The terrain was tough; rain and snow made the task extremely difficult, but, despite many casualties, the Ghataks, followed by the 'Charlie' Company from the north-eastern side and the 'Delta' Company from the eastern side, successfully occupied areas 'Top Knob' and 'Tooth'. Pakistani troops, however, were still entrenched on the reverse slopes of Tiger Hill, including areas 'Collar' and 'V cut'. With the help of 8 Sikh Battalion, the Tiger Hill complex was now isolated from the north, south and east, but the enemy was in control of the whole ridge on the west. The western side could not be isolated, as Indians were forbidden to cross the Line of Control; the Indian Army could not attack these enemy positions from the rear, to cut their lines of supply and communication.

Two PVC receipients - Subedar Yogendra Yadav (left) with Naib Subedar Sanjay Kumar (right)-Courtesy HT

Subedar Yogendra Yadav being felicitated by Mr Arun Jaitley (then Defence Minister)

'Superman' Yogender

Yogender narrated his group's mission: "It had taken us 2 nights and part of 1 day to make an almost vertical climb to 16,000 feet. The way was narrow, and we often had to support each other or tie ropes to proceed, with the darkness and the icy winds making our task even more difficult. Yet we climbed upwards, step by inexorable step. By the time we established our MMG fire-base at 16,000 feet, it was already early morning on 4 July. There were three Pakistani-held bunkers to clear, but we would have to wait there and try that night.

"On the night of 4 July, the first night when I had to actually attack the enemy, I was warned by some unseen Power that I would be hit by bullets but wouldn't die. I gained confidence: if I am not hit by bullets in my head or chest, then I'll live. Even if they cut off my hands and legs, I'll still live. I was filled with the idea that I have to do the work entrusted to me, at any cost.

"We resumed our ascent. There was another scout in my group, a giant of a man, who had exactly the same name as I. When I was chosen to lead our group, he objected. When asked why, he said, 'You were married only a few weeks back. So I should be given the more dangerous task.' I retorted, 'If death is destined, then a bullet can hit somebody in the middle or behind, leaving the person in front untouched. So don't worry about me.' He insisted, nonetheless, on walking beside me. At 5:30 a.m., we came to a steep rock. I climbed the rock-face, fixing ropes for my comrades. We were climbing by the side of a *nala* – a small, drain-like crevasse. There were enemy bunkers just 10 metres above us, on both sides of the *nala*. We were careful not to make the least sound, and the enemy didn't know of our advance till we neared the top. But suddenly – there was the muffled sound of a dislodged stone rolling down. At once, the Pakistanis began firing heavily from both sides of the *nala* and blocked the advance of our group. 18 of our jawans and officers, including Lt. Balwan, had to retreat.

"Now, we were just seven jawans left near the Pakistani bunkers. We were in a precarious situation: we could neither advance nor retreat.

We had to wait for the right opportunity. By then, the enemy had deployed a company of 135 soldiers on top of Tiger Hill.

"From above, the Pakistanis were spraying machine-gun fire, and from lower down, our mates were providing whatever fire support they could, with an MMG. After the firing stopped, the seven of us slowly began advancing again to capture the Pakistani bunkers just ten metres away. At that moment, I had no fear – I continued to climb that vertical cliff. Three bullets hit me in the groin and shoulders. I drew upon the courage and strength God gave me, and climbed the last 40 feet of that icy slope in the reduced visibility and fog. We crawled up and opened fire at the first enemy bunker, threw some grenades and killed the 4 Pakistani soldiers inside. The first bunker was thus captured quickly. The surviving Pakistanis had fallen back to the other bunkers, higher up – obviously, they assumed that a bigger force had climbed up. Ignoring my wounds, I charged the second bunker with 2 of my colleagues and, in hand-to-hand combat, killed 3 Pakistani soldiers.

"Of the 7 of us now near the bunkers, 1 was a havildar, another was my friend Yogender Singh Yadav, then there was Ananthraman, someone called Raj Kumar, myself, and 2 others whose names I can't recall. We moved forward in the dark towards the third bunker. A little ahead and higher up, I saw 4 shadows – Pakistani soldiers lying in wait. Crawling towards them, I lobbed a grenade. It exploded and I saw them fall. Reaching the spot, I found them lying on the rocky ground, mortally wounded. I picked up one of their guns – it was a Peeka – and shot them all. I moved forward, firing as I climbed a rock. As soon as we neared the summit, we found the third bunker. There were about 20 of them holed up here. We killed them all with grenade and rifle fire and took the bunker.

"The enemy's main post on top of Tiger Hill was only about 40 metres from that point. They mounted a fierce attack on us from there with grenades and automatic weapons. We retaliated as well, but our supply line was severed and the enemy fire was heavier. They rained stones and bullets on us as they neared us, damaging our light machine gun (LMG). Our Havildar told me to bring the LMG so that we could repair it. Just then, the enemy launched a grenade attack on us. One grenade burst between me and the other Yogender, blowing off one of the fingers on his right hand. I gave him first aid, then lifted the LMG and carried it to the Havildar. He asked me to go to another position. As I reached there, the enemy threw a grenade at me, its splinters wounding my leg. While I was bandaging it, they threw another grenade, which caused deep wounds on my face, especially my nose. I could not see anymore; I tried to open my eyes but couldn't. By the time I could, my dress was wet with blood. I asked a soldier to bandage my nose. Just as he was tearing a bandage to do so, a bullet killed him. I said to another soldier, 'He has been hit by a bullet.' He barely exclaimed, 'What?' when he too was shot. I told my commander, Havildar Udai Singh, that 2 of us had been killed.

"We were only 5 now, but we didn't lose heart. Our battle with the enemy lasted a full 5 hours. At about 10:30 a.m., the enemy on top of Tiger Hill sent a party of soldiers to ascertain our numbers. We killed 9 of them as they drew near. Only 2 escaped, but they had seen us. Now the Pakistanis knew how few we were.

"At about 11:30 a.m., once they had made full preparations, the enemy mounted another counter-attack, with more than 60 soldiers. We were only 5, with 2 among us wounded, but the fire of patriotism burned high in our hearts. We attacked the enemy soldiers ferociously, killing about 25 of them. I was wounded repeatedly and almost lost consciousness. Just then, the Pakistanis surrounded us from three sides and started to rain bullets on us. All my friends were killed in a moment. I was the only one left. I had carried up 25 kg of ammunition with me and almost all of it was exhausted; it was impossible to have it replenished right then. In those critical moments, there was no time to think. A bullet had torn my face, and I had been hit in my arm, leg, and several other places, but I was so pumped up with adrenalin that I didn't feel any pain. I moved ahead, struggling to stay conscious. Then I too fell down. I was the sole survivor, with 6 of my colleagues already dead, and I was lying, half unconscious, amid the corpses of Indian and Pakistani soldiers.

"The Pakistani troops assumed they had destroyed all the Indian Army troops on the summit of Tiger Hill. They took us for dead and began hurling abuse on us. After a while, they rained bullets down on our bodies to make sure we were all dead. 3 lodged in my left hand and 3 in my right leg. I wasn't fully conscious, but I could still somehow discern the actions of the enemy." Bullets had been pumped again and again into Yogender's body, breaking the bones in his left arm so much that they protruded out of the skin, but this Param Vir did not cry out or move. Exercising supreme self-control, he lay still as death.

Once the hail of bullets stopped, the Pakistanis sent a wireless order to their comrades at Mushkoh Valley to prepare to attack the Indian MMG post. "This post, near the Mushkoh Valley, was where we'd begun our ascent from, that night," Yogender clarified. "I remember thinking, in my semi-conscious state: If they attack the MMG Post, our friends who'd retreated due to crossfire will also be killed. But I was surrounded by enemies. What could I do alone? Then I remembered the mantra *'Josh ke beech hosh'* and continued to pretend I was dead."

"After an hour, the enemy commander ordered his soldiers to take away our weapons," Yogender continued. "One of the enemy soldiers shot us again to make sure that we were dead and the other picked up our weapons. Last of all, he shot me again in my hands, legs, and then in the chest, aiming for my heart. I had sustained about 15 gunshot injuries in all by this time, on my legs, arms, chest, thigh, groin, and other parts of my body. A splinter had hit my nose and I was bleeding heavily. When I felt the impact of the bullet in my heart, I thought I would die. But our elders have rightly said, 'Nobody can kill the one whom the Lord saves.' My purse was in my chest pocket (above the heart), exactly where the Pakistani soldier had shot me. In my purse were some 5-rupee coins, which had all collected in one place and the bullet struck them and ricocheted aside. Then the other soldier, who was collecting our weapons, turned away after picking up my AK-47 rifle, not seeing the grenade in my pocket."

The story of the 5-rupee coins which saved Yogender's life is strange indeed. Before scaling up the 16,000-feet-high icy cliff-face of Tiger

Hill, to keep themselves as light as possible, the Indian troops had thrown away every object that was not absolutely necessary, as any extra weight would make the climb many times more difficult. What, then, were these coins doing in Yogender's pocket? How is it that his purse had not fallen out of his pocket on that vertical climb when he must have, time and again, crouched, lain flat to escape detection or bullets, rolled over to save himself, then stood up and run? Fate works in inexplicable ways indeed. Those coins were the armour which destiny had placed in his pocket to ward off that bullet which could have been fatal.

Param Vir Yogender continued his tale: "My eyes opened. I discovered that I was still alive. Then I felt: If I haven't died even after all this, then I cannot die. The Pakistani soldiers were walking away. They were descending a slope. I realised I still had one grenade.

"Things moved very quickly after that. I took out my grenade, pulled the pin and threw it at the last enemy soldier. It fell in his cap, which was hanging behind his neck, and exploded before he could react. His body was blown to pieces in the air, plunging the Pakistan Army camp into confusion. The dead Pakistani soldier's automatic rifle had fallen to the side in the explosion. I crawled forward, picked it up, and fired burst after burst of automatic fire upon the enemy. They were badly shaken – they had believed us all dead. They had no idea who was attacking them. They must have wondered if another group of Indian soldiers had been hiding somewhere nearby. I killed 5 of them and wounded others; the rest ran away. I crawled for 15 metres and kept firing at them. From there, I observed their main post minutely. I heard the order on their wireless to retreat from Tiger Hill, and also the instruction to attack the Indian MMG-base 500 metres below Tiger Hill. Then I crawled back to my comrades to check if any of them was still miraculously alive, but, alas, all of them were dead. I sat near them and wept and wept. But then, I realised that they had sacrificed themselves for the country, and I resolved to not allow this sacrifice to be wasted."

It is pertinent to mention here what Yogender's parents revealed: "It was almost impossible to make Yogender weep." In fact, no one in his family has ever seen him do so, not even when he was hospitalized for 16 months after the Kargil war, with nearly fatal wounds, nor when his father died in 2004.

"Now my aim was to save the MMG post," Yogender revealed. "My first thought was to go there, but I asked myself: At night, when we climbed up with the support of ropes, my hands and legs were not wounded and it was still so difficult; now one leg and one hand have become useless – how will I descend? In my half-conscious state and in that fog, I didn't even know which way led to the Indian side. And I had no strength left.

"But my elders had taught me that if someone doing a noble, disinterested work calls to even a stone for help, he will get it. When a work is begun with a true heart and the aim is high, God helps fulfil that aim. It was then that a Divine Power, neither male nor female, and clad in white, materialized in front of me. I couldn't see its face clearly in that fog. This Divine Being filled me with a supernatural strength, showed me the path towards the Indian side, and instructed me in Hindi to roll down. Bones were protruding out of my left arm. I tried to break them off but couldn't, because the skin was still joined. Then I tied the arm with my belt to my body. I couldn't stand, so I began to crawl and roll my way down. After covering a long distance, I suddenly came to a drain. I hung onto that drain with one arm. I wondered if I had, unwittingly, come to the Pakistani side. But when I glanced down, I saw that my comrades, who had been unable to climb up due to the crossfire, were returning to the MMG post. I called to them; they came and took me down. Seeing my tattered and bloodied clothes, they grew nervous. I assured them that nothing would happen to me and that they should rush me to the MMG post. They carried me to the Ghatak Platoon commander, Lt. Balwan Singh. I informed him that there would be an attack on the MMG post that very night. He relayed all the information to the battalion commander, Col. Khushhal Chand Thakur. After being given some first aid, I was carried to the Colonel. I reached there at about 8 p.m. By then, I couldn't see any more, but I could still speak. I calmly told the colonel all I knew about the planned attack on the MMG post.

"He saw how heavily I was wounded. 'How do you feel?' he asked.

" 'Sahib, I am fine,' I replied.

" 'You do not look well at all. I am going to send you down.'

" 'No, I want to go back,' I protested. 'There is one more enemy post left.'

" 'There is not much left in you. How will you fight?' Col. Thakur asked.

"Small splinters were stuck to my vest and I was still bleeding; I don't know how I hadn't passed out. I was given some glucose, and I remember being injected with a painkiller. My wounds were bandaged about 8 hours after I'd sustained the first ones. I was taken down to Haliwal on a stretcher. I don't know what happened next, for I lost consciousness. 3 days later, I regained consciousness in the Base Hospital.

"Our Colonel Sahib had sent our reserve B Company to attack Tiger Hill and the C Company to defend the MMG post. That night, when the Pakistanis attacked the MMG post as expected, the alert C Company soldiers mowed them down. The battle was finally over. On 5 July, the soldiers of B Company planted our victorious Tricolour on Tiger Hill.

"In the Kargil operation, the 18 Grenadiers lost 2 officers, 2 JCOs and 32 jawans. Our battalion won 1 Param Vir Chakra, 2 Mahavir Chakras, 36 Vir Chakras, 1 War Seva Medal, 1 Shaurya Chakra, and 19 Sena Medals."

Asked later by this author how he could have remained absolutely still while bullets were being pumped into his body, Yogender replied, "As a child, I would watch the TV serial 'Mahabharata'. When the bullets hit me, I asked myself: If Bhishma *pitamaha* could remain still after his body was pierced by countless arrows, why can't I do it? In comparison to him, I was hit with only 15 bullets!"

Yogender Singh had to remain in the hospital for 16 months after the war. Even in 2005, he had not fully recovered the use of his left arm, whose bones he had tried to break and throw away during the war. But a better fate was in store for an arm that had accomplished so much: today, it is fully healed and ready to serve the country again.

A great honour befell Yogender while he recuperated. The Chief of Army Staff, General V. P. Malik, came to the hospital to see him. An Army clerk had mistakenly entered the identification number of the other Yogender Singh Yadav as that of the recipient of the Param Vir Chakra. Our hero thus thought that the Param Vir Chakra was being awarded posthumously to his friend, the other Yogender Singh Yadav. General Malik was the first to inform him that it was he who had won the Param Vir Chakra, not the other Yogender. Strange coincidence indeed! 2 jawans of the same unit had had exactly the same name and surname, had fought in the same battle side by side, had climbed the icy, vertical slopes of Tiger Hill together, but one was shot dead – and the other lived to win the Param Vir Chakra.

Citation

Grenadier Yogender Singh Yadav

18 Grenadiers (2690572)

Grenadier Yogender Singh Yadav was part of the leading team of a Ghatak Platoon tasked to capture Tiger Hill on the night of 3/4 July 1999. The approach to the top was steep, snowbound and rocky. Grenadier Yogender Singh, unmindful of the danger involved, volunteered to be the lead and fixed the rope for his team to climb up. On seeing the team, the enemy opened intense automatic grenade, rocket and artillery fire, killing the Commander and two of his colleagues, and the platoon was stalled. Realizing the gravity of the situation, Grenadier Yogender Singh Yadav crawled up to the enemy position to silence it and in the process sustained multiple bullet injuries. Unmindful of his injuries and in the hail of enemy bullets, Grenadier Yogender Yadav continued climbing towards the enemy positions, lobbed grenades, continued firing from his weapons and killed four enemy soldiers in close combat and silenced the automatic fire. Despite multiple bullet wounds, he refused to be evacuated and continued the charge. Inspired by his gallant act, the platoon charged on to the other positions with renewed punch and captured Tiger Hill Top.

Grenadier Yogender Singh Yadav displayed the most conspicuous courage, indomitable gallantry, grit and determination under extreme, adverse circumstances.

Gazette of India Notification

No. 16 – Press/2000

Awarded India's highest military honour, the Param Vir Chakra, for his acts of almost inconceivable bravery, Yogender Singh Yadav is now a man for whom even the President of India must rise, never mind the higher ranks of the defence forces. And rightly so, because the PVC is awarded for acts of such incredible bravery that it is, more often than not, a posthumous award. Havildar Yogender Singh Yadav received the Param Vir Chakra from President K. R. Narayanan at the age of 19, the youngest recipient of the award. Yet he remains an unassuming soldier. When on leave, he is to be found working in his fields. Apt for him is the slogan coined by our former Prime Minister, the late Lal Bahadur Shastri: *"Jai Jawan, Jai Kisan!"* (Victory to the Soldier, Victory to the Farmer!)

In a tribute straight from the heart, journalist Srinjoy Chowdhury writes about Yogender's exploits: "Bollywood's most outrageous film-makers wouldn't have got their leading man to do for the cameras what Grenadier Yadav did over those few hours. If they had, they might have been laughed out of town. In the chilly darkness on the snow-covered rocks, surrounded by dead comrades, a 19-year-old boy with a wispy moustache and a severe crew-cut would become Superman. Grenadier Yadav's story seemed to come from the Commando war comics – full of children of Achilles blowing away the enemy.

"We threw away those comics, telling ourselves that such men could not exist; that such 'kill everyone before me'–courage was impossible.

And then, those comics, those tame black-and-white illustrations, became a man with an arm in a sling. Grenadier Yadav was as real as I was. Did he have the warrior gene, I wondered" (*Despatches from Kargil*, 56-57, 60).

Indian Air Force

This victory would not have been possible without the daring of the Indian Air Force. They rose to the occasion and did the near-impossible. It would have proved very costly, in terms of lives lost, for the infantry to fight alone. The planes of the Air Force were flown to heights for which they were not made. Their fighter planes made 580 sorties, the helicopters about 2500 flights, and the transport planes several supply missions. So intense was the activity of Indian planes in that area that the Pakistanis did not dare provide air support to their trapped troops.

In the beginning, attempts were made to pinpoint the positions of the enemy with the help of satellites, but the imagery was hazy, so we had to depend on aerial reconnaissance. India's Tiger 1 Squadron made an important contribution – this squadron of Mirages, posted at Ambala airport for the operation called 'White Sea', flew 234 sorties, some at night. A few planes were also posted at Jodhpur, to be prepared in case Pakistan opened another front in Rajasthan. From there, these planes flew another 153 sorties to Kargil. They dominated the skies completely. (Vinayak Parab, quoted by Heera Lal Yadav, *Salam Sainik*, 30)

The Cost of Victory

25 officers and 436 jawans of the Indian Army died on the Kargil slopes. 54 officers and 629 jawans were wounded and disabled, some for life. It was a battle beamed to every home by national television networks. Indian forces fought ferociously, as there was this added motivation that their families – indeed, the whole country – was watching and cheering for them.

Indian gunners, behind those famous Bofors guns, also did a splendid job. There was perfect synergy between the Air Force and the Army. Their valour unnerved the Pakistanis, whose belief in the certainty of victory vanished like a mirage.

The Pakistani government panicked. As early as June, they sensed defeat staring them in the face, and began to petition the American president to broker a ceasefire. President Clinton took his stand on truth: unlike what America had done in the past, he refused to support Pakistani aggression and made it clear that they had to withdraw their troops behind the Line of Control.

On 4 July 1999, a panicked Nawaz Sharif hurried to Washington and begged Bill Clinton to broker a ceasefire, sparing Pakistan further humiliation. Bruce Riedel, former Special Assistant to the U.S. President and Senior Director for Near East and South Asia Affairs in the National Security Council at the White House (1997–2001), has written a graphic description of this meeting.

As in 1948 in Kashmir and in the Siachen conflict of 1987, the Pakistani government tried, in the Kargil war of 1999 as well, to claim that the attackers were Kashmiri freedom fighters; however, the papers, diaries, insignias, weapons and soldiers of Pakistan's Northern Light Infantry captured at Kargil provided ample proof of the falsity of this claim. Sadly, to keep up this pretence, Pakistan did not even claim some of the dead bodies of the 45 Pakistani officers and 700 soldiers who had died in Kargil.

"The Pakistanis were fighting for their country as we were for ours," said PVC Yogender Singh Yadav. "We were enemies in the battlefield, but we have always said that there can be no enmity after death. The Pakistanis gouged out the eyes and nails of Saurav Kalia and his five soldiers and dismembered them in order to terrorize us, to warn us: 'If you come near us, we will do this to you.' In contrast, we brought their dead soldiers down with honour and buried them properly (when they were not claimed by Pakistan)."

The Present

PVC Yogender Singh is part of a joint family. His father, Karan Singh Yadav, was proud of his son's bravery and the honour it brought to his family. He died on 9 September 2004. Yogender's younger brother lives in their village with their mother, Santara Devi. After the Kargil war, UP Chief Minister Mulayam Singh Yadav rewarded PVC Yogender Singh Yadav with a plot of land in Ghaziabad. His wife, Reena, lives there at present with their two sons, Prashant Kumar and Vishant Yadav. Earlier, the state government used to give a mere extra thousand rupees as annual pension to a PVC. In 2008, Chief Minister Mayawati enhanced it to Rs. 1,50,000 annually. Laudable, but there is an inexplicable rider: the PVC will receive it only for 30 years from the date of the PVC award. It is difficult to fathom the intention of such a provision, especially when one considers that it is in old age that such monetary help would be most useful!

As with all Chakra Award winners, the central government has given Yogender a free railway pass; his landline phone usage and medical care are also free. For domestic air travel, a PVC-recipient pays only 25% of the fare.

On 1 April 2010, PVC Yogender Singh was promoted to the rank of Naib Subedar. Discussing the grave problem of the paucity of officers and the lack of enthusiasm amongst the country's youth to serve in the Army, PVC Yogender Singh opined, "If out of four members of a family, three are elsewhere, the remaining one has to do the work of all the four. That is similar to the situation in the Army – each officer and jawan is doing the work of several persons. It affects even their mental balance.

"It is true that selfishness is increasing in the country and patriotism is on the wane. Young people do not want to join the Army because of higher salaries elsewhere. But those who are patriotic will not think of money alone. If they read the history of our freedom movement, they will see that Chandra Shekhar 'Azad' and 'Shaheed' Bhagat Singh did not join the Army. Their only aim was to serve the country, to liberate it, to sacrifice themselves for **Bharatmata**.

If we think only of money, there will be no patriotism. Today, the mentality of most people in our country is such that, if terrorists attack their neighbours, they'll say, 'Let us close our doors and save ourselves.' If we unite and face terrorism and aggression together, then we will achieve true solidarity.

"Indians do not lack patriotism. It only needs to be rekindled. Shyam Kumari's scheme – 'Let Each School Adopt a Hero' – should be taken up from the nursery stage. If children learn every day about our national heroes and about the present perils to our country, then they will inevitably become patriotic. For me and my peers, Chandra Shekhar 'Azad', 'Shaheed' Bhagat Singh and Subhash Chandra Bose were the heroic ideals; that is how we could accomplish so much. All Indians have the capacity and strength to do something as extraordinary as we did. But they are not aware of it. We must help them discover their own strength – we must convince them that they too can become heroes."1 (see appendix 9)

PVC Yogender Singh Yadav being felicitated by the members of Indian War Heroes Felicitation Committee, Villupuram.

Indian War Heroes Felicitation Committee, Villupuram, school children honouring PVC Yogender Singh Yadav

A Homage: Yogender Singh, the Lion

That day on the jagged, steep slopes of Tiger Hill
When the task ahead seemed impossible,
When hail of bullets, snow and sleet covered the rocks
And made the odds against India seem insurmountable,
When Pakistan had the advantage of the heights,
And Indian soldiers were in the enemy's gun sights, -

Regardless of that unceasing rain of bullets,
For which he became a perfect target,
Sprinted up a brave youth, still in his teens,
And blew the enemy snipers to smithereens.
Our Hero Yogender was then only nineteen.
The Pakis peppered him with bullets fifteen,
And also pumped fatal bullets into his six buddies.
A final shot they fired aimed at wounded Yogender's heart.
Thus in the war-arena having played their diabolical part,
Collecting their weapons, having done their worst,
The Pakis left, sure all were dead, after that final burst.
But the high Gods of India had willed otherwise,
That last bullet ricocheted against some coins,
Placed by the Goddess of Fate in his purse.
On India's enemies was that day laid a curse.
The diabolical designs of the enemy thus to thwart,
Was saved, Yogender, the brave heart.
Instead, at his hands, soon the attackers would die.

For, even with fifteen bullets pumped into his body,
Somehow Yogender would live, would survive.
Yes, though the enemy had left him for dead,
Though barely, yet our super hero was alive.
He tried to break his arm's protruding bones,
So that he could roll down the jagged stones
To warn his friends. Guided by Durga, who guards India,
Down the slope he would roll, crawl and slide.
To save his comrades he held death at bay,
Steeled himself, for India's sake, to stay
Alive, to sojourn in this house of clay.
But how to find the way?
Then the Goddess came, to show the way to her child,
She descended there, on her lion astride.
Indomitable his courage, firm his resolve
To save India's medium machine-gun post,
To help his comrades, whatever the cost.
To conquer Tiger Hill and on its top to unfurl
The flag of India, our beloved Tricolour.

To do this brave deed unparalleled
Was born a hero in an Indian village,
Of valour, who was a living image.
Bathed in his own blood, yet with fire in his soul,
He cut the enemy soldiers to pieces, made their bodies roll,
Down the Tiger Hill slopes. Where he was
To write an amazing chapter of bravery,
To do deeds beyond imagination, to snatch victory.

O raging torrent, O Himalayan peak of courage,
To you, O Yogender, we pay homage.
Because, O Hero, you had stepped upon them,
For your blood had flowed upon them,
Today each stone of Tiger Hill is a sacred gem.
The impossible you dared and endured and won
Yogender! We bow down to you – India's hero son.

–Shyam Kumari

Appendices

Appendix 1

Forgotten By History

1. Kashmir's accession to India: Sardar Vallabhbhai Patel's Masterstroke:

Narendra Sehgal, in his Hindi book *Vyathit Jammu & Kashmir* published in 2013 (Publisher: Sarsahitya Prakashan, 205-B Chawri Bazar, Delhi-110006), has revealed some startling and hither-to almost unknown facts and facets about Kashmir's accession to India.

It is well known that Jawaharlal Nehru and Sardar Vallabhbhai Patel had divergent views on many crucial issues. Maharaja Hari Singh was hesitating about Kashmir's accession to India. Many of the Maharaja's ministers and court officials tried their best to persuade him to accede to India. Sardar Patel and Acharya J. B. Kriplani also tried but because of Pandit Nehru's known partiality for Sheikh Abdullah, whom he freed from prison and declared the future ruler of Kashmir, Maharaja Hari Singh did not want to accede to India. That Sheikh Abdullah vehemently opposed Maharaja Hari Singh is a well-known fact.

Then Sardar Patel, as a last resort, unbeknown to Nehru, requested Mehr Chand Mahajan, who had taken charge as Prime Minister of Jammu and Kashmir, to invite Sangh Sarchalak Guru Golwarkar Ji, whom Maharaja Hari Singh held in high esteem, to Srinagar to meet the Maharaja and persuade him to accede to India. Sri Guruji at once cancelled all his programmes and from Nagpur took a plane to Delhi and from Delhi to Srinagar. Pandit Prem Nath Dogra and Mehr Chand Mahajan felicitated this meeting. (Details of this meeting have been published in the chapter on *Guruji and Jammu & Kashmir* of the book *Shri Guruji Samagra Darshan* Part 1, P. 172.) Guruji reached Srinagar on 17 October 1947 and met the Maharaja on 18th

October. Maharaja Hari Singh told Guruji that his state was fully dependent on Pakistan. Since all the connecting roads to Kashmir were from Sialkot and Rawalpindi, accession to India would not be practical.

Sri Guruji answered him that as he was a Hindu Raja, if he acceded to Pakistan his Hindu subjects would be in great danger. It would be in his and his subject's interest if he joined India. The work of road connectivity to India would be taken up on priority basis. Mehr Chand Mahajan, who was present during the meeting, also endorsed the views of Guruji. Maharaja was still undecided. On 19 October Shri Guruji returned to Delhi and reported the Maharaja's views to Sardar Patel. Forced by the Pakistani invasion of Kashmir, on 26 October, the Maharaja signed the instrument of accession to India. (*Vyathit Jammu and Kashmir*, Narendra Sehgal P. 67.)

Facing the Enemy in the Interregnum

Some months before the accession of Kashmir to India, two of the prominent *pracharks* of RSS, in Jammu and Kashmir, Harish Bhanot and Mangal Sen, had posed as Muslims and established contact with Pakistani Army officers. Clandestinely they were giving information about the activities and movements of the Pakistani Army to RSS leader of Jammu & Kashmir, Shri Balraj Madhok. They even supplied the date and route of the impending attack by Pakistani *lashkars*. Shri Madhok passed on all the information to Maharaja Hari Singh.

Breaking the 'Standstill Agreement' with the Maharaja, the Pakistani Army invaded Kashmir. There was a gap of two crucial days before the Indian troops landed in Kashmir. How to keep the invaders at bay till the Indian troops arrived was the question haunting Maharaja Hari Singh. He called Balraj Madhok and requested him to gather 200 volunteers.

At midnight 200 *swayamsevaks* of RSS, mostly students, were informed about the urgent need of volunteers to stop the invaders from reaching Srinagar. It was a work fraught with danger and death for these youngsters who had never even held a rifle. But ready to lay down their lives for the motherland, never caring for the risk involved, these 200 volunteers reached the Arya Samaj Mandir Srinagar at 6 a.m., where some military trucks ferried them to Badami Bag Cantonment. There some soldiers immediately began to teach these novices how to use rifles. For two days these brave volunteers kept the Pakistani invaders at bay.

The Runway of Srinagar Aerodrome

During those days when Kashmir's safety hung in the balance, in the absence of road connectivity with India, the safety of Srinagar aerodrome was of utmost importance.

Previously, the Srinagar aerodrome was only used for the Maharaja's personal aircraft. There was only an earthen landing strip, no cemented runway, nor any safety landing devices, nor fire fighting facilities. But now, in this hour of peril, there was an urgent need to repair and maintain this airstrip. Due to the turbulence and pro-Pakistan tendency in the majority Muslim community, it was impossible to get sufficient labourers for this task at such a short notice. The Maharaja contacted some office-bearers of the RSS. Thousands of volunteers came forward for the construction and upkeep of airstrips at Srinagar, Jammu and Poonch. Working day and night, they removed tons of ice from the Srinagar runway, levelled and firmed it up. Truly they did a commendable, almost unbelievable work. These volunteers brought their own food and implements for digging. They did it, without any payment, for the service of the Motherland.

Everyone wondered how scores of Indian Dakotas, loaded with troops and war material, made hundreds of sorties, landing and taking off from that mud strip of Srinagar aerodrome without any mishap! Therein lies the story of the selfless service and untiring labour of these volunteers of RSS, who tirelessly worked 24 hours a day to keep the landing strip firm and fit for these aeroplanes ferrying in the Indian troops and their ammunition. There being no road connectivity with India, each bullet and every rifle had to be flown in by aeroplanes. It is sad that their contribution has not been acknowledged by historians.

Lest We Forget: The Martyrs

In those early crucial days Indian troops were short of arms and ammunition. Every bullet, every grenade was being brought by air. Some of the boxes of ammunition paradropped by Indian Dakotas fell in the area which came within the firing range of Pakistani Army. How to bring them back? Who will bring them back?

The Army approached the head of Kotli Branch of RSS, Shri Chandra Prakash, and asked for volunteers to bring back the boxes of ammunition. Chandra Prakash heard the commander's request and asked him how many volunteers were needed for this work. "Eight" answered the officer. Chandra Prakash said, "All right. I am the first volunteer and will come back with another seven in half an hour. Please wait here." He went to the city. Not seven, but thirty volunteered for this dangerous task. Chandra Prakash had great difficulty in selecting only seven, because each of the thirty wanted to undertake this work and if necessary, sacrifice his life for the Motherland. He selected seven and "ordered" the others not to insist. As in the military, in RSS an "order" has to be obeyed.

The commander explained what they had to do. Soon the eight volunteers reached the front with the Army commander and swiftly swam across the fast flowing waters of the rivulet on whose other bank lay the four ammunition boxes. Each of them picked up a box and swam back. But in spite of utmost silence, the Pakistanis became aware about their presence and rained bullets in the direction of the noise. Two of the volunteers, Chandra Prakash and Ved Prakash, were badly wounded. Their six comrades steeled their hearts and leaving their two wounded comrades behind, came back with the ammunition boxes. After giving the boxes to the Commander, four of them went back to bring back their two wounded comrades. In the meanwhile the two wounded bled to death. Their comrades lifted their bodies and turned back. But alas, by then the rain of bullets had intensified. On the way two more of the rescuers were hit by bullets and died. Their comrades brought back the four martyr's bodies. Alas, Indian history has forgotten them. (*Ibid*, pp. 79-81)

Appendix 2

PVC Som Nath Sharma Remembered By His Sister (Late) Major Dr. Kamla Tewari

When my eldest brother, Major Som Nath Sharma, the first recipient of the Param Vir Chakra, was killed in action in Kashmir in 1947, I was only 20 years old then and knew very little about spirituality. The fact of his death came as a sort of a powerful spiritual experience, although at the time I could not understand or believe in it.

He was by nature full of life, very cheerful, extremely popular and absolutely fearless. He had a hero soul's deep conviction that every bullet or shrapnel in war has a name inscribed on it and would find its target whenever and wherever it might be. This was the answer he gave to those who pleaded with him that he was not fit to go to war. During World War II he told his mother that he would get the Victoria Cross and that if he survived the war, he would rise to the highest post in the Army. He would talk about a 'break in his lifeline' at the age of 25, implying that he might not survive.

When Pakistan invaded the Kashmir valley in October 1947, so soon after India's independence, Indian troops had to be flown in at short notice. Som's unit was then deployed in Delhi on internal security duties and his company was one of the first to be flown in. His left hand was in plaster up to the elbow due to a sport injury and under normal circumstances he would not have been allowed to go into battle but he insisted that he must go with his men. He pleaded with his commanding officer that until then he had fought in Burma and Malaya for the British and now that he had a chance to fight for free India, he should not be denied the privilege and opportunity to lead his men.

During the disturbed period of riots in Delhi after independence, Lady Hardinge Medical College, where I was studying, was put under curfew and after a few days we began to feel the pinch of the lack of food supplies. I mentioned the fact to him and he immediately arranged to take me and the college staff responsible for food through the back door lane in his Army vehicle to make the necessary purchases. This endeared him to the whole college.

He flew to Srinagar with his men early in the morning of 30th October and was at once given the responsibility for the defence of the airfield. On 3rd November at about 6 p.m., I had a very oppressive feeling within me that something was not all right about Som. I even shared this feeling with one of my friends when we went to play badminton. She reassured me that Som had just left for Kashmir and that nothing could happen that soon. But this oppressive feeling persisted to the extent that I felt as if his soul was hovering around me and trying to talk to me and there was no way I could understand him. His presence haunted me constantly and yet I felt that I should not accept that he was no more until there was some definite news. And I was afraid to express my uneasy feelings to anyone in case I was wrong.

The confirmation of his demise was received only a day later, on 4th November, when I was told by Maj. K. K. Tewari, who would become my husband, about it. I was stunned and shocked into silence. The feeling of his being around me lasted until all the *pujas* and *havans* had been done as per the customs. This confirmed the fact that these customary *pujas* and *havans* had helped his soul to rest in peace. This incident had such a deep impact upon me that I could not share it with anyone. Even my own children did not know anything about their uncle from me, till after the TV serial on Param Vir Chakra recipients was aired, which helped me to cry out my emotions.

Appendix 3

PVC A. B. Tarapore Remembered By His Daughter Zarin Boyce

When I try to remember my Dad, the clouds seem to part, and I can clearly see a well-built, handsome man with a commanding personality, in front of my eyes. It is almost 46 years since his heroic demise, but it seems like just yesterday! One knows that he was an exceptional commander – that is history – but there were some inbuilt personal traits that made him so. As a young girl, what I remember as his most outstanding quality was his passion for truth. All things were either black or white for him, no shades of grey! Something was right or it was wrong, no excuses. He always told my brother and me, "Do not mind what others say. You should be your own judge. If you can look yourself straight in the eye in the mirror, every morning, you know that life is on the correct track. The day you can't, look over your actions to see what went wrong!"

As a family man, for him, my mother Perin, my brother Xerxes and I meant the world. This sense of responsibility included his extended family – his Regiment. He always said that he would never expect his men to do what he would not do himself. And this can be clearly seen from the fact that he always led the regiment from the front, with his tank copula open, so that he could inspire the men under his command. I once read an article in a book written by a Pakistani general who had fought in the Phillora sector – he mentioned my father by name and he felt it was a privilege to have such a fine solider and thorough gentleman as an opponent – truly a great compliment from the enemy!

Even in peacetime, my father led his men by example. I remember an incident from when I was about 13 years old, in Babina, where dad was posted. Some of my mother's relatives – all civilians – were visiting us. It was past 6 pm and my dad was not back from an exercise he was on. He came in later that evening, covered from head to toe in slush. The jeep, his driver Swaroop Singh and his operator were in a similar state. One of our guests asked, "What happened?" and my father answered, "The jeep got stuck in the slush of Gurari Nala (a stream near Babina) so we all had to push." To which our guest (the MD of a company) said, "Why did you have to do this? Weren't the men there?" My father just looked at him and said, "Why, am I made of sugar or salt that I'll melt? What's so special about me that I cannot do what the men under me have to do?" This was his guiding principle in life too.

Family legend has it that we are the direct descendants of General Ratanjiba, who held a *mansab* under Shivaji, for which he was given 100 villages, the largest of them being Tarapore, hence the family name. Stories of valour and chivalry towards women were our daily fare at night. Although we were in boarding school, whenever we were at home for our vacations, my father always told us a bedtime story and ended by telling my brother that respecting women was the sign of a true man. My father used to say, "There is good in everyone. There is so much bad in the best of us and so much good in the worst of us, it hardly behoves any of us to speak ill of the rest of us." Once, somebody came to him and started to speak ill of a mutual acquaintance. My father told him, "How do you know in what circumstances he did it? He is a very good man. If you treat others well, they will treat you well." He was very kind to everyone, one of the reasons why his Regiment reveres him to this day. I remember, when I had sunstroke and cholera at the age of 10 in Babina, with the closest hospital at Jhansi, my father sat up the whole night changing the cold-compress cloth on my forehead so that my mother could get some rest, as she had been by my side all day.

After his posting to England in 1950, the gifts he brought back for me and Xerxes were all carefully and thoughtfully selected so that we got not only joy from them but some education too – education meant the world to him. He was a highly religious person who prayed daily. If he was awakened at night to meet someone, he would finish his work, and then, before sleeping, he would again take a bath and offer prayers. His *sevakdar* told us later that, even on the battlefield, he would not sleep until he had washed up and said his prayers. When wounded too, this was his routine. Though badly wounded, he refused to be evacuated, as he would not leave his men. His trust and belief in the Almighty was unshakeable.

I remember that night in April 1965 when they left from Babina for the front. There was a celebration party at the mess as the Poona Horse had won the shooting competition during the training. While I was dancing with him, his adjutant came and called him aside. Dad left and soon, one by one, all the officers in order of seniority left to confer in the next room. All the ladies were then asked to go home. We knew something was afoot, but what? All night, we could hear the sound of the tanks driving to the loading flats at the station. Early next morning, he returned home and told us they were moving to the front. We were in shock, but dad said that, as a soldier, he was getting the greatest possible honour, as he was going to lead his regiment in battle and he could not ask for finer men. If something were to happen, he asked us to be brave and remember that there is no finer end for the valiant than to die doing their duty for the motherland. The rest is history. I can never thank the Almighty enough for blessing me with such an exceptional, loving and kind father who was truly a mentor to be proud of.

When my father died, I was only 15 years old. If my grandfather had not been so rich, and my mother had not been his only child, we would have been in great difficulty. But, many times, it seemed to me that nobody appreciated my father's sacrifice. Was it worth dying for a nation which does not even remember its martyrs, leave aside honouring them?

On 21-22 February 2009, inspired by Shyam Kumari's scheme 'Let Us Honour Our Soldiers' two great patriots, C. B. Singh and Surendra Rai of Jhansi, arranged a memorable function ('The Great Congregation of Great Warriors') to honour some of our living Param Vir Chakra–recipients and the families of some of those PVCs who had received the award posthumously. My father, PVC A. B. Tarapore, was also honoured on this occasion. I flew in from Jordan, cutting short my holiday to participate in this function.

I remember an incident from this occasion: when the victory procession with its life-size cut-outs of the PVC heroes stopped at a place where garlands were offered, a man came by and asked me, "Madam, what is a Param Vir?" When I explained it to him, the man bowed reverentially before the cut-out of my father. I was so moved that tears flowed from my eyes throughout the victory procession.

In 44 years, I felt, it was the first time, there in Jhansi, that the public of the country had honoured him. That day, I felt that his martyrdom was vindicated, that the country remembers him with gratitude, after all.

"My Dad, who I am so proud of" – PVC A. B. Tarapore Remembered By His Son Xerxes Tarapore

At the time my Dad was killed in action in the Indo-Pakistani conflict of 1965, I was a teenager. His death caused immense grief, dismay and loss to my mother, my sister and me. We had a difficult time adjusting to the new reality that he was not around us anymore to give us the love, advice and support we were so used to. However, even after such a tragedy, life goes on. I think, in retrospect, my Dad would have been very happy to see that both my sister and I mastered the tragedy well and grew up to be responsible adults who passed college/university, took on challenging assignments in our professional lives, got married, started our respective families, raised our children well, and also reached a level of moderate prosperity.

The one incident that I remember well about my father was from when I was about 6 years old and my parents had decided that both my sister and I would go to boarding school in Nainital, UP. They had got admission for me at St. Joseph's College, and for my sister at St. Mary's Convent, both in Nainital. On the day my parents brought me to boarding school, I cried bitterly and just didn't want to remain there. Everything there was new and different for me and I felt very uncomfortable. I remember my mother was also feeling terrible and this is when my Dad took me aside and spoke to me. He said: "Son, what we are doing for you also requires an immense sacrifice from your mother and me. If you stayed with us, you would not get the good education we want you to have. The Regiment is often located at the frontier or at sites where there are no good schools and this can have a negative impact on your education and your upbringing. Even though it means that you are separated from your parents, we want you to have the best schooling possible, so that, later, when you are grown up, you can build on this education and become a responsible person in society."

At that time, I don't think I completely understood what my father was trying to say to me. However, today when I think back about my school days at St. Joseph's College, I must say my father was very correct in what he said. I got a good school education and also learnt to take the initiative to overcome obstacles and resolve problems. This has helped me a lot in my university days and in my professional life.

My Dad will always remain in my memories as a person who loved his family and who took decisions that he assessed to be correct, even though they required a major sacrifice from him.

Appendix 4

PVC Arun Khetarpal Remembered By His Brother Mukesh Khetarpal

[*In An Address To the Students of Vidya Niketan in Pondicherry on 30 October 2010*]

Though Arun was only a year older, I always felt protected at school because of him. I remember that Arun always acceded to my demands. Once, when he was seven or eight years old, our mother bought a new cardigan for Arun. He put it on and went to school. When he returned from school, he was not wearing his new cardigan. Mom was surprised and asked where it was. He replied that he had left it in the school. Naturally, Mom was annoyed and scolded him for being careless. She asked him to bring it back from school the next day. The following day, Arun wore his old cardigan to school. On his return Mom asked him whether he'd brought back his new cardigan. Arun replied that he had not been able to find it. So he was scolded again.

Some years later, I went to the school canteen and ordered some snacks. After eating, I went to the counter and asked for my bill. The young man behind the counter looked at me and enquired whether I was the brother of Arun Khetarpal. When I replied in the affirmative, the young man refused to take any money. I was bewildered and asked, "Why not?"

The young man replied, "Some years ago, during the winter, I had no cardigan; I was a poor boy. One day as I sat shivering on the pavement, your brother saw me and gave me his new cardigan. How can I take payment from you?"

Appendix 5

The Ice Warriors of Siachen Glacier

According to Indian scriptures, all areas above the tree line are unfit for human living. They are ascended by humans at the end of their 'van-prasth' stage to seek salvation, as was done by the Pandavas. Such a premise is also supported scientifically. Lack of flora and fauna, coupled with acute shortage of oxygen and excessive intensity of ultra-violet rays make areas above tree line highly unsuitable for habitation. Leaving aside snow and boulders, there are no local resources available. Every single item for sustenance has to be brought in at enormous effort. Peculiarities of the challenges faced can be gauged from the fact that disposal of human excreta has been defying all solutions – chemical, biological and physical. Due to extremely low temperatures, it just does not decompose and remains unchanged for ever, posing major hygiene problems.

Siachen Glacier at a height of over 18,000 feet is the world's highest battlefield. Enormity of effort required for living and fighting at that altitude can be judged from the fact that the highest mountain in Alps is Mont Blanc at 15,774 ft and climbers carry oxygen with them. Ironically, Siachen means 'places of the wild roses' in local lore. In addition to the hostile activities of the enemy, soldiers endure treacherous environment – avalanches, snow storms and crevasses make for a deadly combination. Frost bites result in loss of limbs in numerous cases.

Thousands of soldiers have perished due to pulmonary oedema and other high altitude diseases while defending this inhospitable terrain. As Western countries do not face such an environment, very little medical research has been carried out in the world as regards long and short term effects of high altitude areas. In case a man is taken directly from plains to Siachen, he is unlikely to survive. His lungs will fail to trap enough air to get required supply of oxygen and he will, in all probability, succumb to accumulation of fluids in his lungs. Therefore, soldiers have to undergo elaborate acclimatization programme before induction, spanning over 4 weeks and even more.

Snowstorms last for weeks and temperatures dip down to minus 60 degrees centigrade. Helicopters, the sole means of quick de-induction, become inoperative and the area remains cut-off for prolonged periods. Construction and maintenance of helipads is a huge challenge. If constructed in summers, they get buried under heavy winter snow. On the other hand, in case they are prepared in winters, snow around them melts in summers and they get perched on tall snow pillars.

Psychological Effects

One thing is certain that no human can ever remain unaffected by a tenure on the glacier. Oxygen-deprivation, exposure to ultra-violet rays, prolonged isolation and constant threat to life have varied effects on soldiers. Severe psychological pressures change their personality, thinking and approach to life. Response depends on individual threshold of tolerance and coping mechanism. In some cases body's defence mechanism is unable to withstand stress and reaches breaking point. Normal functioning is replaced by erratic demeanour.

Many soldiers suffer from acute psychosomatic and mental stress. Frequent loss of lives and fatal injuries show them frailty of human life, driving them to become highly philosophical – trying to decipher ultimate purpose of life. They start relating to God and his omnipresence. They become overly religious and seek solace in prayers. There have been cases where soldiers have sought premature retirement after completing glacier tenure to join some *ashram* in search of peace of mind, their personality having undergone complete transformation.

Such an environment also makes many soldiers excessively god fearing, bordering on becoming superstitious. Most stop drinking liquor and eating meat, some for personal fulfilment and some to placate the gods. Some soldiers tend to assign usual natural occurrences to supernatural phenomena. Hallucinations blur the difference between fact and imagination.

Though not proved medically, there is a general apprehension in the minds of troops that prolonged exposure to ultra-violet rays in oxygen-starved environment makes men impotent. Despite repeated reassurances to the contrary by commanders and doctors, this fear stays with almost all soldiers. It has been a major cause of concern for the organisation.

Behavioural Changes

Soldiers by nature are very emotional. Every letter received from home means excitement and instant morale boost, more so if it contains photographs of wife and children. But lack of oxygen on the glacier has a strange effect on normal mental orientation of some soldiers. They display a distinct indifference to normal human emotions. Some soldiers have been seen carrying unopened letters in their pockets for days, showing a distinct lack of enthusiasm to read them.

In a few cases, sense of isolation results in a feeling of being overwhelmed, forcing soldiers to withdraw into their shells. Some go into depression. At times, indecisiveness, pessimism and inability to concentrate result in cognitive impairment and memory problems. Anxiety, tension and restlessness cause mood swings and short tempers.

Due to rarefied atmosphere, soldiers lose appetite and avoid eating meals, resulting in debilitation which further reduces urge to eat. They thus get trapped in a vicious cycle. The Government has tried to provide attractive food items like dry fruits and chocolates but with little effect. Soldiers have been seen to throw food away rather than eat it.

Challenges of Command

Command of troops in such environment is an extreme test of leadership traits. In addition to managing troops, commanders have to ensure that their own temperament and deportment remain unaffected. Irrational and erratic behaviour by a commander is a sure recipe for the breakdown of normal functioning of a military unit. Therefore, it is essential that they be trained to read signs of their own inconsistent behaviour to be able to exercise caution. It is only then that they can monitor mental and physical health of their troops.

The problem of isolation in the case of officers is far more acute as almost all posts are manned by a solitary officer with his men. He has no one around to share his feelings and thoughts. Therefore, every officer in the glacier has to be physically and mentally robust.

Commanders have to be on the look out for possible behavioural changes amongst troops and handle them with empathy. They should be able to identify symptoms of extreme duress and take timely curative action. Instead of commanding troops through issuance of orders, they have to modify their style of leadership. Less authoritarian approach and display of compassion invariably prove more effective.

Most officers assume the mantle of being a father figure to their troops. They make them eat their meals sitting in front of them. Periodic 'letter parades' are held where all troops are ordered to write letters to their homes conveying their welfare. Soldiers are engaged in informal conversation and encouraged subtly to share their concerns.

The Brave Hearts with Never-Say-Die Spirit

The very fact that during the last three decades of Indian Army's deployment on Siachen Glacier, there has not been a single incident of transgression bears testimony to the mental and physical robustness of Indian soldiers and the high quality of leadership. To date, no Indian soldier has ever sought exemption from serving on the glacier. It is considered a cowardly and 'unsoldierlike' act. On the contrary, many officers and men hide their medical infirmities lest they be prevented from being with their units on the glacier. Group cohesion and peer support sustain soldiers on the glacier. Their light hearted banter and sense of humour enliven their stay.

There are numerous acts of individual and collective heroism every day – risking own lives to rescue colleagues trapped in hazardous snow avalanches or to save a soldier lying crippled at the base of a deep crevasse. A soldier offered to jump down from a hovering helicopter at a post located at 20,000 feet altitude to prepare a makeshift helipad with shovel to help evacuate a casualty. Army helicopter pilots have been flouting all norms of flight safety while volunteering to fly out seriously sick soldiers in sub-optimal and perilous flying conditions.

Finally, one is reminded of the famous counsel of Kautilya to Chandragupta, "*Pataliputra reposes each night in peaceful comfort secure in the belief that the distant borders of Magadha are inviolate, thanks only to the Mauryan Army standing vigil with naked swords and eyes peeled for action, day and night, in weather fair and foul, all eight praharas (round the clock), quite unmindful of personal discomfort and hardship, all through the year, year after year. While the citizenry of the State contributes to see that the State prospers and flourishes, the soldier guarantees it continues to exist as a State.*"

Our *Unsung Heroes of Siachen Glacier* defy nature to stand vigil in the most inhospitable environs of the glacier to guard national frontiers. They brave extreme physical and mental privations so that India remains secure and their countrymen can sleep in peace. They do deserve nation's recognition and support.

A Vignette

Somnath and **Jagir** were close to completing their tenure on Siachen Glacier. A report was received that a soldier had got trapped at a place at 14,000 feet altitude and was losing consciousness due to extreme cold and oxygen deficiency. He needed immediate evacuation by helicopter. Unfortunately, no helipad existed close by. Possibility of carrying two persons who could jump from a hovering helicopter and beat down the snow to prepare a makeshift helipad was being discussed. That appeared to be the sole way to save the injured soldier. However, jumping from a hovering helicopter in blizzard like environment on unprobed ground could prove fatal. Fall in a concealed crevice could mean certain death.

Even before the discussion could be concluded, Somnath and Jagir appeared fully dressed with shovels and helipad markers. They were apprised of the risks involved. On their insistence, they were given quick briefing and carried in a helicopter. They did the task admirably and saved the life of the stranded soldier. However, Jagir suffered frostbite injuries and lost a toe. He does not regret his decision. Strangely, they neither knew nor cared to find out as to who the injured soldier was. For them, every Indian soldier deserved help.

Major General Mrinal Suman, AVSM, VSM, PhD

Appendix 6

PVC Manoj Kumar Pandey Remembered By His Mother Brijmohini Pandey

Manoj did everything before time. He grew up at a fast pace. He had his first teeth when he was five months old. At seven months he could stand and walk holding the wall. When he was two and a half years old, I took him to a fair and asked him to choose some toy. He asked to buy a flute, which cost only one rupee at the time. Manoj would try to play tunes on the flute. After he joined Sainik School at the age of twelve and a half, whenever he came home he would take down his flute from the nail (where it hung by a piece of cord) and play on it. Once a child saw the flute and asked to play on it. After she finished playing on the flute I placed the flute in a cupboard instead of hanging it back in its place on the hook. When Manoj came home on leave he missed the flute and asked for it and played upon it. He took such good care of everything that today, even after a gap of about forty-five years, his flute looks like new.

Manoj was a pure and straightforward person. Greed, falsehood, prevarication or cheating were all absolutely foreign to his nature. If he told us that he will come at a particular time and due to unavoidable circumstances could not make it, he would take great pains to inform us of it.

In February 1999 he came home on one month's leave. When I expressed disappointment that his leave was for just one month, instead of the usual two months, he replied, "Ma, I will come back again for one month on Dewali (which usually falls at the beginning of November)." I replied, "But Dewali is so far." He said, "All right, I will surely come in July."

He kept his word but came back wrapped in the tricolour. We are extremely proud of him but also extremely sad. We will pass all our life with the joy of his sacrifice and sorrow of his parting.

Appendix 7

Homage to PVC Vikram Batra By His Father, Girdhari Lal Batra

To sacrifice one's life in the prime of youth, to achieve martyrdom for the protection of one's Motherland, is the highest of human sacrifices. Martyrs are blessed with the virtues of selfless and true love, for their people, their country and humanity at large. I believe it is a godly instinct.

Holy scriptures say that the ultimate goal of human life is Nirvana or Moksha. Lord Krishna has said in the Bhagavad Gita that whosoever sacrifices his life in the battlefield for the establishment of the truth and righteousness directly comes to me and achieves liberation (Moksha).

हतो वा प्राप्स्यसि स्वर्गं जित्वा वा भोक्ष्यसे महीम्।

तस्मादुत्तिष्ठ कौन्तेय युद्धाय कृतनिश्चयः ।।

Slain thou shalt win heaven, victorious thou shalt enjoy the earth; therefore arise, O Son of Kunti, resolved upon battle. (2-37)

He has also said to Arjuna:

यदृच्छया चोपपन्नं स्वर्गद्वारमपावृत्तम्।

सुखिनः क्षत्रियाः पार्थ लभन्ते युद्धमीदृशम्।।

Arjuna, happy are the Kshatriyas who get such an unsolicited opportunity for war; which opens the door to heaven. (2-32)

Martyrs are part incarnation of gods and are graced with godly virtues. They are always prepared for the supreme sacrifice for the protection of the Motherland. What better way to serve the nation other than to sacrifice one's life for the Motherland and our people.

I, not as a father but being a teacher, have observed Vikram keenly and found him totally different. From his childhood he had a heavenly glow on his face He was brilliant and signs of his doing something extraordinary were visible. He has proved a worthy son. He had given us honour and pride and made our present life worthy. Thousands of salutations to him. He is always with us.

Appendix 8

The Param Vir Chakra

The Param Vir Chakra, India's highest award for bravery is given to the 'bravest of the brave'. Since the President of India instituted these awards on 26th January 1950, up to now only 21 defence personnel have received this award, 14 of them posthumously.

The Designer of the Param Vir Chakra

After India's Independence Major General Hira Lal Atal was given the task of designing and naming independent India's military decorations. General Atal entrusted the work to Major General Vikram Khanolkar's wife Savitri Bai. Gen. Atal has to be congratulated for his choice. A brief perusal of Mrs Savitri Bai's story will show that she had a deep knowledge of India's mythology.

Destination India

Eva Yvonne Linda Madayde Maros was born on 20 July 1913 in Switzerland. Her mother was a Russian and father a Hungarian. But Eva's soul was surely Indian. Since her childhood India and things Indian attracted her. And on a skiing trip in 1929 Eva's Indian destiny awaited her. She met a handsome Indian, Vikram Khanolkar, who was a cadet at Sandhurst. They fell in love and after some initial hesitation her parents consented to their marriage. She came to India in 1932 and converted to Hinduism. She took the name Savitri Bai and married the dashing young Captain Vikram Khanolkar who had in the meanwhile joined the Sikh Regiment.

Savitri Bai was so thirsty to know all things Indian that within a few years she absorbed an astounding amount of knowledge about Indian scriptures, mythology, traditions, culture and languages. She enrolled at Patna University to learn Sanskrit and Hindi. She learnt Hindustani music and Kathakali dance. She had the good fortune to learn Indian classical dance from the renowned dancer Uday Shankar and became proficient in all of the classical dance forms. Being a talented painter, Savitri Bai made a series of paintings about the basic principles of Vedanta. She wrote several books. Amongst her published books are, a *Sanskrit Dictionary of Names* and *Saints of Maharastra*.

The Design

Savitri Bai responded enthusiastically to the work of designing the emblem for the Highest Award of Bravery in the Indian Army. The Param Vir Chakra medal is made of bronze and is circular in shape. Mythology says that the demon Vrtra was menacing the gods, but they could not defeat him. It was found that a weapon made from the bones of sage Dadhichi, who had done extreme penance, could kill the demon Vrtra. For the welfare of the gods, the sage donated his bones to Indra, the king of the gods. From the thigh bones of sage Dadhichi, Indra fashioned his *Vajra* (thunderbolt) and killed the demon Vrtra with it. Thus the Vajra represents a Victory of Gods over Demons. Savitri Bai chose the *Vajra* for the Param Vir Chakra.

On the front of the medal are four images of the infallible weapon of Indra: the *Vajra*. On either side of the four *Vajras* are replicas of Shivaji's famous sword *Bhawani*. In the centre of the medal is embossed the State emblem of India which has the four lions of Ashoka facing in four directions with the motto of India: *satyamev jayate* in Devanagari script at the bottom.

On the reverse side of the medal are embossed the words: Param Vir Chakra, both in Devanagari and in English with two lotus flowers between the words. The recipient should wear the medal on the left side of the breast, suspended with a purple ribbon of one and a quarter inches width. In case a recipient receives another Param Vir Chakra a bar will be attached to the ribbon.

This award is presented on Indian Republic Day, 26th January, by the President of India to the recipient, or if granted posthumously, to the recipient's widow or father/mother. All ranks of the Indian armed forces, right from the highest officer to a simple soldier, are eligible to win this award.

Appendix 9

Three Schemes By Shyam Kumari

1. 'Honour Our Soldiers'

A nation, if it wants to retain its freedom, must honour its martyrs and soldiers. We Indians have been guilty of grave neglect of our martyrs, ex-servicemen, soldiers and their families. We hardly remember those who have given their lives or limbs for the country. The perfunctory homage paid on Independence Day and other such occasions is not enough. Awarding a salary or a pension, and granting a piece of land or the dealership of a petrol pump are not sufficient compensation for the loss of a dear son, brother or husband.

Our soldiers fight and die for the honour of our country, yet we forget them after a few months or years. For example, on July 2006, the death anniversary function of Kargil War hero, Param Vir Chakra recipient Captain Manoj Pandey, was attended, apart from the hero's family, only by some members of an NGO. And this is the case of someone who was awarded the highest honour of India and whose statue has been installed in a public park named after him. What of those who died fighting for us yet did not win any bravery awards? I came to know of four families whose only sons have sacrificed their lives fighting for India. Their families are lonely and desolate. The public neither knows about them nor remembers them.

A soldier loves his family. While he is fighting for us, his family is left to face the innumerable difficulties of life alone. Should we not make committees to visit the soldiers' families and help them cope with the problems of life in the absence of the head of the family? Such a move will give solace and strength to our soldiers. Assured that their families are being looked after, they will be able to give their full attention to the task of protecting the country.

We, the citizens of India, must pay our debt of gratitude to these soldiers, ex-servicemen and martyrs' families. Should not the Nation integrate these families and shower love and respect on them? If we honour them we will be honouring Mother India through them. Because of them we and our children sleep in peace. Here is a simple scheme to accomplish this:

We should get the names from the District Soldiers Boards of each district the names of all the serving soldiers, ex-servicemen and martyrs of that district. Let the schools invite and honour these soldiers, ex-servicemen and their families, as well as the martyrs' families of all ranks, in their 15 August, 26 January and Annual Day functions. They may be presented with flowers or cards. They should be requested to narrate to the students and other participants the stories of their bravery and valour. Hopefully, they may be invited by Lions Clubs, the Rotarians, the Arya Samaj Schools, and the Ramakrishna Vidyalayas etc.

Later, as the movement spreads, the more conscious amongst the public may invite them to their family functions. This scheme is immensely advantageous. Through its implementation the public will become conscious of the safety aspect of the country and of the sad reality of martyrdom. Through this simple scheme our students will imbibe bravery and patriotism and our hearts will become larger and break out of the cage of narrow self-interest.

Thus we can pay our debt of gratitude to those whose valiantly guard our frontiers. Let us know them, love them and cherish them.

Pondicherry has pioneered this scheme. In February 2007 we invited Param Vir Chakra recipients Hon. Captain Bana Singh and Grenadier Yogender Singh Yadav to Pondicherry and held many grand functions in their honour. We also invited and honoured Maj. General Ian Cardozo, Maj. General Raj Mehta, Mukesh Khetarpal, brother of martyr PVC Arun Khetarpal, Col. Ashok Chandra Tara and Commander Vinayak Agashe. These heroes interacted with and inspired thousands of students of many educational institutes. I am happy that these functions were followed by numerous functions at different places in India.

Let us pay our debt of gratitude to the defenders of our country.

2. Let each class of each school/college/institute adopt a hero.

Sri Aurobindo has written:

"Every child is a lover of interesting narrative, a hero-worshipper and a patriot. Appeal to these qualities in him and through them let him master without knowing it the living and human parts of his nation's history."

Let us introduce students from a young age to the true heroes of the country. I am writing and publishing the stories of all those who have won the Param Vir Chakra, as well as of the great revolutionaries such as Chandrashekhar 'Azad', Khudi Ram and countless others for schools. Books with the stories of the two great revolutionaries Chandrashekhar 'Azad' and Kanailal Dutt, and of 13 Param Vir Chakra winners: Major Somnath Sharma, Second Lieutenant Ram Raghoba Rane, Major Shaitan Singh, Colonel Dhan Singh Thapa, Company Quartermaster Havildar Abdul Hamid, Lieutenant Colonel A.B. Tarapore, Second Lieutenant Arun Khetarpal, Hon. Captain Bana Singh, Captain Manoj Kumar Pandey, Captain Vikram Batra, Grenadier Yogender Singh Yadav, Rifleman Sanjay Kumar and Lance Naik Albert Ekka are ready in Hindi and English. The story of will come out soon. Each book costs only Rs. 30.

1: Every year each school in India will select a new hero from amongst the heroes, whose stories and photographs we have to provide. Beautiful photographs of all these heroes are ready. Each 12 x 10 inches photograph will cost Rs. 30 only. Some schools have adopted different heroes for some classes.

2: A framed photograph of their hero will be installed by each school/college /institute.

3: Every year on 15th August and 26th January each school will read out the story of their hero before the whole school. The photograph of the adopted hero will be put on a decorated platform and one by one the whole gathering will either offer flowers in front of the photograph or will simply do pranam with folded hands. This will be followed by a programme of patriotic songs, poems, plays, preferably mentioning the hero. Thought provoking questions should be posed during the debate such as:

a: Who is greater – a rich man or one who has laid down his life for the country?

b: Is it better to defend the country or to lead a comfortable life?

c: If we are conquered will not our wealth be taken away by the victors?

It should be mandatory for the parents to attend this function, so that they too may realize that freedom can be lost again.

4 : All the prizes, which schools routinely give throughout the year, will be named after the hero they have selected i.e. "Captain Manoj Pandey Prize" for best student or best athlete etc. The winners will be given tiny badges with the photograph of their hero to wear proudly.

5: The school stationary will bear the stamp size photograph of the hero with a caption like: Our hero Param Vir Chakra Vijeta Major Somnath Sharma.

6: After 2-3 years of participating in such functions the students of each school will know the story of their hero. Then inter-school programmes about their respective heroes should be held.

When school children hear these stories year after year for 10-12 years, when they bow before the photograph of a brave-hearted soldier or revolutionary martyr and tell the life stories of these revolutionary and military heroes they will gradually become suffused with the spirit of patriotism and would like to fight for, and if need be, lay down their lives for Mother India. Then there will be a surfeit, instead of a shortage of men and officers for our armed forces.

This scheme will not entail much expenditure for the schools except the cost of a framed photograph, the making of some badges, and adding one line to their stationary. Each student will have to spend

Rs. 30/- for a book with the hero's story and his beautiful photograph on the cover.

It will make our children brave, patriotic and willing to live and die for the country. If this scheme is presented to a million students and even one per cent of them decide to pursue a military career, the country will be well defended.

3. "Make Our Children Hero Warriors"

It is a matter for concern that our education system does not sufficiently stress physical fitness. Too many of our students are weak and meek. To infuse strength in our students, our schools must start a solid and scientific programme of physical culture. Physical culture must be given at least as much importance as mental education. Even for a brilliant mental development, a strong body is necessary.

Due to the lack of physical fitness, nervous strength and resilience, we are witnessing the phenomenon of "burning out" by mid-thirties of our software experts. On the contrary, when the body is fit and supple and the nervous system strong, one can be fully active even in the eighties.

This programme of physical culture should begin right from the kindergarten, and should be taught every day. Its aim should be to make our students strong to defend and strong to attack. For centuries we have been slaves to foreign invaders. To protect our freedom we need strong citizens.

There are two things which may be deemed to be in short supply — time and money. It is true that in the modern competitive world, students have to learn many subjects. But to make time for physical education, the usual eight periods can be shortened by five minutes each. Thus at hardly any loss to general education, 40 minutes can be made available for physical culture.

Even those schools which do not have the elaborate equipment, facilities and grounds to enable them to have a full-fledged scientific and exhaustive physical culture, can have running (running on the spot on rainy days), skipping, Judo, Karate, wrestling, Asanas and Pranayam. These inexpensive exercises will make our students strong enough to defend their honour and their country's honour.

But to achieve some degree of success, if possible this training should be given every day.

Namaste

Author

Shyam Kumari was born in Muzaffarnagar, U.P., in 1934. There she studied in the Vedic Putri Pathshala and S. D. Degree College up to her B.A. In 1965, she passed her M.A. from Lucknow University. She has read widely in Hindi and English literature, as well as religious and spiritual books.

Since her childhood she yearned to find God. In 1969, the Divine Mother accepted her in Sri Aurobindo Ashram and appointed her a teacher in the Sri Aurobindo International Centre of Education.

Hundreds of her poems, lyrics, stories, plays, literary and social essays, both in English and Hindi, have appeared in national and international journals. She has also written and published more than 70 books, some running into several reprints. Many of her books have been translated into Hindi, Oriya, Tamil, Bengali, Marathi and Gujarati. She has written path-breaking rhymes and story books for children. In 1998 she launched a Hindi quarterly magazine, Swarna Hansa which she, single-handedly, wrote, edited and published for 20 years.

In 1998, she established Vraja Trust, a public charitable trust, and is at present its managing trustee. In 2001, she started *Sri Aravinda Sanskrit Vidyalaya,* in Pondicherry, India, to impart free Sanskrit education to children and adults alike and she is its Chairperson. In 2005, she launched the "Let Each School Adopt a Hero" scheme. In 2006, she launched the "Let Us Honour Our Soldiers" and "Let each child become a Hero Warrior" schemes.

www.ingramcontent.com/pod-product-compliance
Lightning Source LLC
Chambersburg PA
CBHW021146160426
43194CB00007B/712